TAMBA
CHILD SOLDIER

MARION ACHARD
WRITER

YANN DÉGRUEL
ART

nbm GRAPHIC NOVELS

Nantier • Beall • Minoustchine
NEW YORK

I'd like to thank Thierry and Yann for giving me this amazing opportunity to enter the world of comics.
A big thank you to Salomé for her invaluable proofreading, to Kidi and Caro for being there, for Shemsi, Maélia, Leila and Farid for their patience.
And thank you, Pablo, for believing in this project from day one, when this comic book was supposed to be a novel. You supported me every step of the way for four years by offering your help in my moments of doubt and lengthy reflection.
Marion Achard

Thank you, Marion, for sharing your story with me, and thank you,
Thierry, for your faith in us.
Yann Dégruel

We have over 200 graphic novels
See more at:
NBMPUB.COM

NBM
160 Broadway, Suite 700, East Wing
New York, NY 10038
Catalog upon request

ISBN 9781681122366
© 2018 Editions Delcourt.
© 2019 NBM for the English translation
Library of Congress Control Number: 2019945416
Translation by Montana Kane
Lettering by Ortho

Printed in China
1st printing October 2019

This book is also available wherever e-books are sold

GRAPHIC NOVELS
Comics Biographies

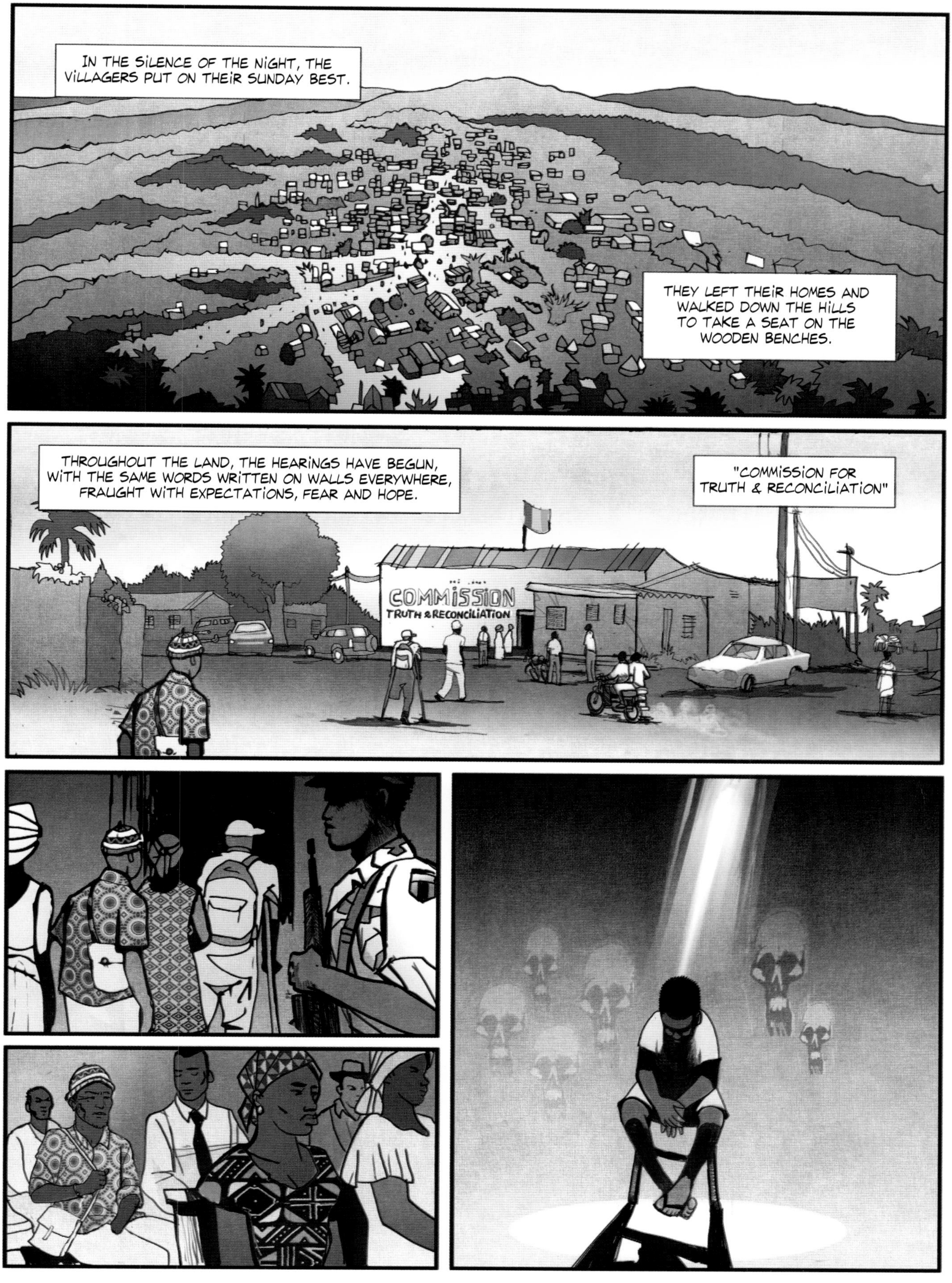
IN THE SILENCE OF THE NIGHT, THE VILLAGERS PUT ON THEIR SUNDAY BEST.
THEY LEFT THEIR HOMES AND WALKED DOWN THE HILLS TO TAKE A SEAT ON THE WOODEN BENCHES.
THROUGHOUT THE LAND, THE HEARINGS HAVE BEGUN, WITH THE SAME WORDS WRITTEN ON WALLS EVERYWHERE, FRAUGHT WITH EXPECTATIONS, FEAR AND HOPE.
"COMMISSION FOR TRUTH & RECONCILIATION"
COMMISSION
TRUTH & RECONCILIATION

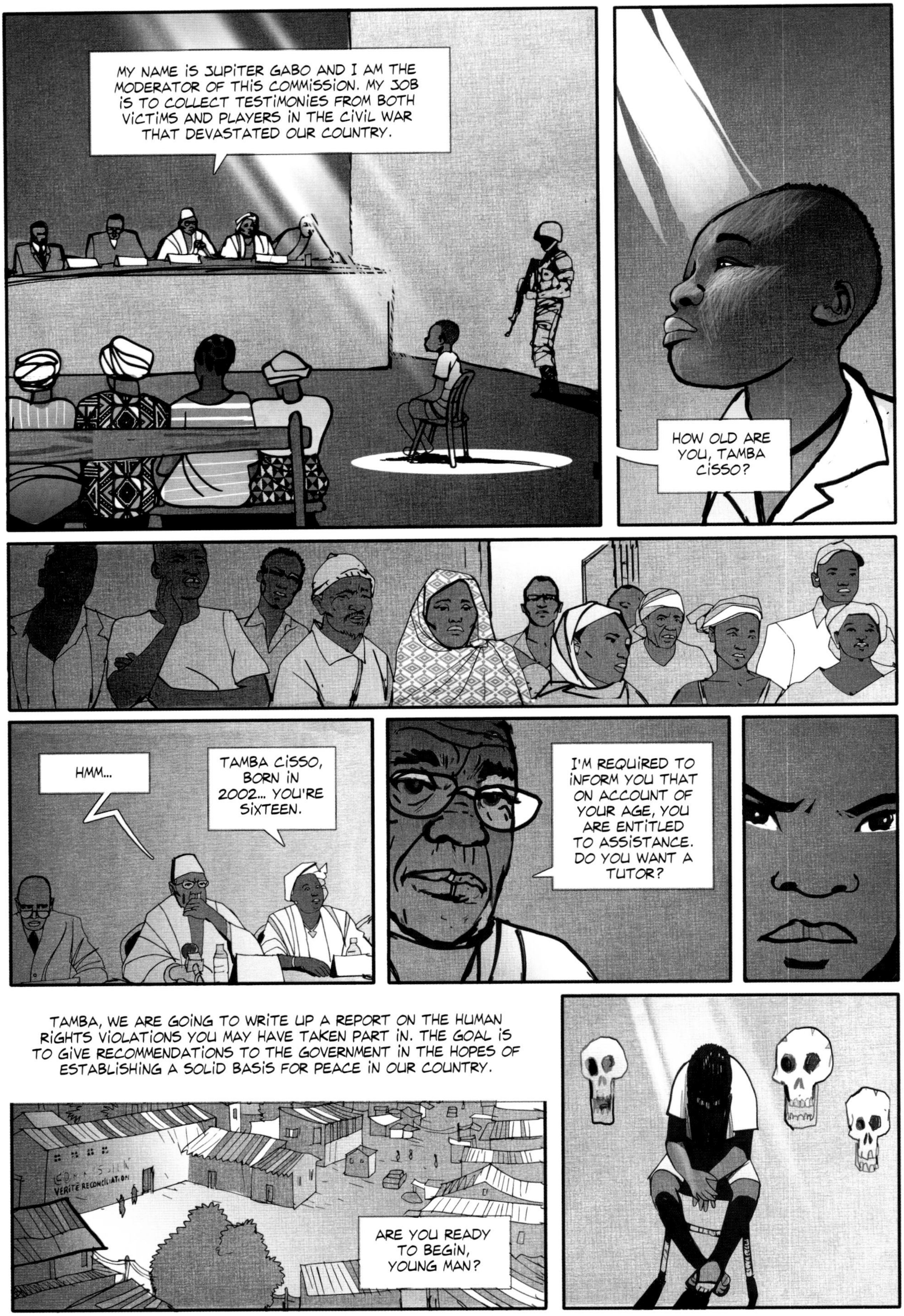
MY NAME IS JUPITER GABO AND I AM THE MODERATOR OF THIS COMMISSION. MY JOB IS TO COLLECT TESTIMONIES FROM BOTH VICTIMS AND PLAYERS IN THE CIVIL WAR THAT DEVASTATED OUR COUNTRY.
HOW OLD ARE YOU, TAMBA CISSO?
HMM...
TAMBA CISSO, BORN IN 2002... YOU'RE SIXTEEN.
I'M REQUIRED TO INFORM YOU THAT ON ACCOUNT OF YOUR AGE, YOU ARE ENTITLED TO ASSISTANCE. DO YOU WANT A TUTOR?
TAMBA, WE ARE GOING TO WRITE UP A REPORT ON THE HUMAN RIGHTS VIOLATIONS YOU MAY HAVE TAKEN PART IN. THE GOAL IS TO GIVE RECOMMENDATIONS TO THE GOVERNMENT IN THE HOPES OF ESTABLISHING A SOLID BASIS FOR PEACE IN OUR COUNTRY.
COMMISSION
VERITÉ RECONCILIATION
ARE YOU READY TO BEGIN, YOUNG MAN?

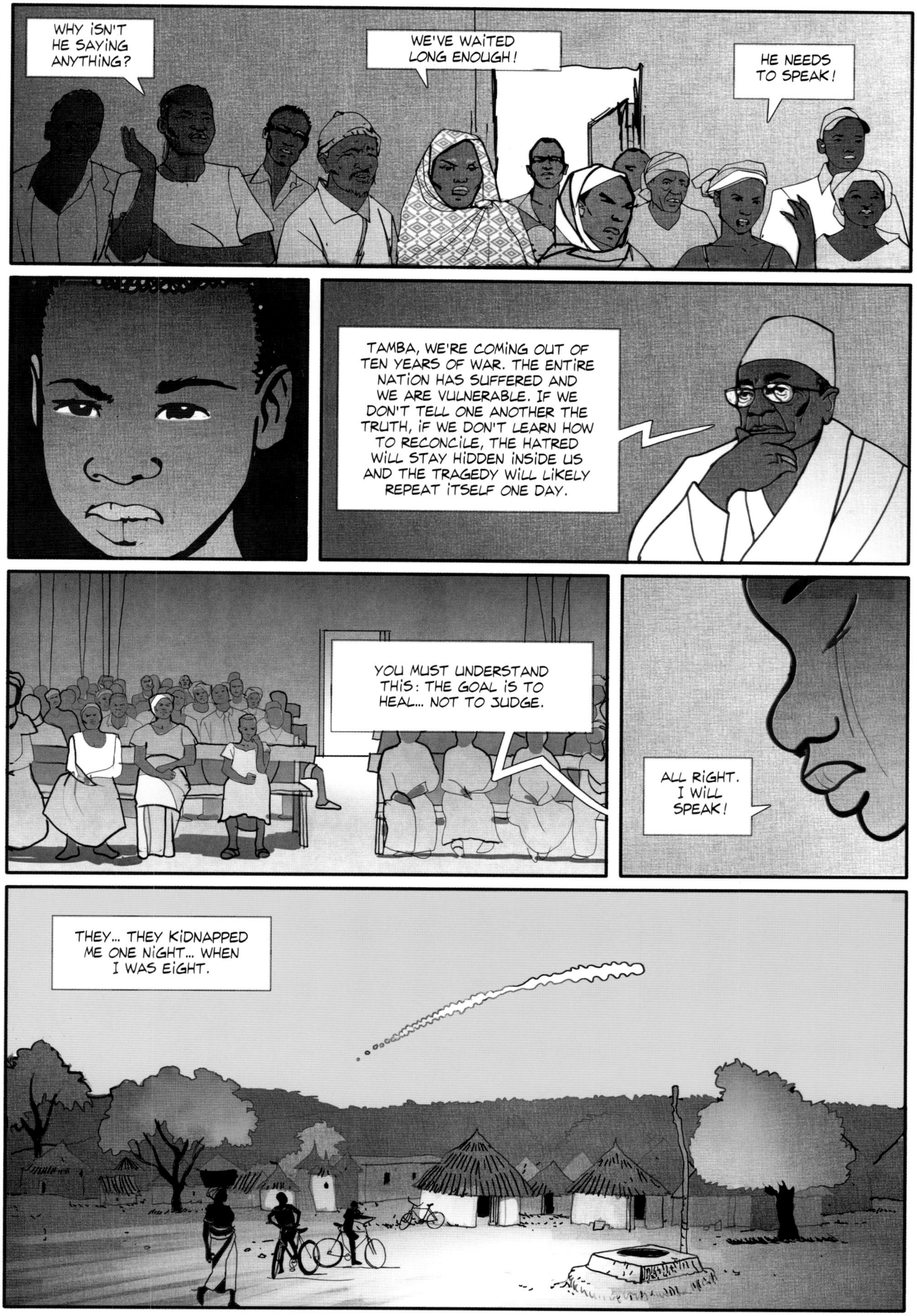
WHY ISN'T HE SAYING ANYTHING?
WE'VE WAITED LONG ENOUGH!
HE NEEDS TO SPEAK!
TAMBA, WE'RE COMING OUT OF TEN YEARS OF WAR. THE ENTIRE NATION HAS SUFFERED AND WE ARE VULNERABLE. IF WE DON'T TELL ONE ANOTHER THE TRUTH, IF WE DON'T LEARN HOW TO RECONCILE, THE HATRED WILL STAY HIDDEN INSIDE US AND THE TRAGEDY WILL LIKELY REPEAT ITSELF ONE DAY.
YOU MUST UNDERSTAND THIS: THE GOAL IS TO HEAL... NOT TO JUDGE.
ALL RIGHT. I WILL SPEAK!
THEY... THEY KIDNAPPED ME ONE NIGHT... WHEN I WAS EIGHT.

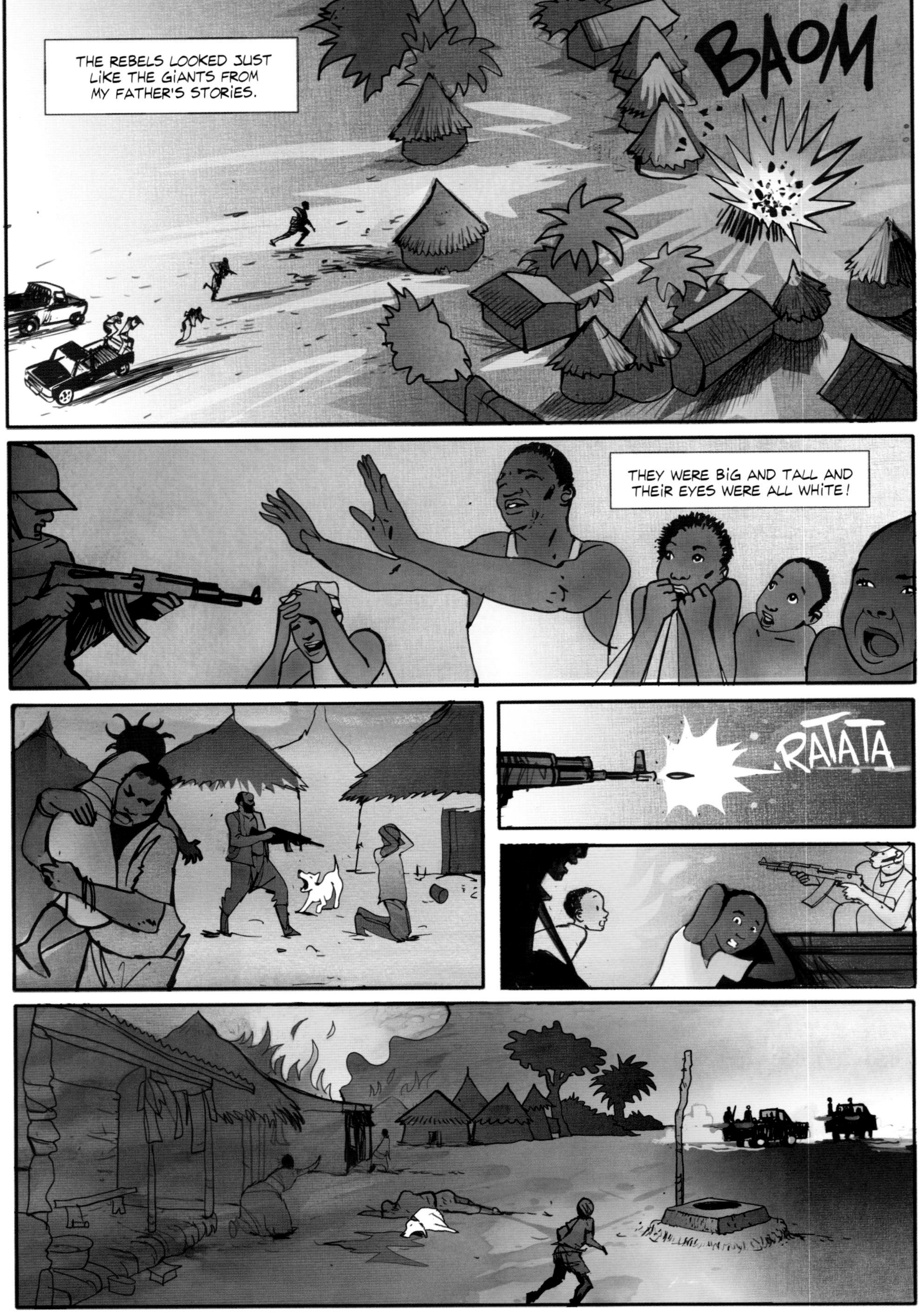
THE REBELS LOOKED JUST LIKE THE GIANTS FROM MY FATHER'S STORIES.
BAOM
THEY WERE BIG AND TALL AND THEIR EYES WERE ALL WHITE!
RATATA

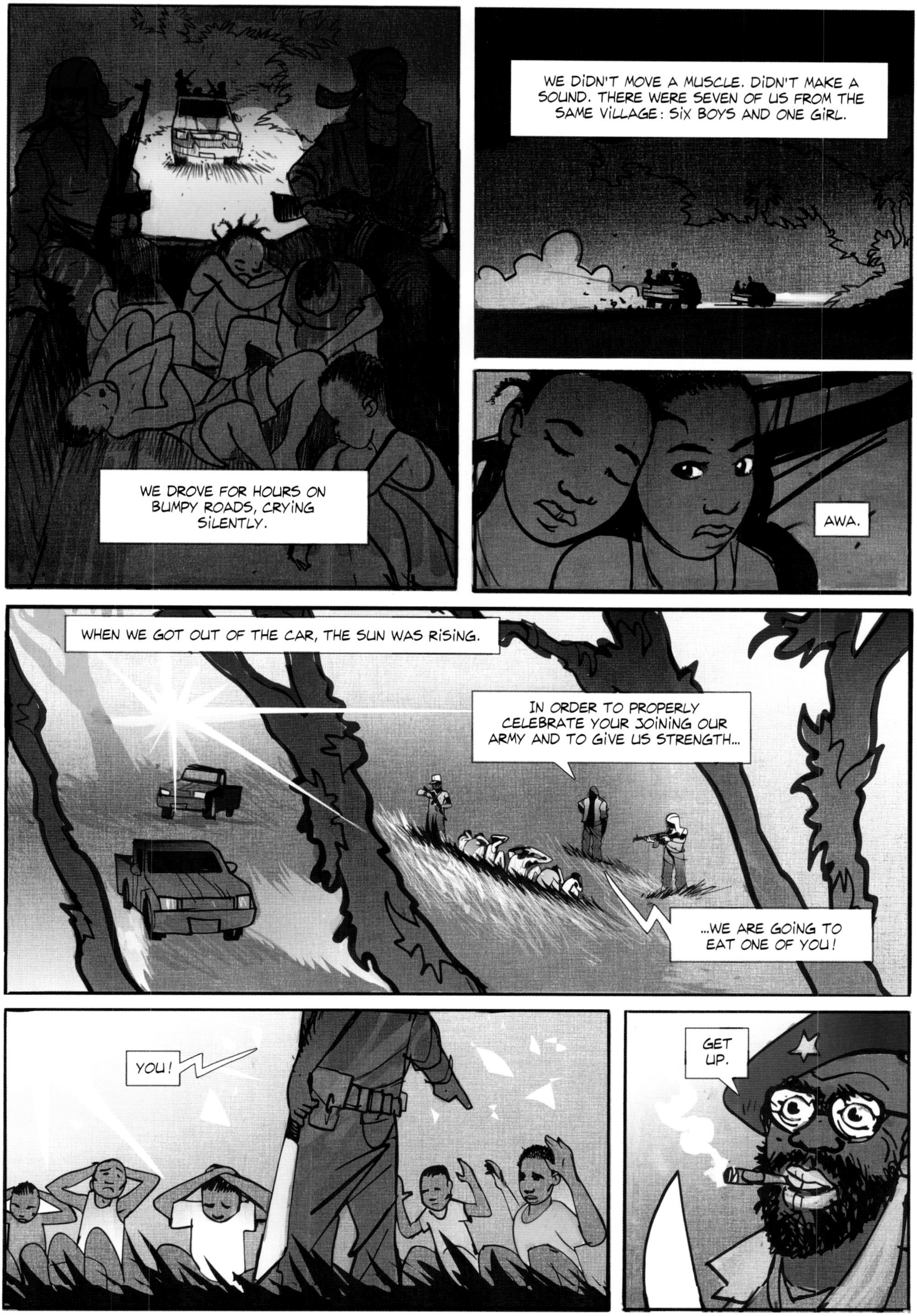
WE DROVE FOR HOURS ON BUMPY ROADS, CRYING SILENTLY.
WE DIDN'T MOVE A MUSCLE. DIDN'T MAKE A SOUND. THERE WERE SEVEN OF US FROM THE SAME VILLAGE: SIX BOYS AND ONE GIRL.
AWA.
WHEN WE GOT OUT OF THE CAR, THE SUN WAS RISING.
IN ORDER TO PROPERLY CELEBRATE YOUR JOINING OUR ARMY AND TO GIVE US STRENGTH...
...WE ARE GOING TO EAT ONE OF YOU!
YOU!
GET UP.

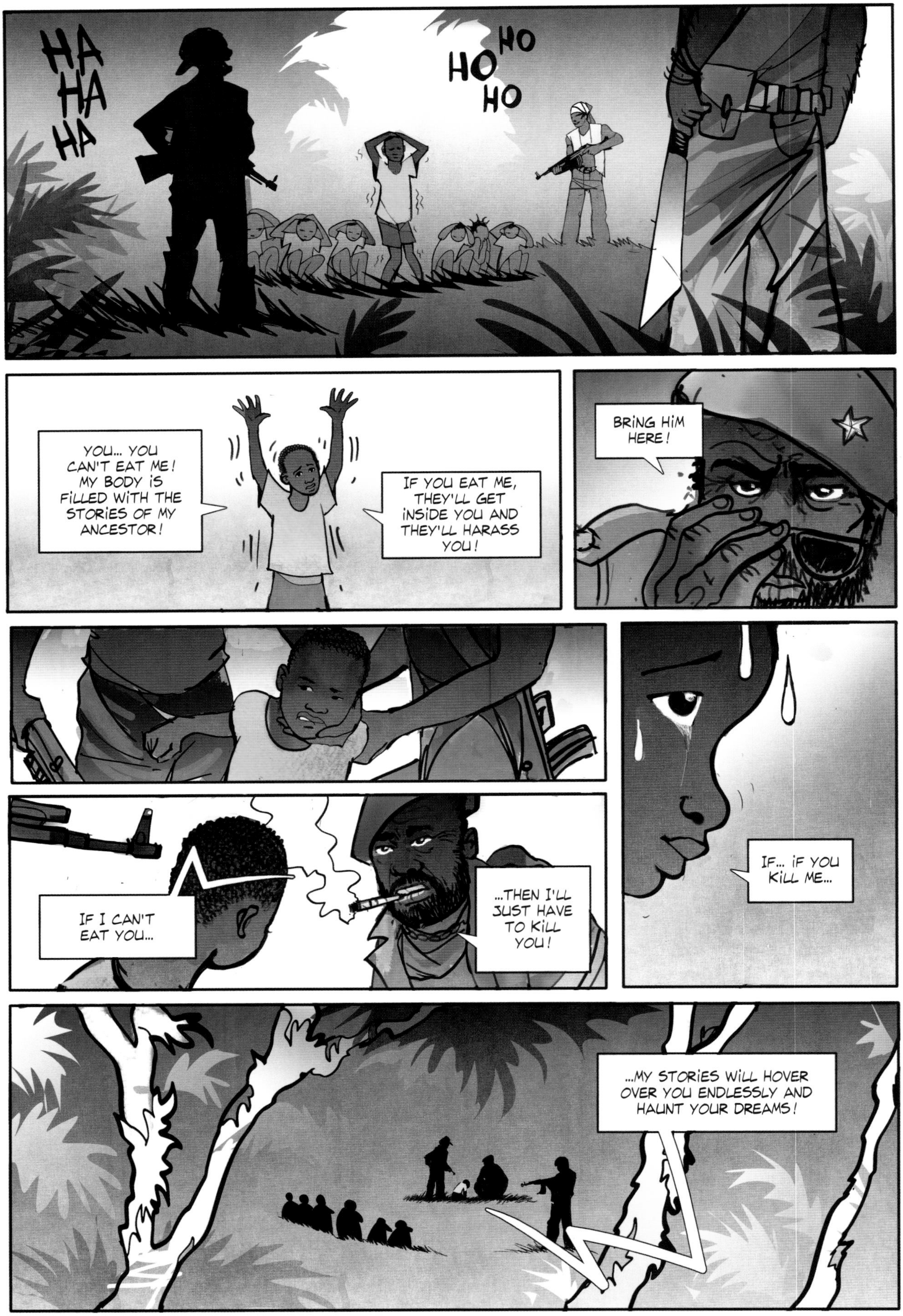
HA HA HA
HO HO HO
YOU... YOU CAN'T EAT ME! MY BODY IS FILLED WITH THE STORIES OF MY ANCESTOR!
IF YOU EAT ME, THEY'LL GET INSIDE YOU AND THEY'LL HARASS YOU!
BRING HIM HERE!
IF I CAN'T EAT YOU...
...THEN I'LL JUST HAVE TO KILL YOU!
IF... IF YOU KILL ME...
...MY STORIES WILL HOVER OVER YOU ENDLESSLY AND HAUNT YOUR DREAMS!

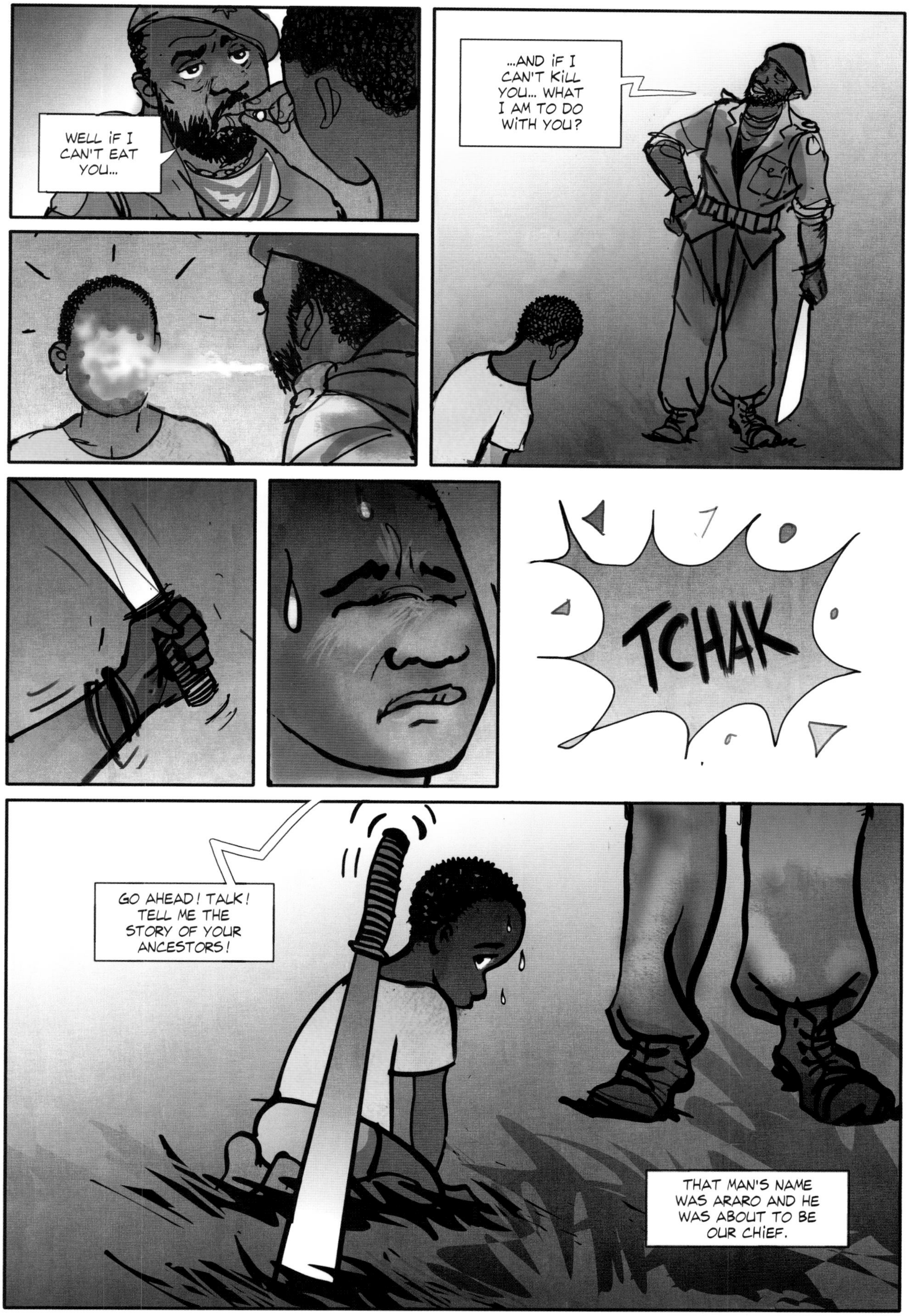
WELL iF I CAN'T EAT YOU...
...AND iF I CAN'T KiLL YOU... WHAT I AM TO DO WiTH YOU?
TCHAK
GO AHEAD! TALK! TELL ME THE STORY OF YOUR ANCESTORS!
THAT MAN'S NAME WAS ARARO AND HE WAS ABOUT TO BE OUR CHiEF.

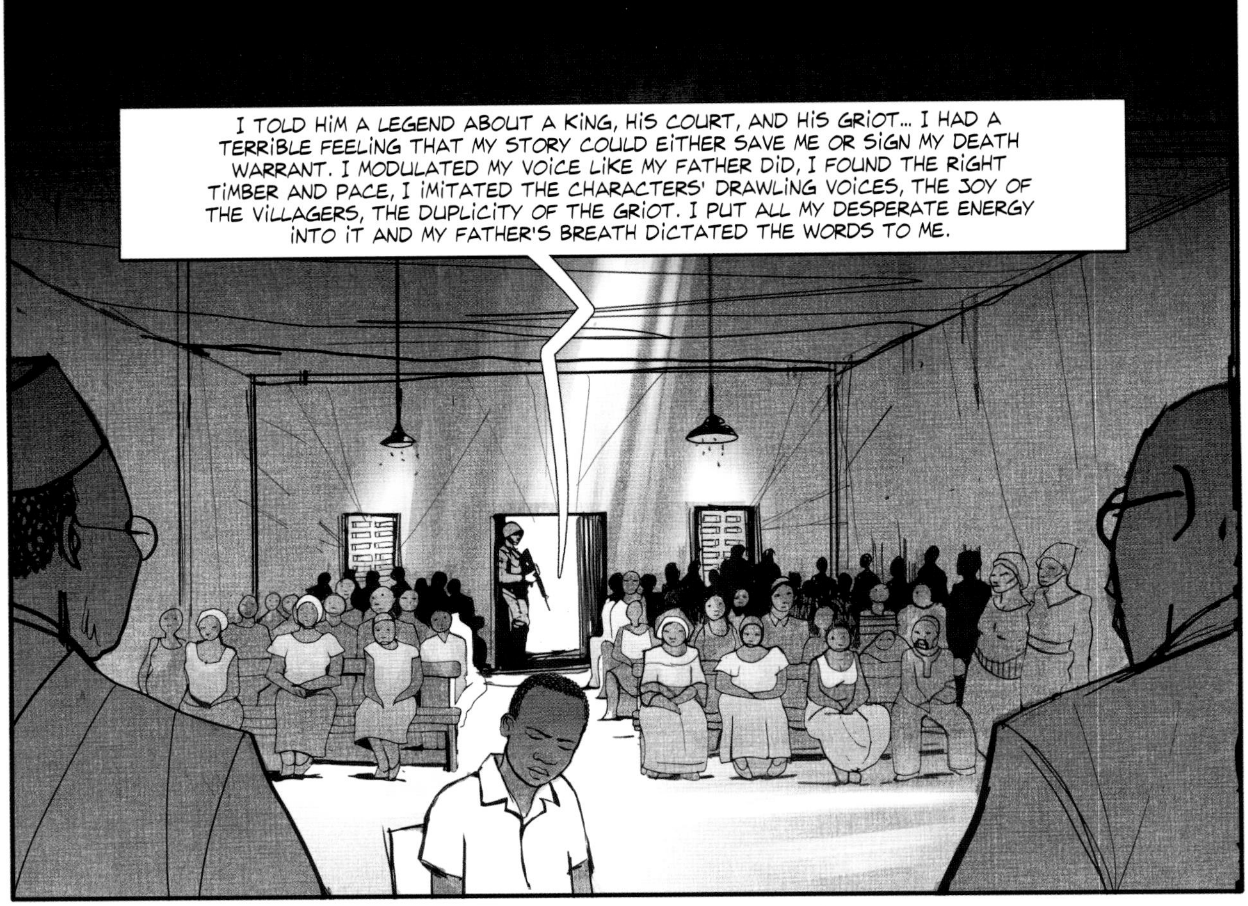
I TOLD HIM A LEGEND ABOUT A KING, HIS COURT, AND HIS GRIOT... I HAD A TERRIBLE FEELING THAT MY STORY COULD EITHER SAVE ME OR SIGN MY DEATH WARRANT. I MODULATED MY VOICE LIKE MY FATHER DID, I FOUND THE RIGHT TIMBER AND PACE, I IMITATED THE CHARACTERS' DRAWLING VOICES, THE JOY OF THE VILLAGERS, THE DUPLICITY OF THE GRIOT. I PUT ALL MY DESPERATE ENERGY INTO IT AND MY FATHER'S BREATH DICTATED THE WORDS TO ME.

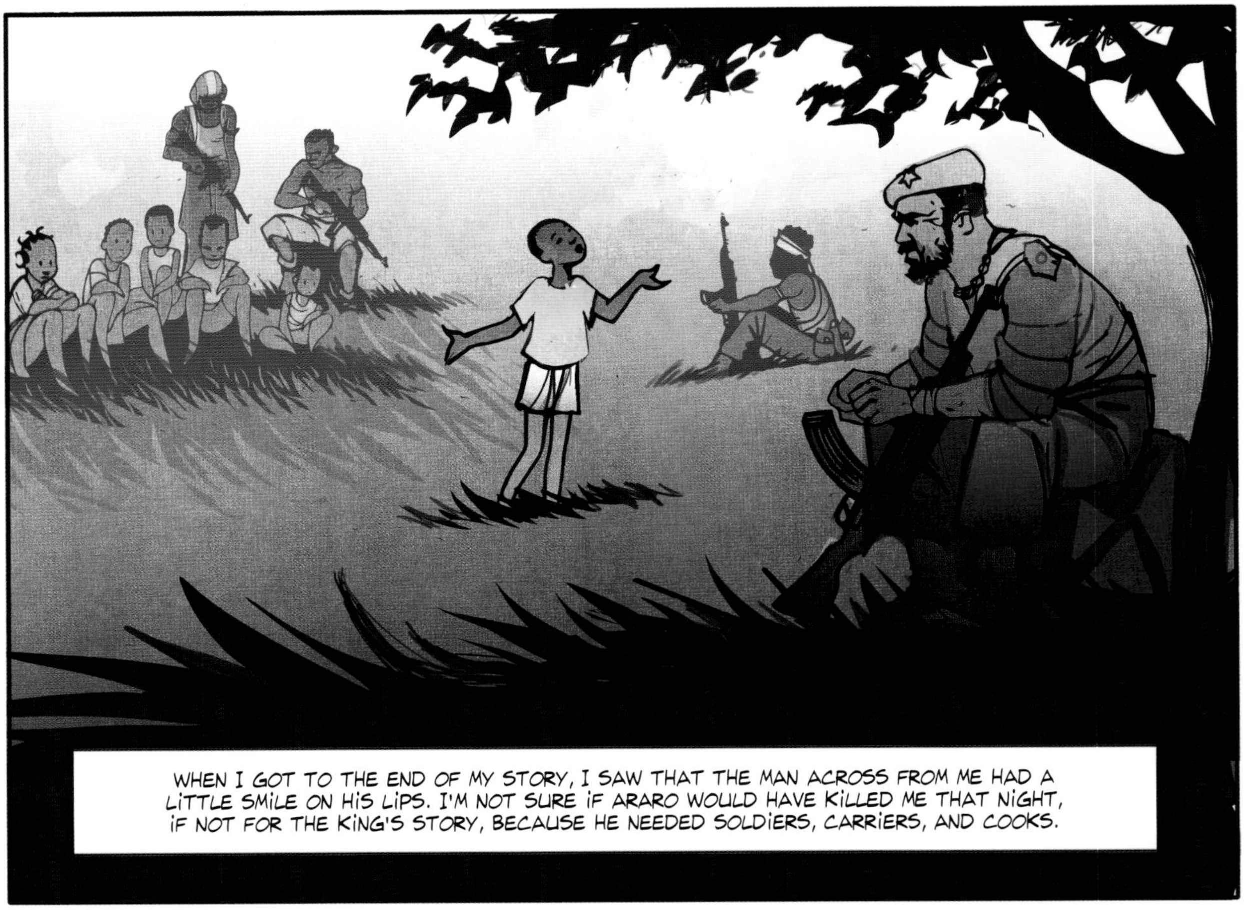
WHEN I GOT TO THE END OF MY STORY, I SAW THAT THE MAN ACROSS FROM ME HAD A LITTLE SMILE ON HIS LIPS. I'M NOT SURE IF ARARO WOULD HAVE KILLED ME THAT NIGHT, IF NOT FOR THE KING'S STORY, BECAUSE HE NEEDED SOLDIERS, CARRIERS, AND COOKS.

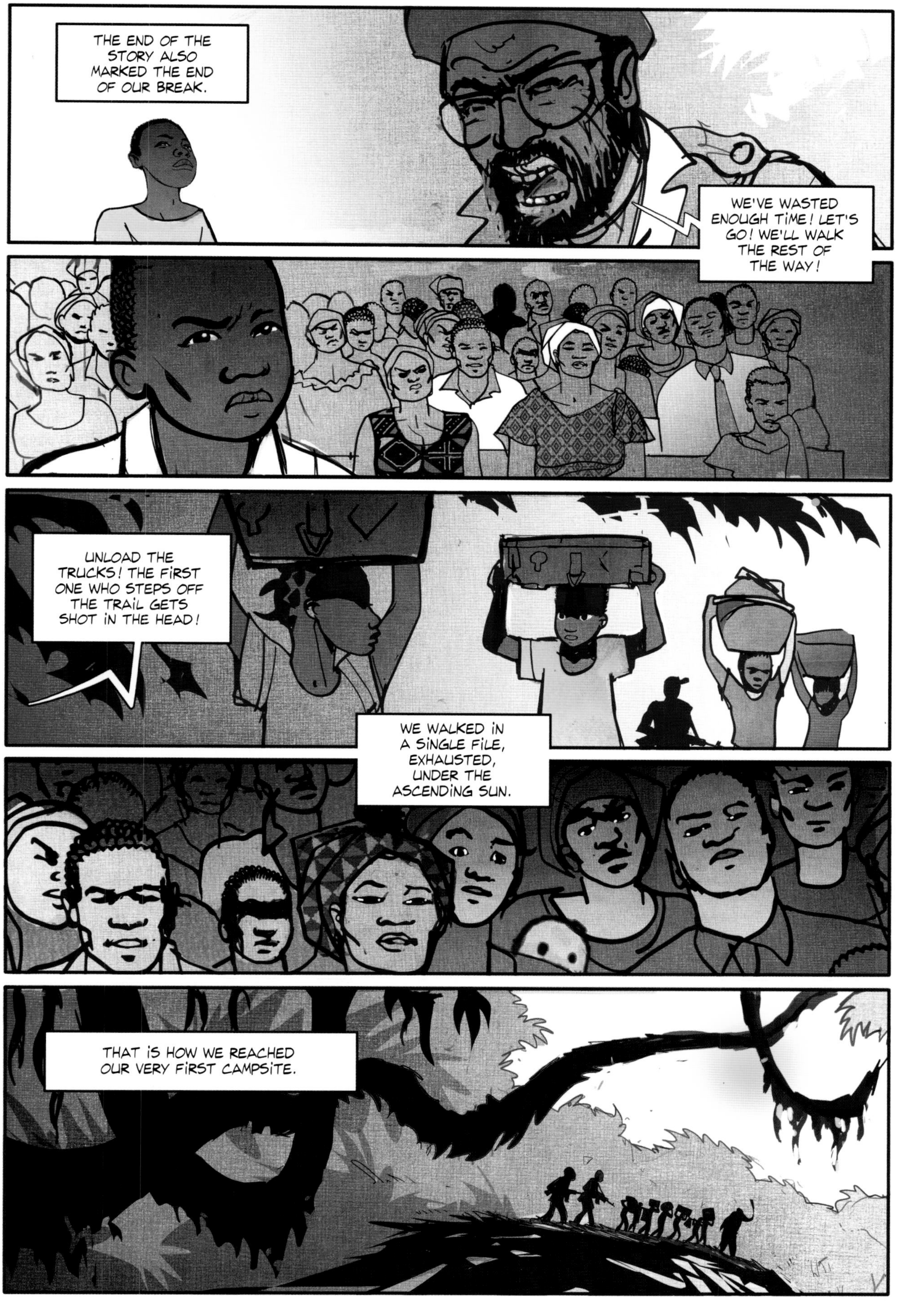
THE END OF THE STORY ALSO MARKED THE END OF OUR BREAK.
WE'VE WASTED ENOUGH TIME! LET'S GO! WE'LL WALK THE REST OF THE WAY!
UNLOAD THE TRUCKS! THE FIRST ONE WHO STEPS OFF THE TRAIL GETS SHOT IN THE HEAD!
WE WALKED IN A SINGLE FILE, EXHAUSTED, UNDER THE ASCENDING SUN.
THAT IS HOW WE REACHED OUR VERY FIRST CAMPSITE.

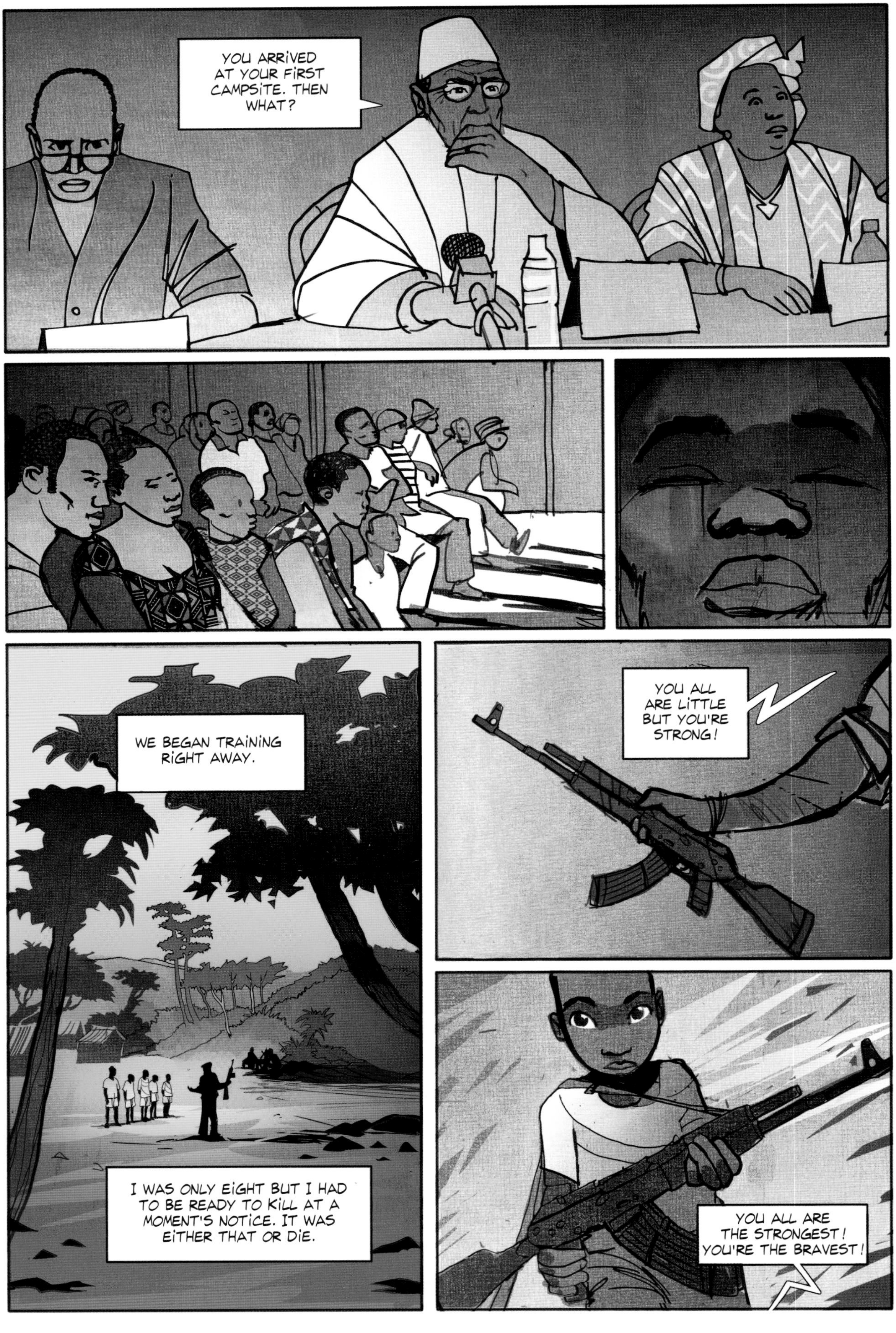
YOU ARRIVED AT YOUR FIRST CAMPSITE. THEN WHAT?
WE BEGAN TRAINING RIGHT AWAY.
I WAS ONLY EIGHT BUT I HAD TO BE READY TO KILL AT A MOMENT'S NOTICE. IT WAS EITHER THAT OR DIE.
YOU ALL ARE LITTLE BUT YOU'RE STRONG!
YOU ALL ARE THE STRONGEST! YOU'RE THE BRAVEST!

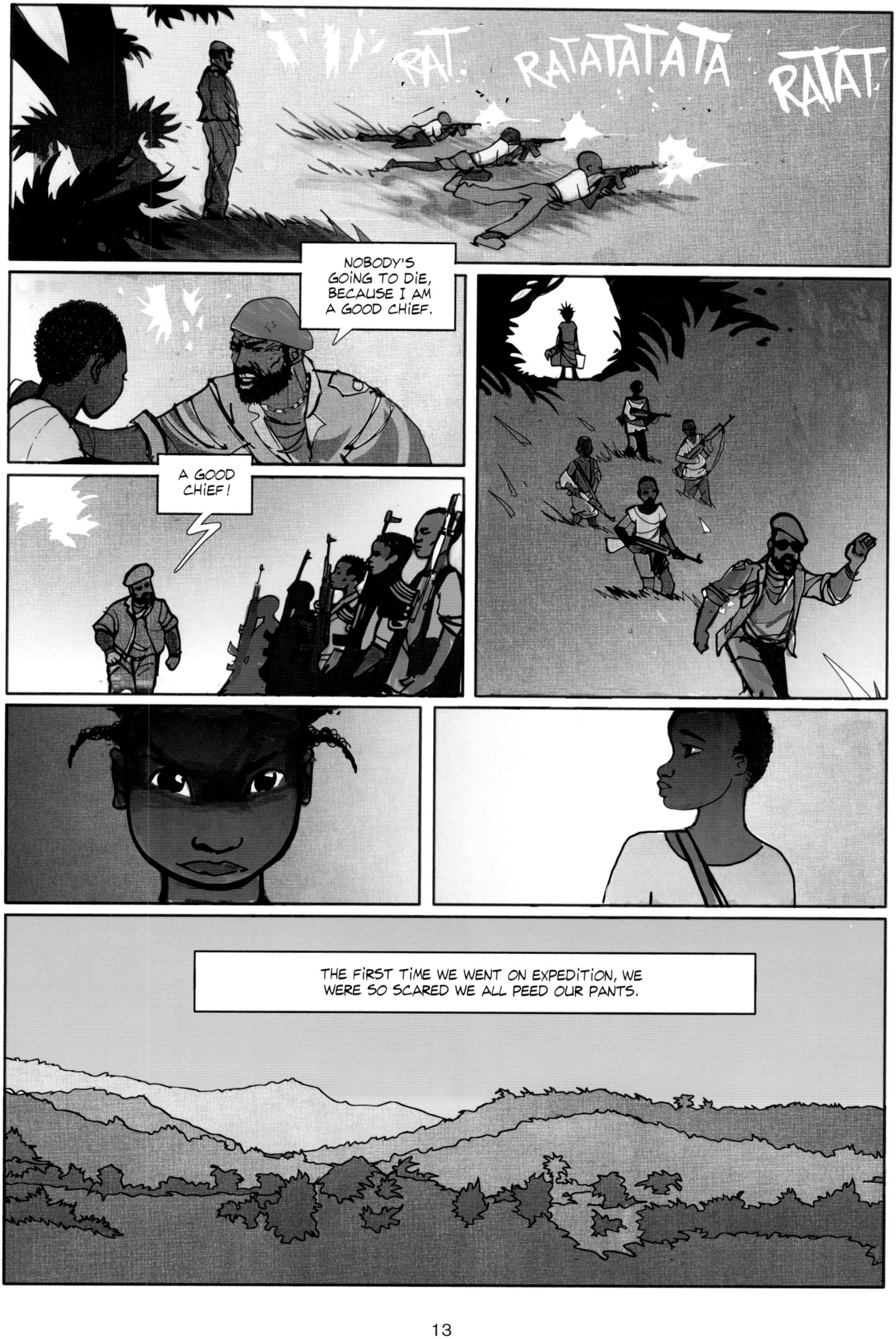
RAT. RATATATATA RATAT.
NOBODY'S GOING TO DIE, BECAUSE I AM A GOOD CHIEF.
A GOOD CHIEF!
THE FIRST TIME WE WENT ON EXPEDITION, WE WERE SO SCARED WE ALL PEED OUR PANTS.

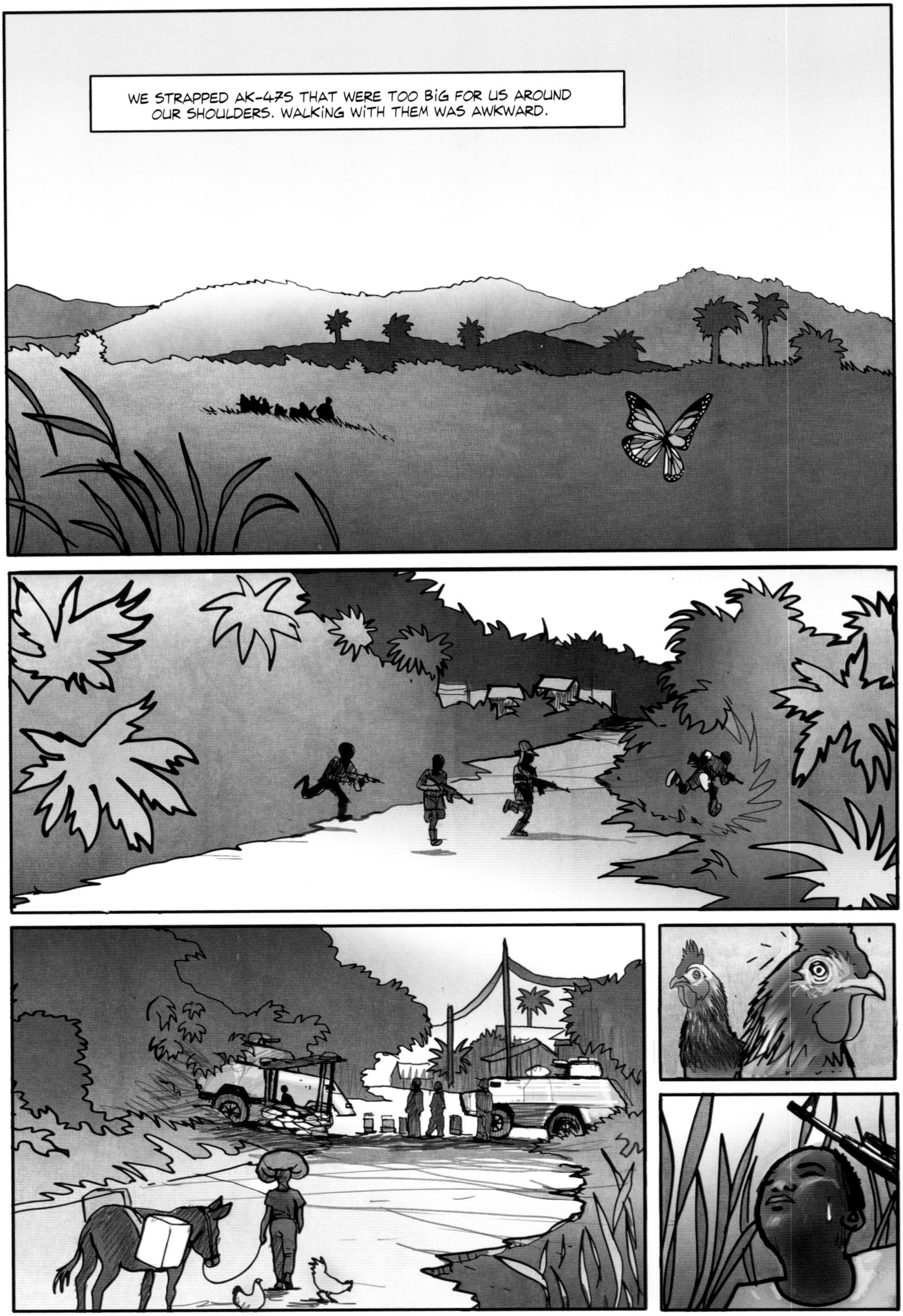
WE STRAPPED AK-47S THAT WERE TOO BIG FOR US AROUND OUR SHOULDERS. WALKING WITH THEM WAS AWKWARD.

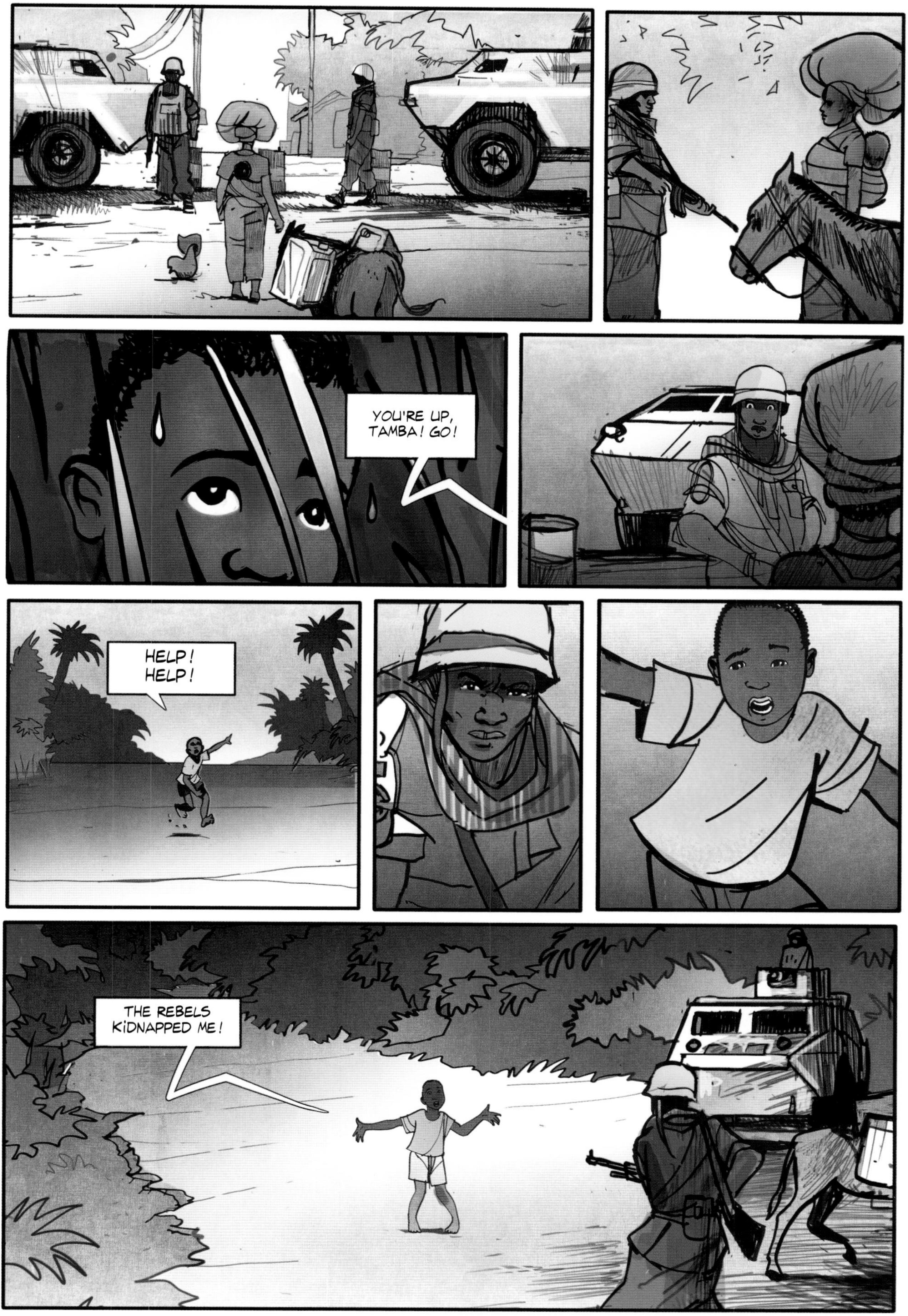
YOU'RE UP, TAMBA! GO!
HELP! HELP!
THE REBELS KIDNAPPED ME!

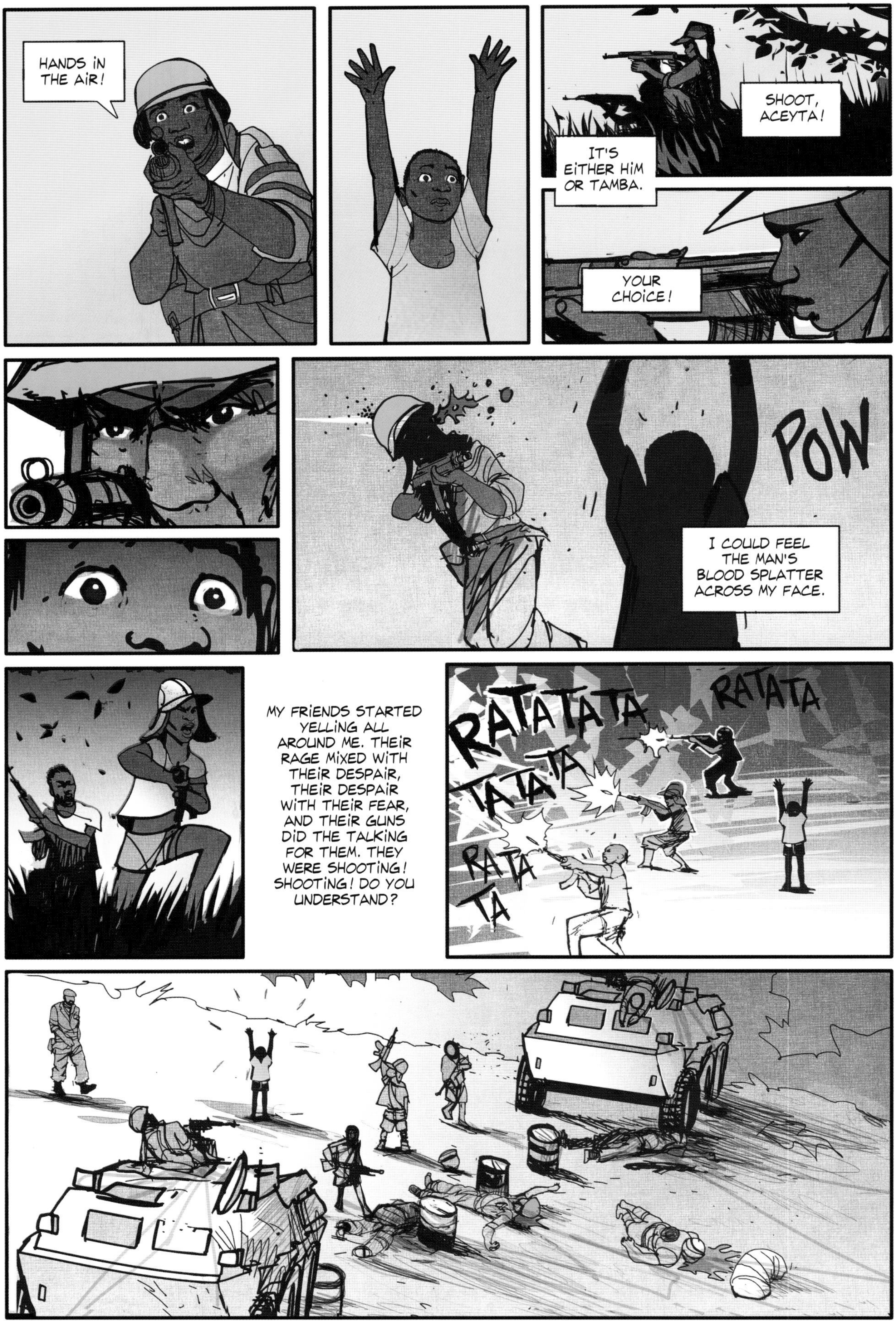
HANDS IN THE AIR!
SHOOT, ACEYTA!
IT'S EITHER HIM OR TAMBA.
YOUR CHOICE!
POW
I COULD FEEL THE MAN'S BLOOD SPLATTER ACROSS MY FACE.
MY FRIENDS STARTED YELLING ALL AROUND ME. THEIR RAGE MIXED WITH THEIR DESPAIR, THEIR DESPAIR WITH THEIR FEAR, AND THEIR GUNS DID THE TALKING FOR THEM. THEY WERE SHOOTING! SHOOTING! DO YOU UNDERSTAND?
RATATATA
RATATA
TATATA
RATATA

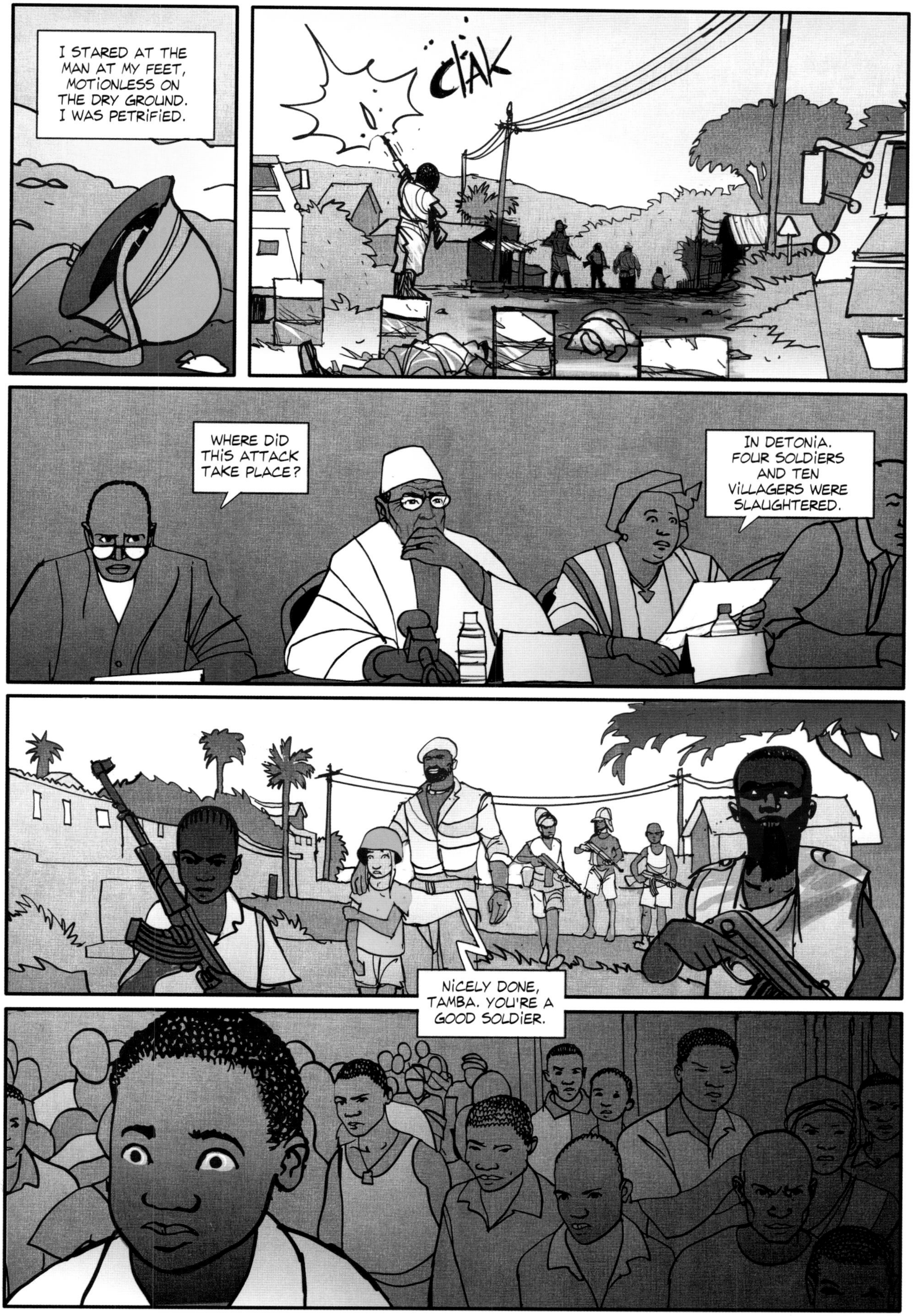
I STARED AT THE MAN AT MY FEET, MOTIONLESS ON THE DRY GROUND. I WAS PETRIFIED.
CIAK
WHERE DID THIS ATTACK TAKE PLACE?
IN DETONIA. FOUR SOLDIERS AND TEN VILLAGERS WERE SLAUGHTERED.
NICELY DONE, TAMBA. YOU'RE A GOOD SOLDIER.

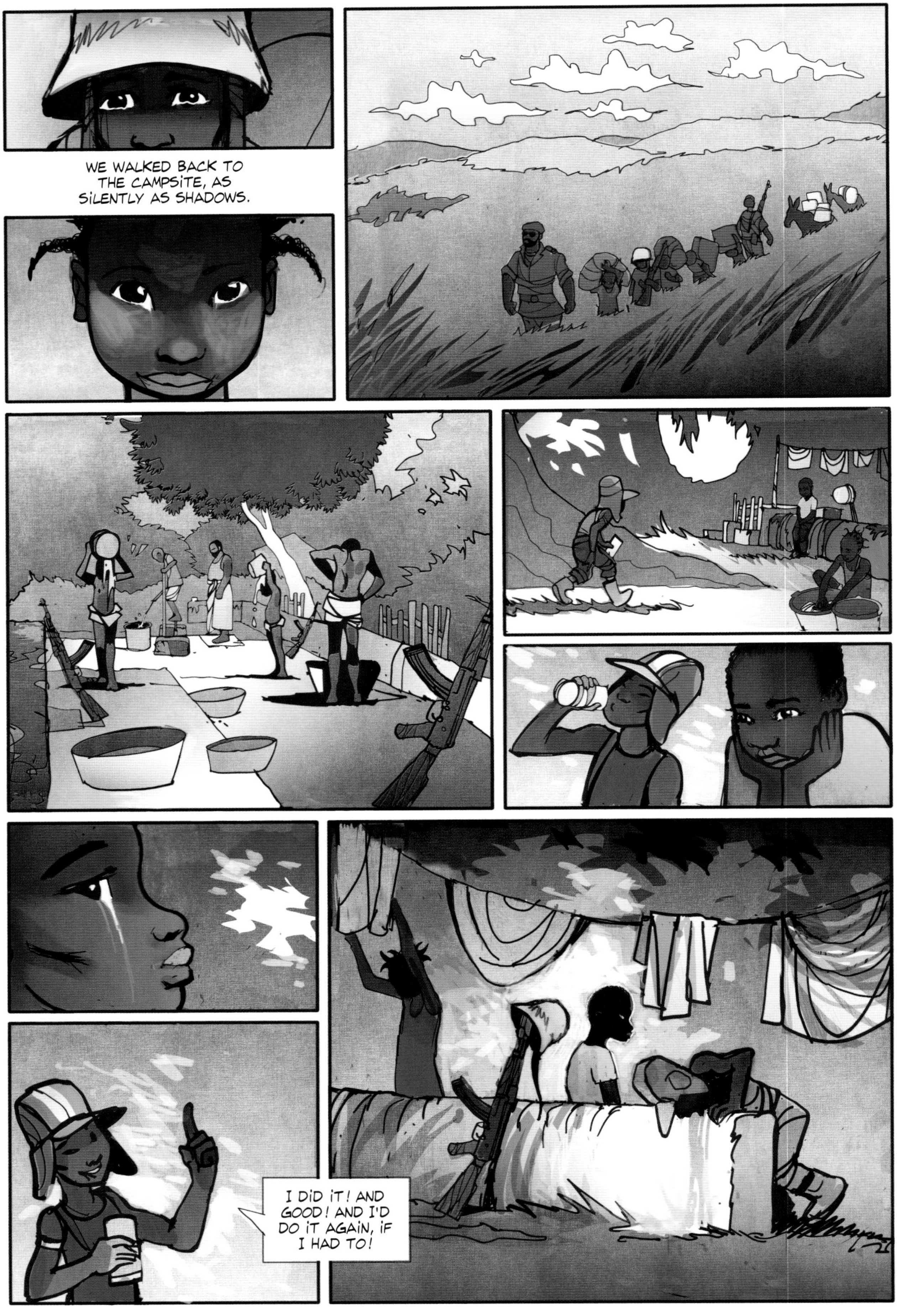
WE WALKED BACK TO THE CAMPSITE, AS SILENTLY AS SHADOWS.
I DID IT! AND GOOD! AND I'D DO IT AGAIN, IF I HAD TO!

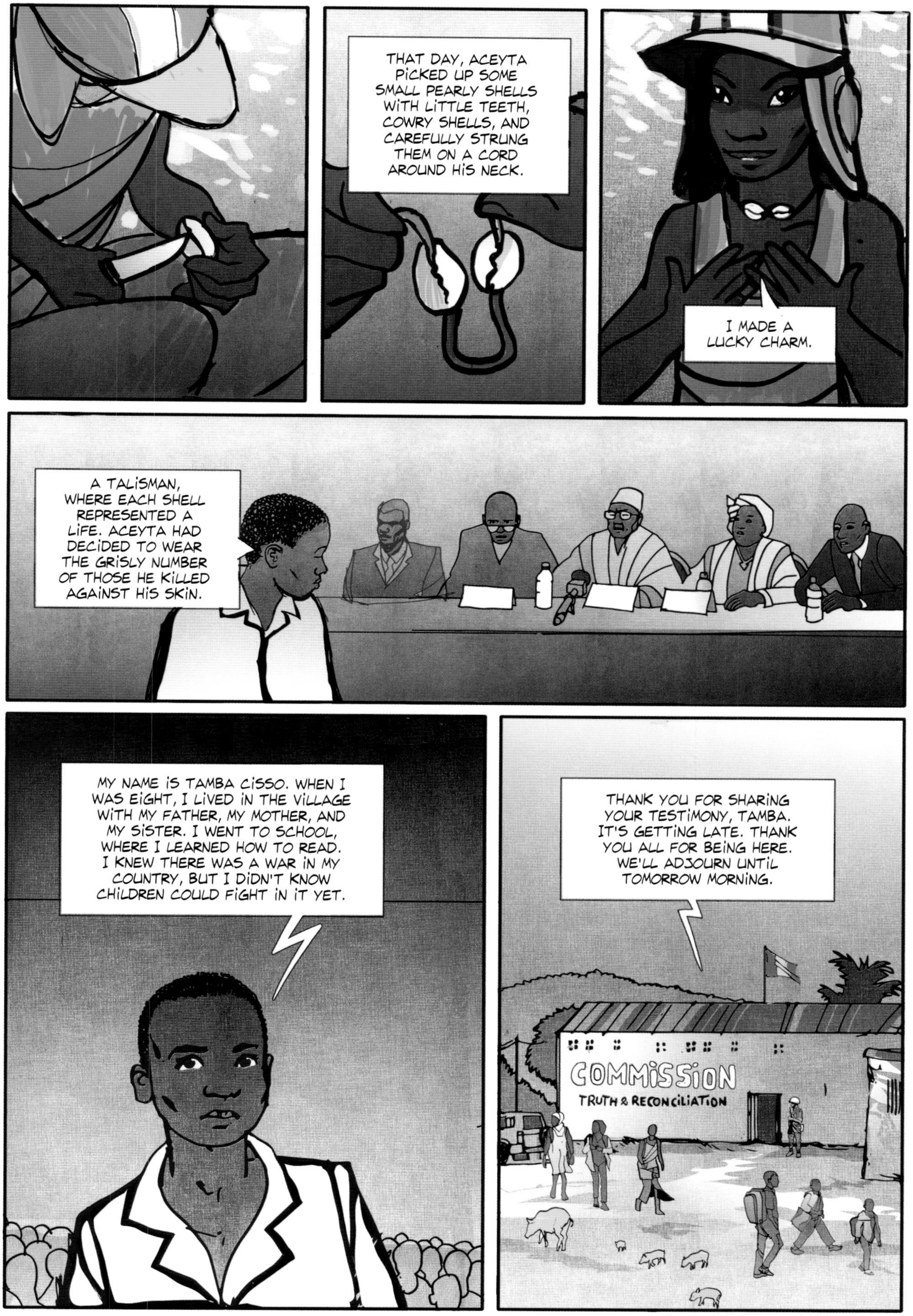
THAT DAY, ACEYTA PICKED UP SOME SMALL PEARLY SHELLS WITH LITTLE TEETH, COWRY SHELLS, AND CAREFULLY STRUNG THEM ON A CORD AROUND HIS NECK.
I MADE A LUCKY CHARM.
A TALISMAN, WHERE EACH SHELL REPRESENTED A LIFE. ACEYTA HAD DECIDED TO WEAR THE GRISLY NUMBER OF THOSE HE KILLED AGAINST HIS SKIN.
MY NAME IS TAMBA CISSO. WHEN I WAS EIGHT, I LIVED IN THE VILLAGE WITH MY FATHER, MY MOTHER, AND MY SISTER. I WENT TO SCHOOL, WHERE I LEARNED HOW TO READ. I KNEW THERE WAS A WAR IN MY COUNTRY, BUT I DIDN'T KNOW CHILDREN COULD FIGHT IN IT YET.
THANK YOU FOR SHARING YOUR TESTIMONY, TAMBA. IT'S GETTING LATE. THANK YOU ALL FOR BEING HERE. WE'LL ADJOURN UNTIL TOMORROW MORNING.
COMMISSION
TRUTH & RECONCILIATION

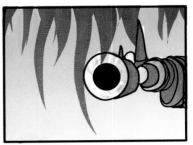

RATAT

GET IT AND TAKE IT TO THE KITCHEN, TAMBA.

TENKI, TAMBA!

STOP IT, AWA! I NEVER WANT TO HEAR MY MOTHER'S LANGUAGE AGAIN!

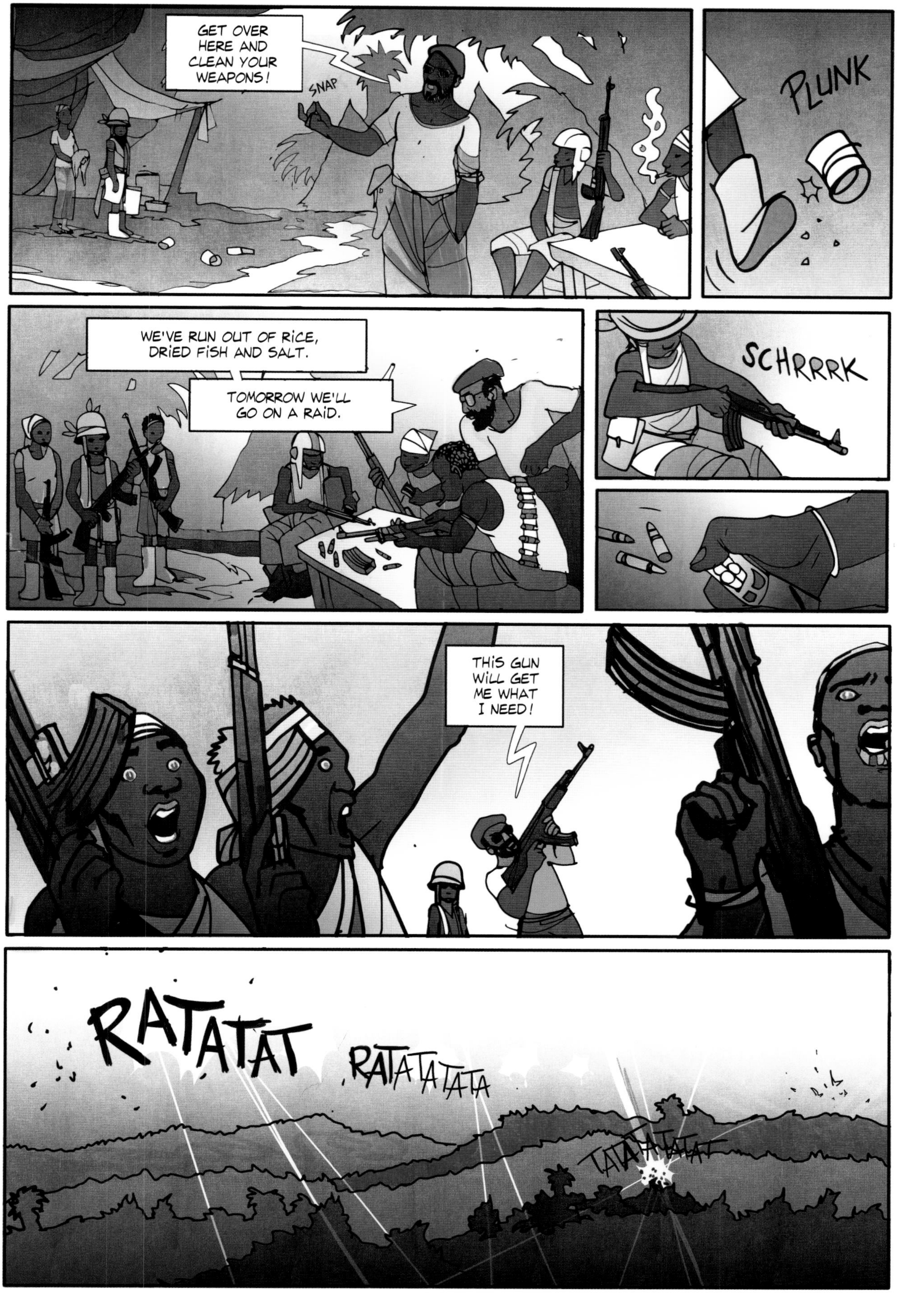
GET OVER HERE AND CLEAN YOUR WEAPONS!
SNAP
PLUNK
WE'VE RUN OUT OF RICE, DRIED FISH AND SALT.
TOMORROW WE'LL GO ON A RAID.
SCHRRRK
THIS GUN WILL GET ME WHAT I NEED!
RATATAT
RATATATATA
TATATATATAT

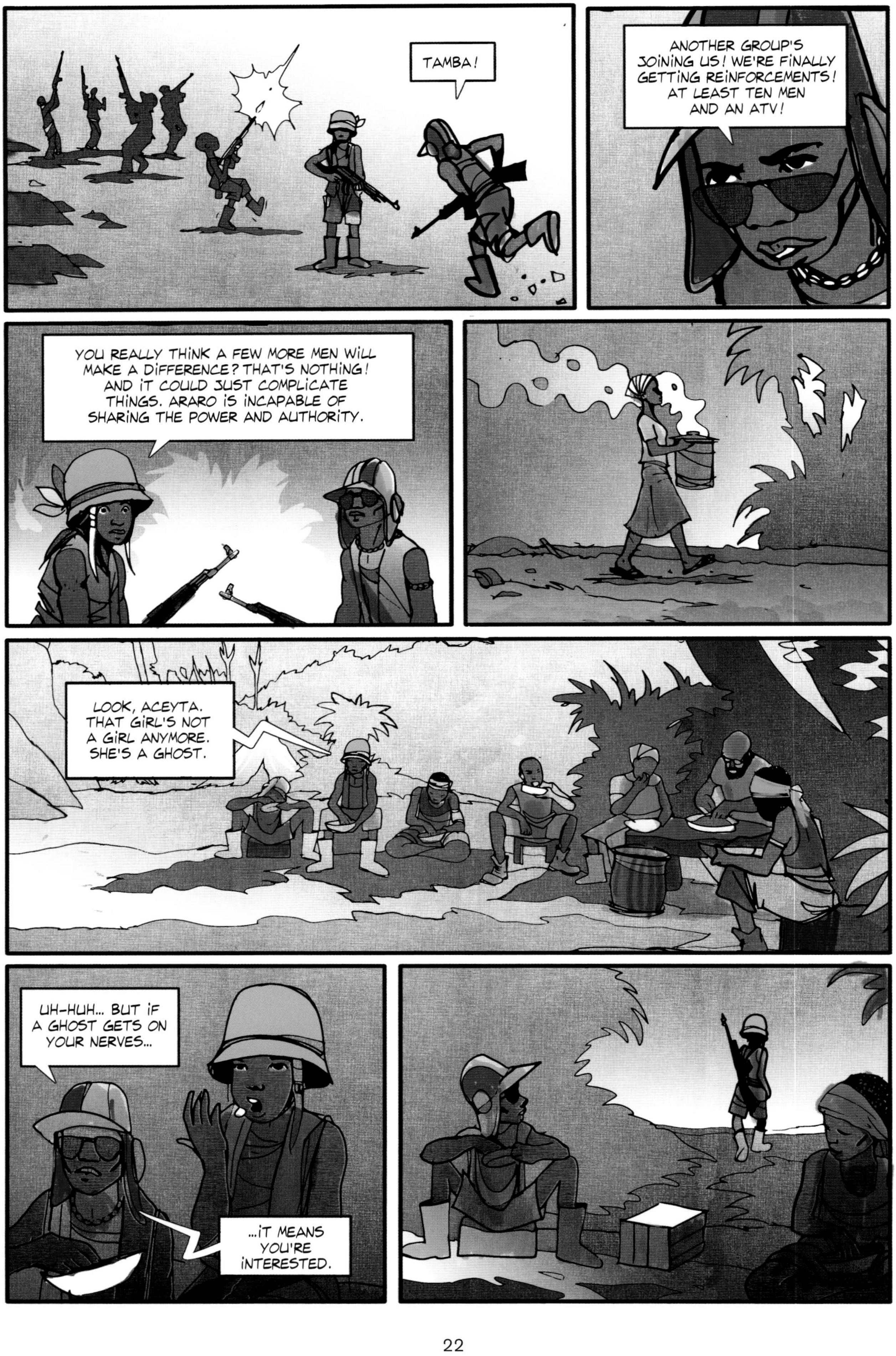
TAMBA!
ANOTHER GROUP'S JOINING US! WE'RE FINALLY GETTING REINFORCEMENTS! AT LEAST TEN MEN AND AN ATV!
YOU REALLY THINK A FEW MORE MEN WILL MAKE A DIFFERENCE? THAT'S NOTHING! AND IT COULD JUST COMPLICATE THINGS. ARARO IS INCAPABLE OF SHARING THE POWER AND AUTHORITY.
LOOK, ACEYTA. THAT GIRL'S NOT A GIRL ANYMORE. SHE'S A GHOST.
UH-HUH... BUT IF A GHOST GETS ON YOUR NERVES...
...IT MEANS YOU'RE INTERESTED.

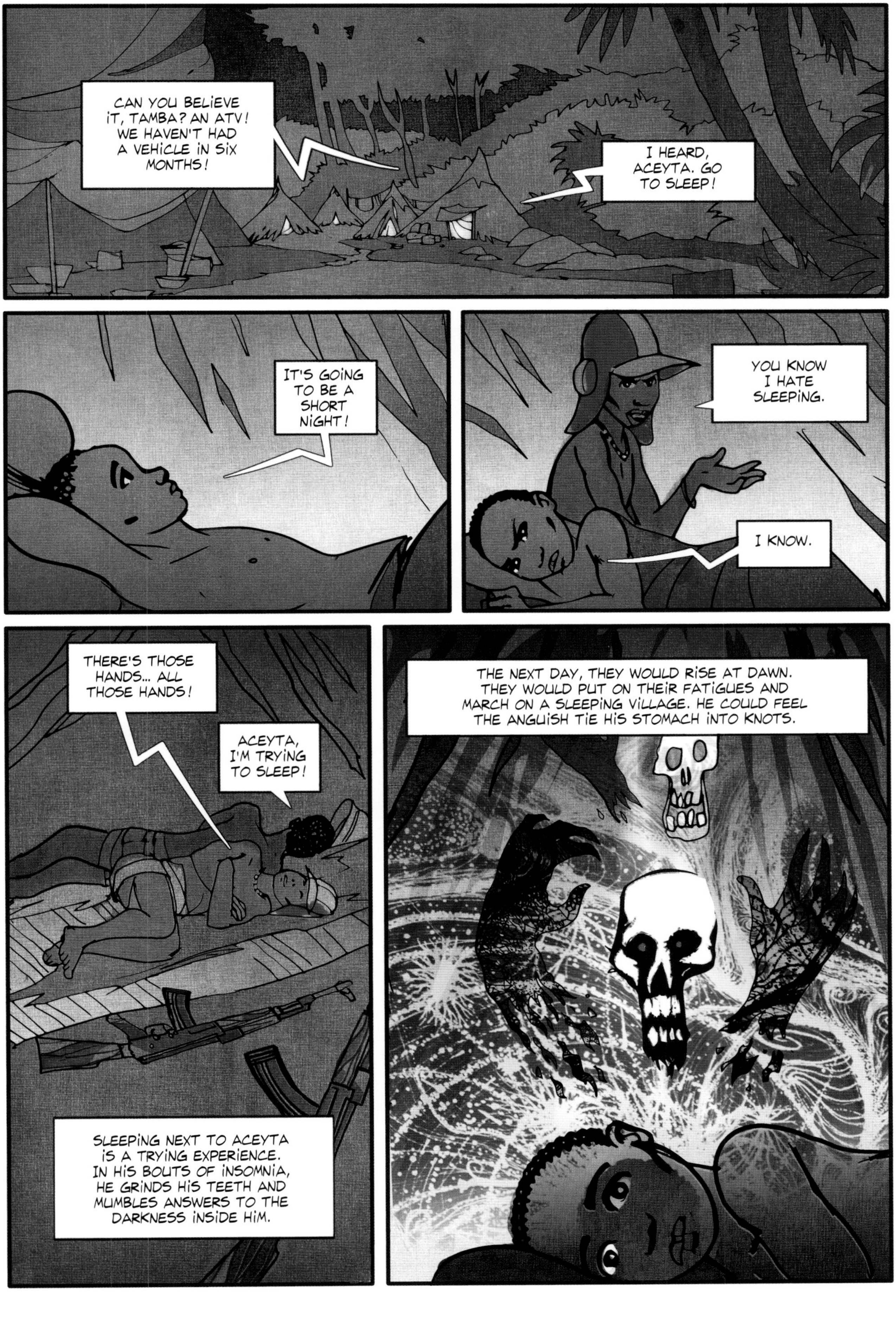
CAN YOU BELIEVE IT, TAMBA? AN ATV! WE HAVEN'T HAD A VEHICLE IN SIX MONTHS!
I HEARD, ACEYTA. GO TO SLEEP!
IT'S GOING TO BE A SHORT NIGHT!
YOU KNOW I HATE SLEEPING.
I KNOW.
THERE'S THOSE HANDS... ALL THOSE HANDS!
ACEYTA, I'M TRYING TO SLEEP!
SLEEPING NEXT TO ACEYTA IS A TRYING EXPERIENCE. IN HIS BOUTS OF INSOMNIA, HE GRINDS HIS TEETH AND MUMBLES ANSWERS TO THE DARKNESS INSIDE HIM.
THE NEXT DAY, THEY WOULD RISE AT DAWN. THEY WOULD PUT ON THEIR FATIGUES AND MARCH ON A SLEEPING VILLAGE. HE COULD FEEL THE ANGUISH TIE HIS STOMACH INTO KNOTS.

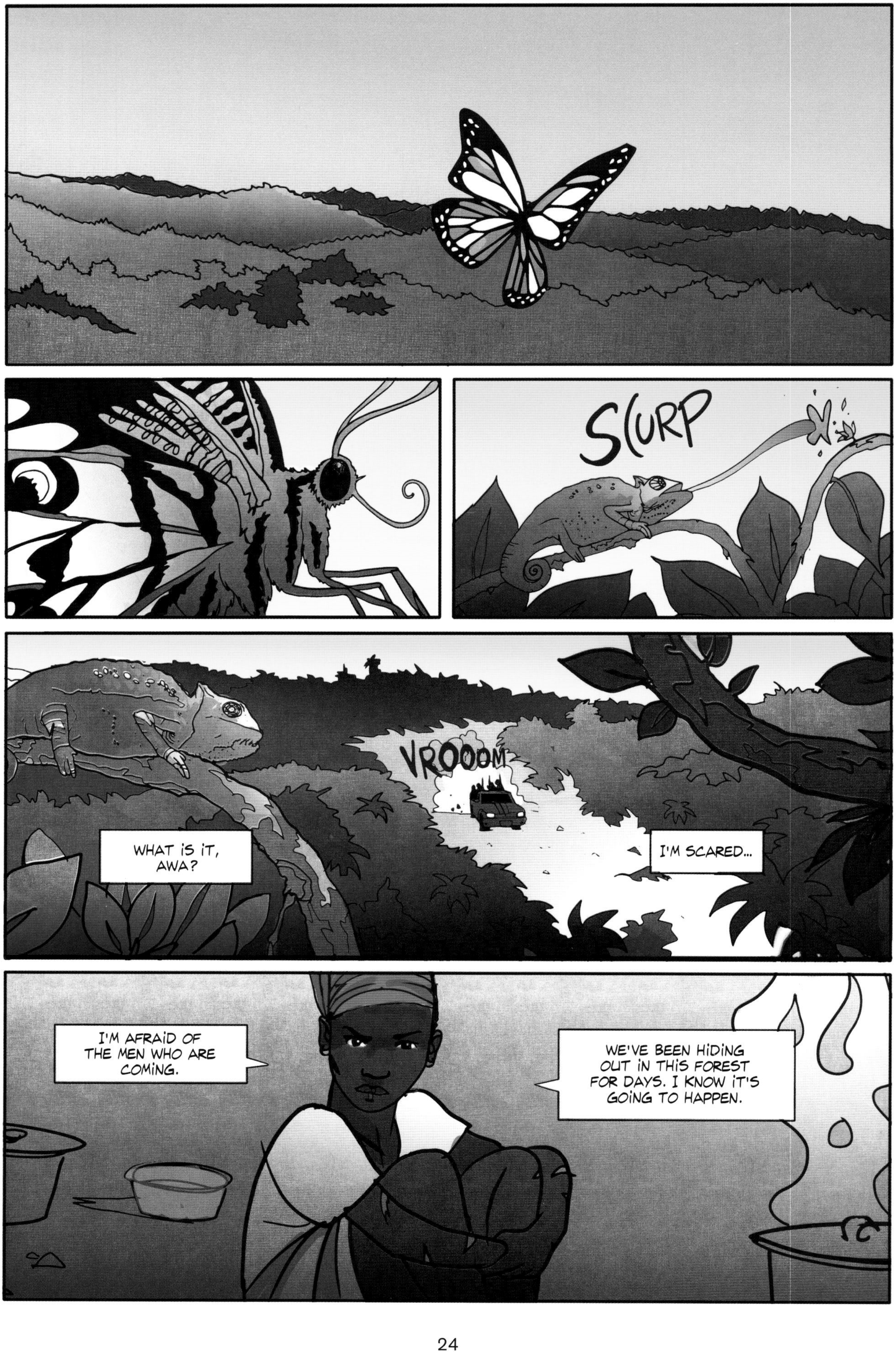
SCURP
VROOOM
WHAT IS IT, AWA?
I'M SCARED...
I'M AFRAID OF THE MEN WHO ARE COMING.
WE'VE BEEN HIDING OUT IN THIS FOREST FOR DAYS. I KNOW IT'S GOING TO HAPPEN.

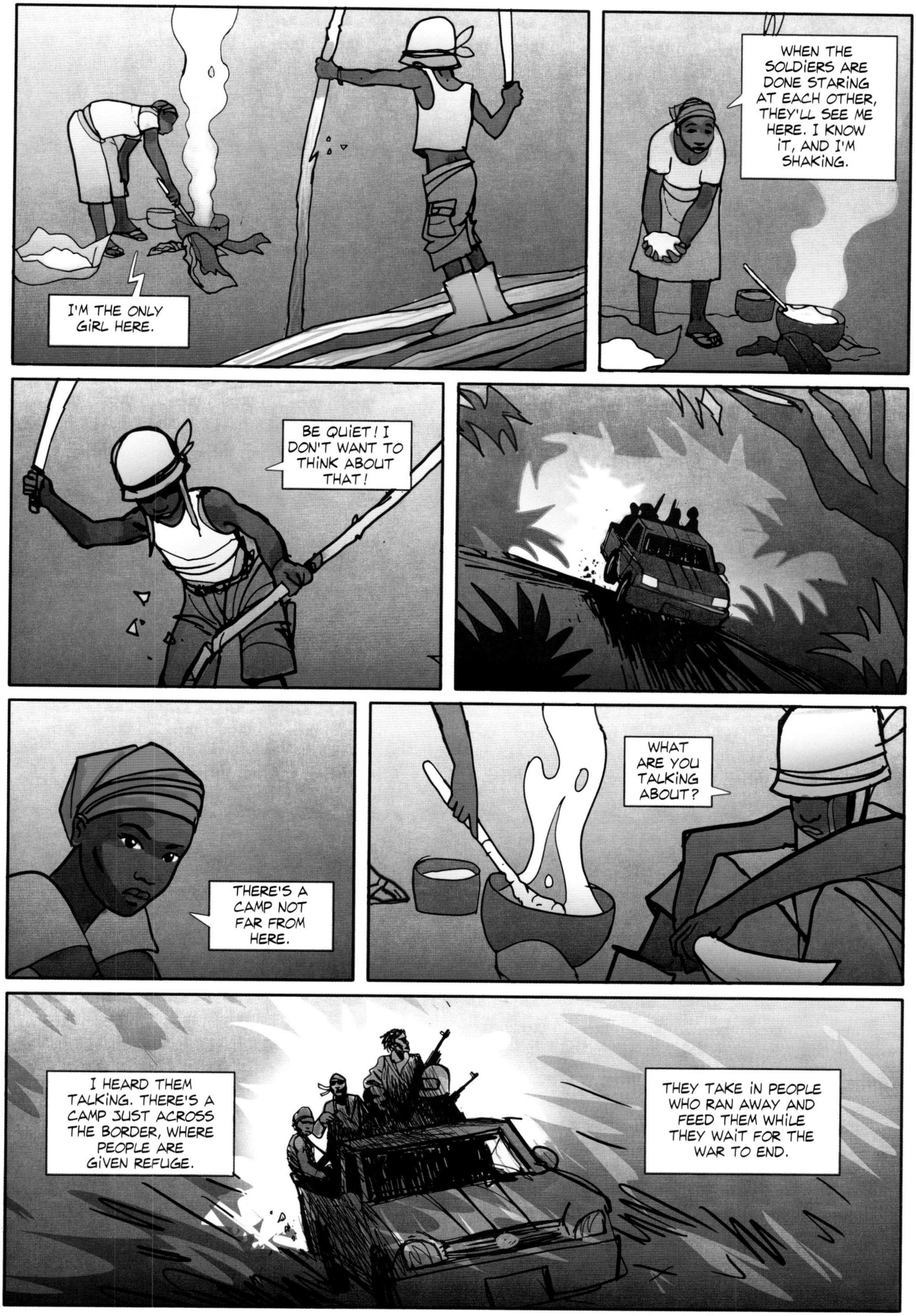
I'M THE ONLY GIRL HERE.
WHEN THE SOLDIERS ARE DONE STARING AT EACH OTHER, THEY'LL SEE ME HERE. I KNOW IT, AND I'M SHAKING.
BE QUIET! I DON'T WANT TO THINK ABOUT THAT!
THERE'S A CAMP NOT FAR FROM HERE.
WHAT ARE YOU TALKING ABOUT?
I HEARD THEM TALKING. THERE'S A CAMP JUST ACROSS THE BORDER, WHERE PEOPLE ARE GIVEN REFUGE.
THEY TAKE IN PEOPLE WHO RAN AWAY AND FEED THEM WHILE THEY WAIT FOR THE WAR TO END.

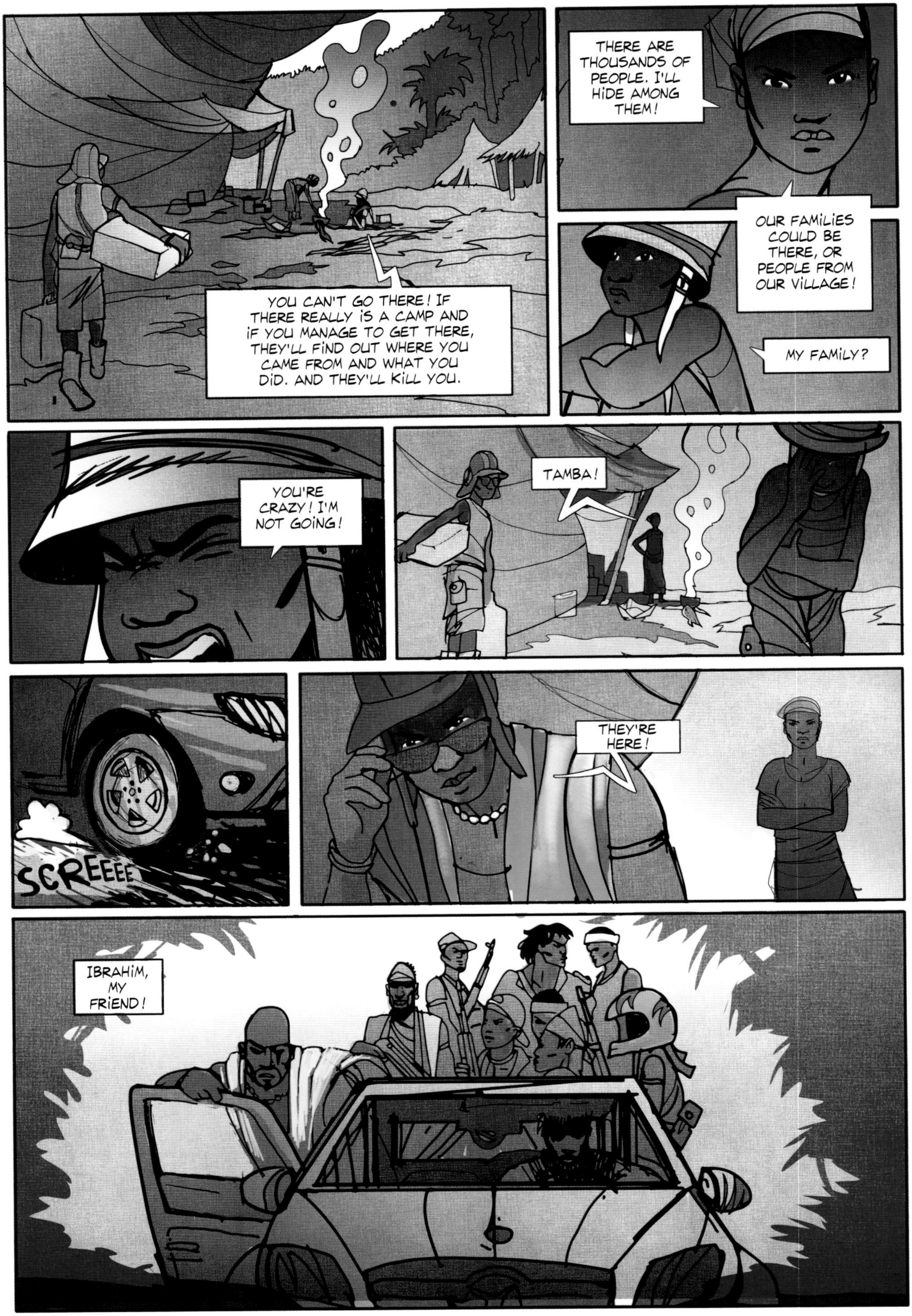
YOU CAN'T GO THERE! IF THERE REALLY IS A CAMP AND IF YOU MANAGE TO GET THERE, THEY'LL FIND OUT WHERE YOU CAME FROM AND WHAT YOU DID. AND THEY'LL KILL YOU.
THERE ARE THOUSANDS OF PEOPLE. I'LL HIDE AMONG THEM!
OUR FAMILIES COULD BE THERE, OR PEOPLE FROM OUR VILLAGE!
MY FAMILY?
YOU'RE CRAZY! I'M NOT GOING!
TAMBA!
SCREEEEE
THEY'RE HERE!
IBRAHIM, MY FRIEND!

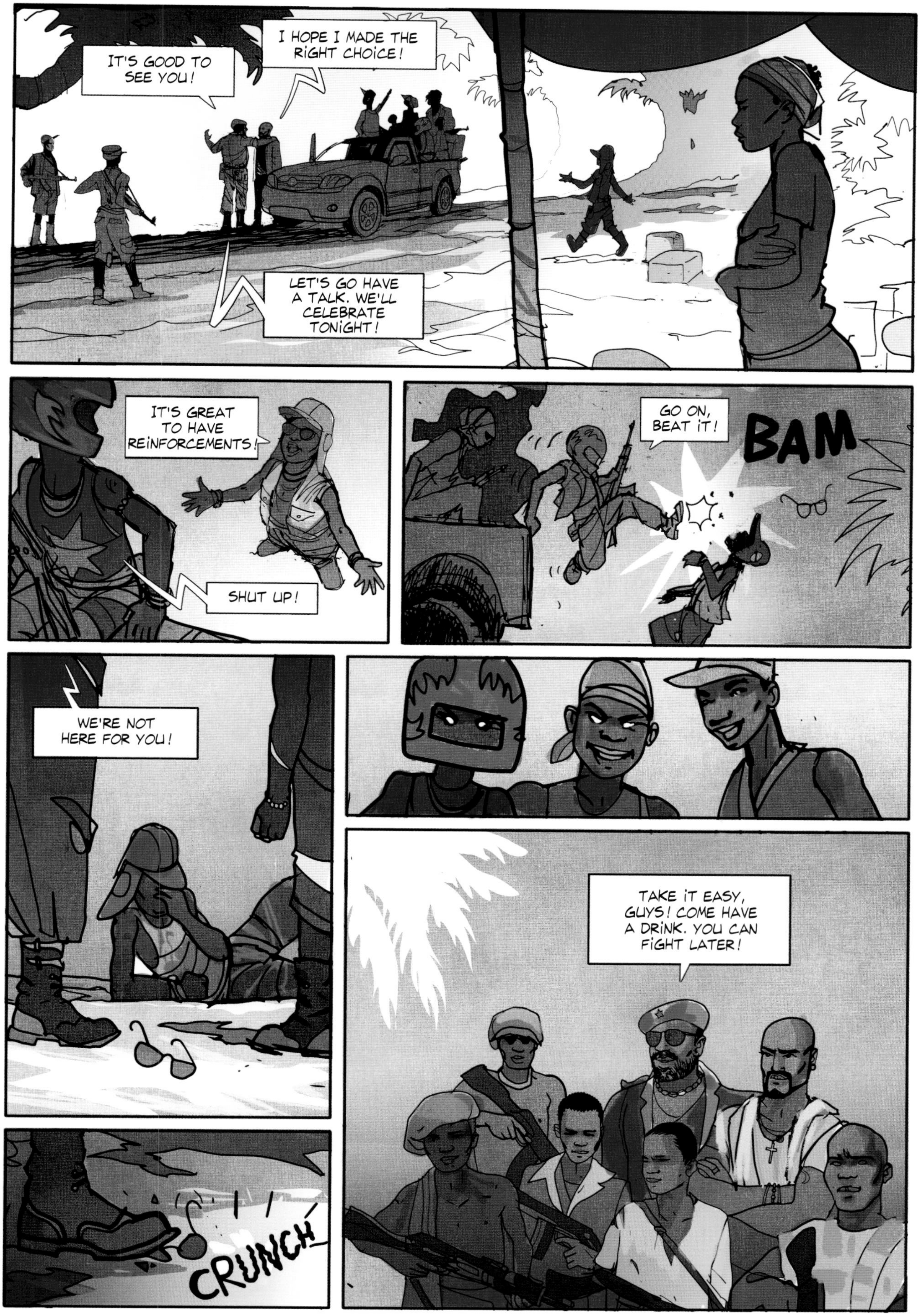

IT'S GOOD TO SEE YOU!
I HOPE I MADE THE RIGHT CHOICE!
LET'S GO HAVE A TALK. WE'LL CELEBRATE TONIGHT!
IT'S GREAT TO HAVE REINFORCEMENTS!
SHUT UP!
GO ON, BEAT IT!
BAM
WE'RE NOT HERE FOR YOU!
CRUNCH
TAKE IT EASY, GUYS! COME HAVE A DRINK. YOU CAN FIGHT LATER!

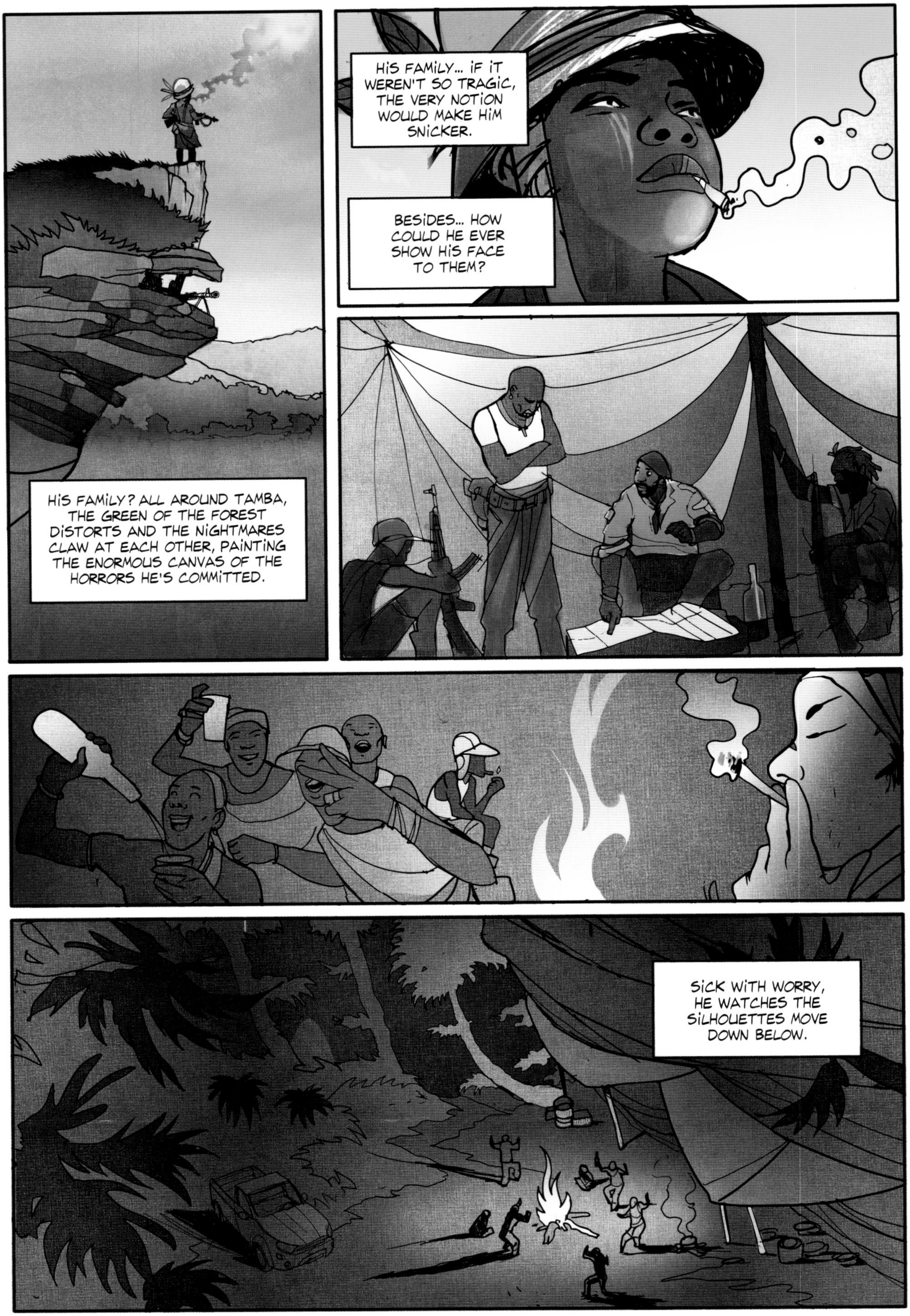
HIS FAMILY... IF IT WEREN'T SO TRAGIC, THE VERY NOTION WOULD MAKE HIM SNICKER.
BESIDES... HOW COULD HE EVER SHOW HIS FACE TO THEM?
HIS FAMILY? ALL AROUND TAMBA, THE GREEN OF THE FOREST DISTORTS AND THE NIGHTMARES CLAW AT EACH OTHER, PAINTING THE ENORMOUS CANVAS OF THE HORRORS HE'S COMMITTED.
SICK WITH WORRY, HE WATCHES THE SILHOUETTES MOVE DOWN BELOW.

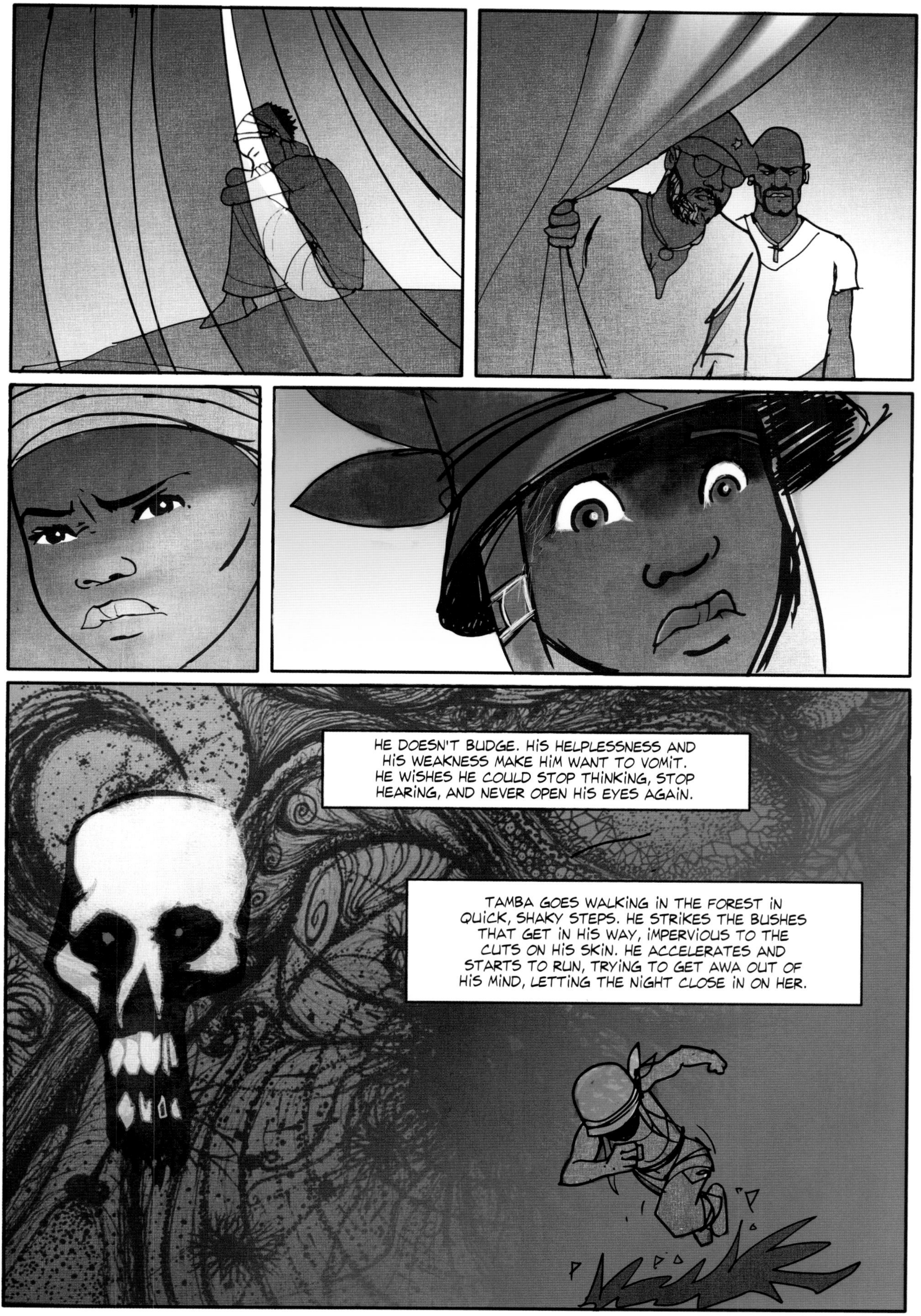
HE DOESN'T BUDGE. HIS HELPLESSNESS AND HIS WEAKNESS MAKE HIM WANT TO VOMIT. HE WISHES HE COULD STOP THINKING, STOP HEARING, AND NEVER OPEN HIS EYES AGAIN.
TAMBA GOES WALKING IN THE FOREST IN QUICK, SHAKY STEPS. HE STRIKES THE BUSHES THAT GET IN HIS WAY, IMPERVIOUS TO THE CUTS ON HIS SKIN. HE ACCELERATES AND STARTS TO RUN, TRYING TO GET AWA OUT OF HIS MIND, LETTING THE NIGHT CLOSE IN ON HER.

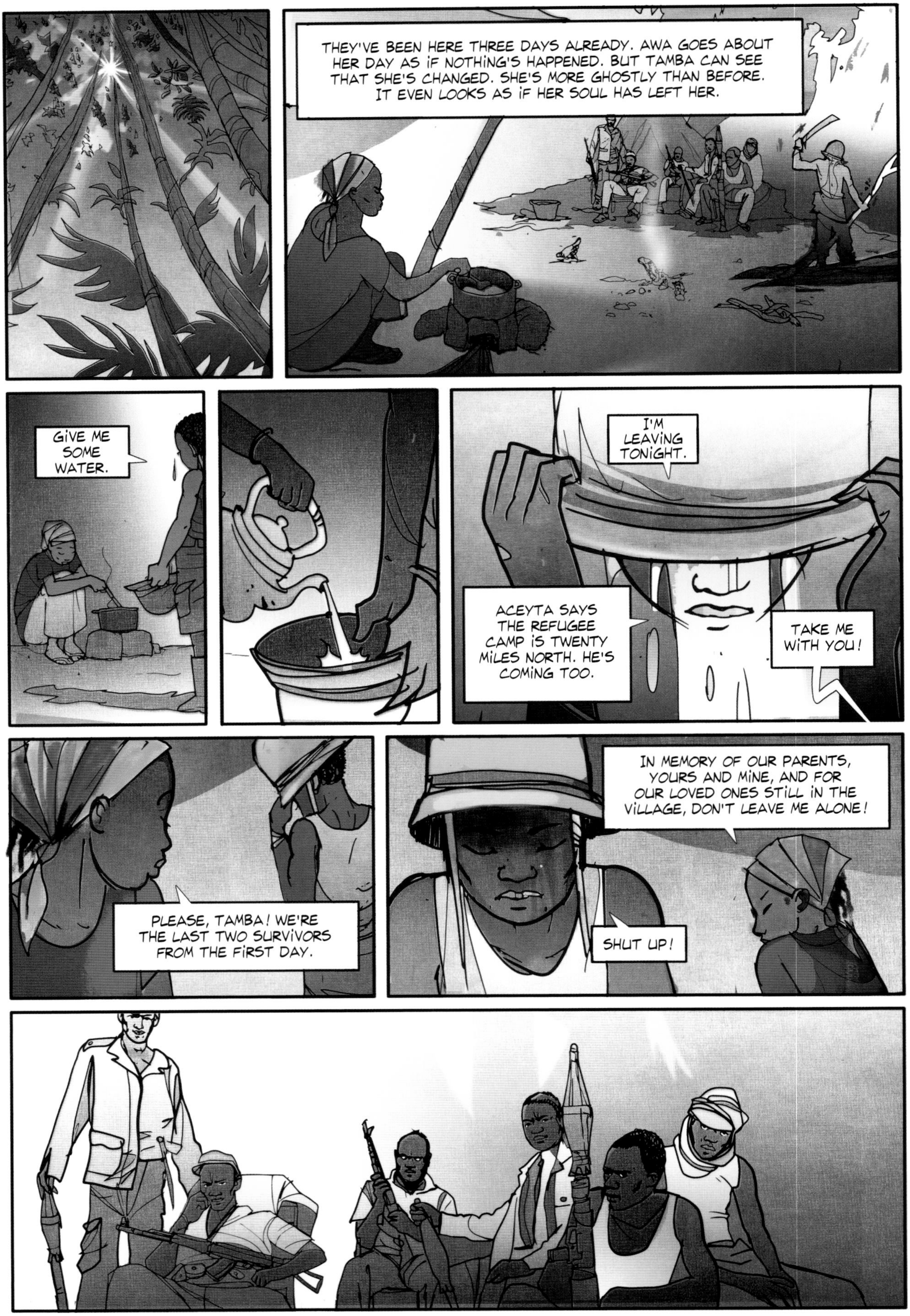
THEY'VE BEEN HERE THREE DAYS ALREADY. AWA GOES ABOUT HER DAY AS IF NOTHING'S HAPPENED. BUT TAMBA CAN SEE THAT SHE'S CHANGED. SHE'S MORE GHOSTLY THAN BEFORE. IT EVEN LOOKS AS IF HER SOUL HAS LEFT HER.
GIVE ME SOME WATER.
I'M LEAVING TONIGHT.
ACEYTA SAYS THE REFUGEE CAMP IS TWENTY MILES NORTH. HE'S COMING TOO.
TAKE ME WITH YOU!
PLEASE, TAMBA! WE'RE THE LAST TWO SURVIVORS FROM THE FIRST DAY.
IN MEMORY OF OUR PARENTS, YOURS AND MINE, AND FOR OUR LOVED ONES STILL IN THE VILLAGE, DON'T LEAVE ME ALONE!
SHUT UP!

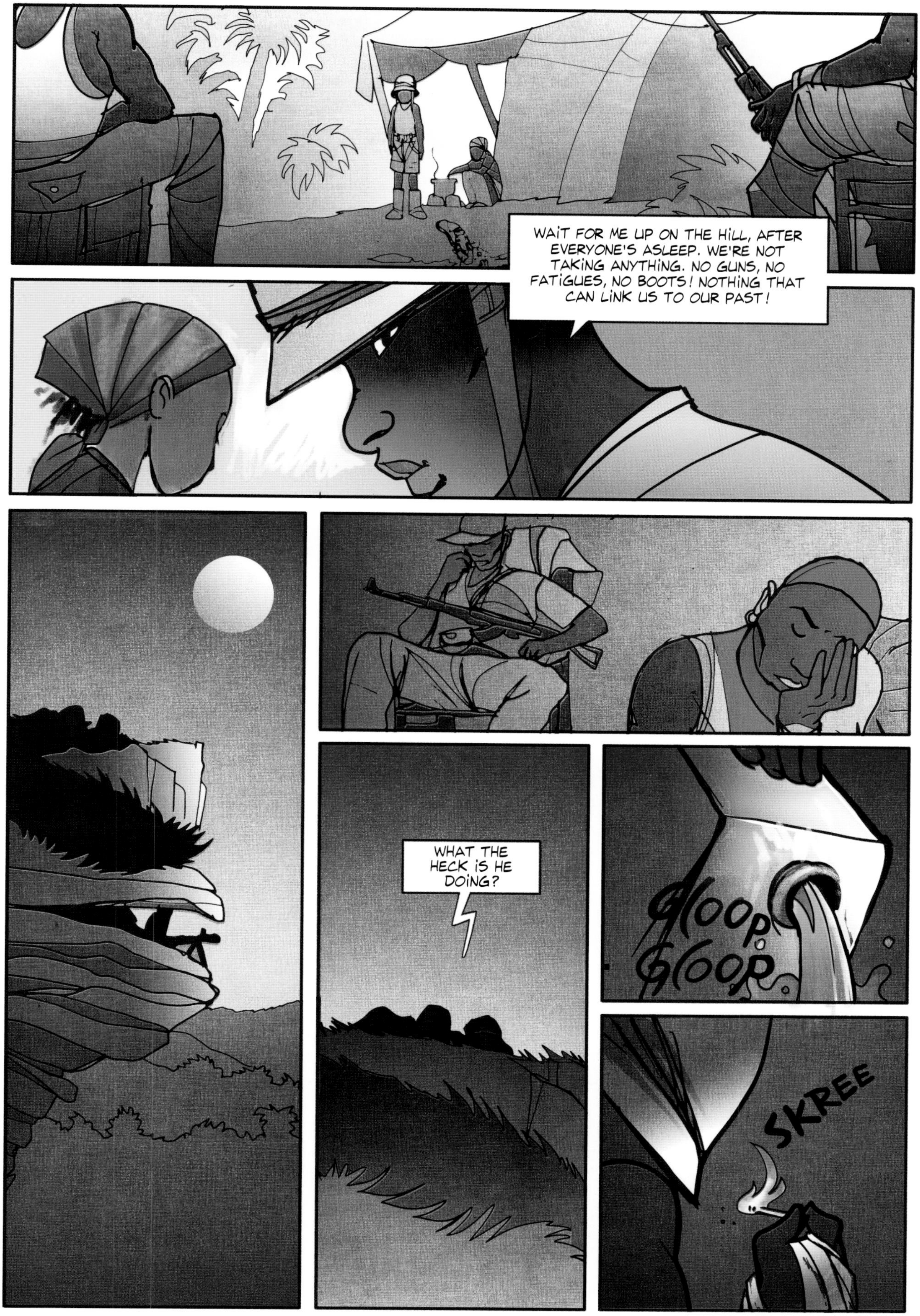
WAIT FOR ME UP ON THE HILL, AFTER EVERYONE'S ASLEEP. WE'RE NOT TAKING ANYTHING. NO GUNS, NO FATIGUES, NO BOOTS! NOTHING THAT CAN LINK US TO OUR PAST!
WHAT THE HECK IS HE DOING?
GLOOP GLOOP
SKREE

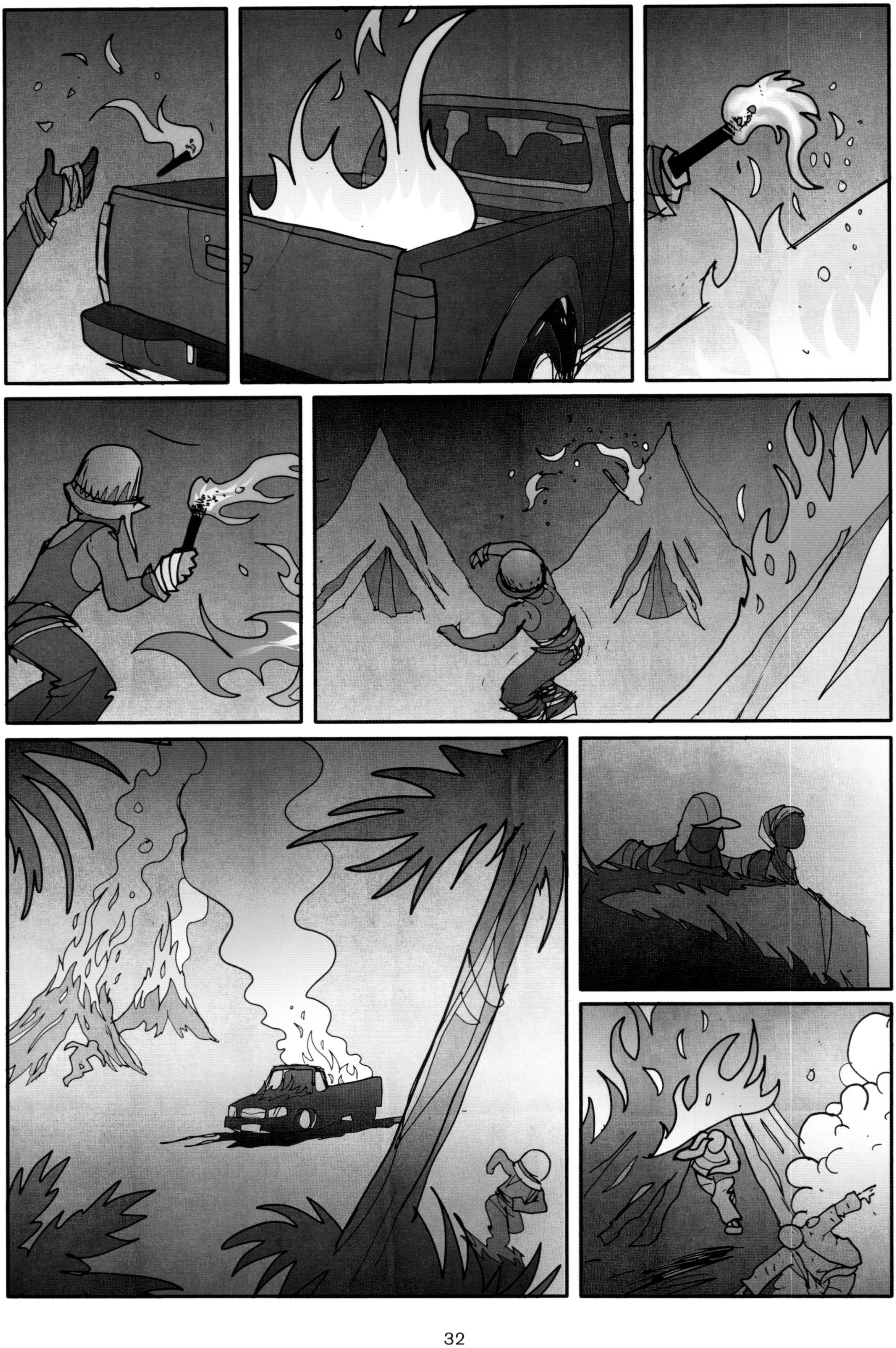

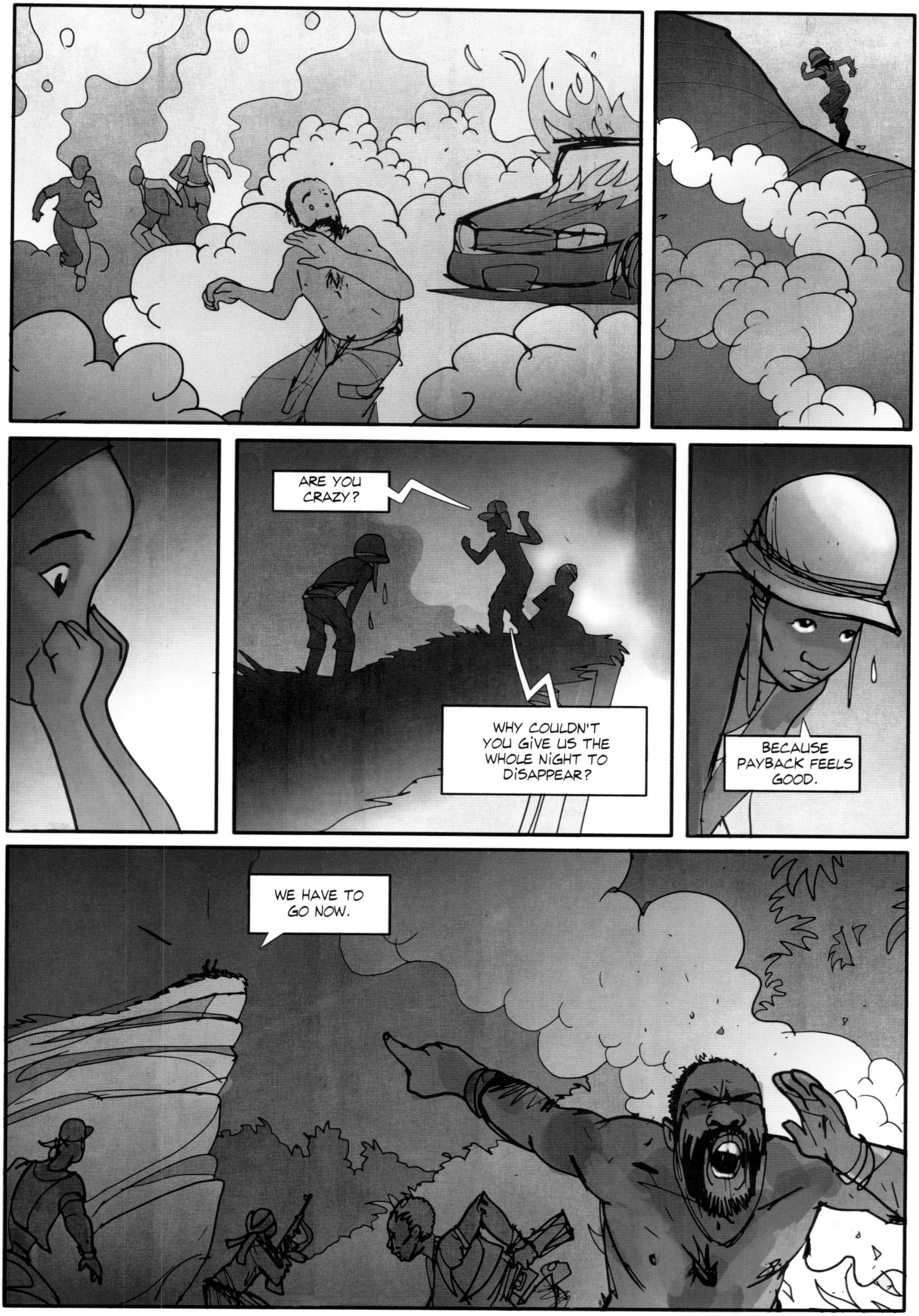
ARE YOU CRAZY?
WHY COULDN'T YOU GIVE US THE WHOLE NIGHT TO DISAPPEAR?
BECAUSE PAYBACK FEELS GOOD.
WE HAVE TO GO NOW.

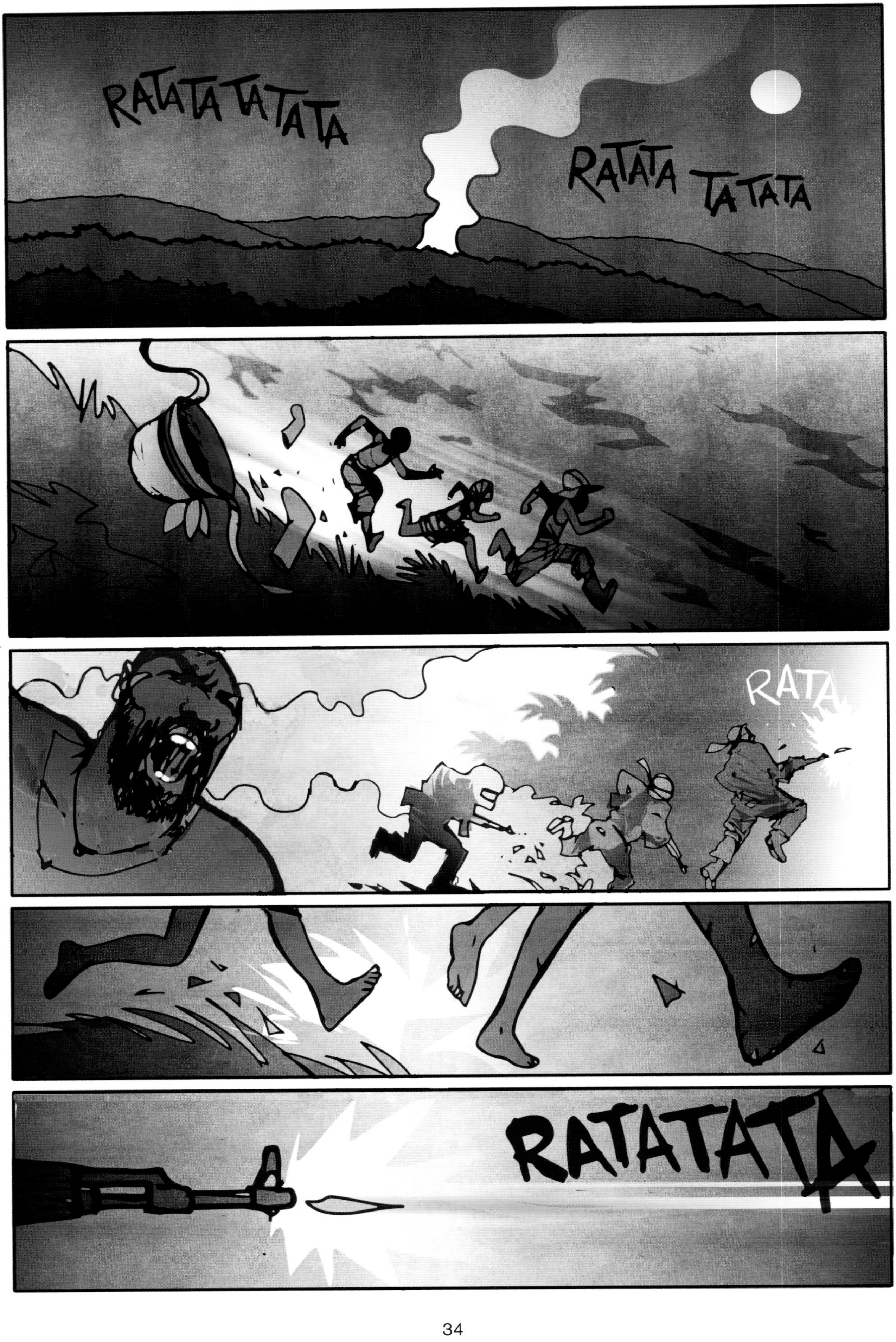
RATATA TATATA
RATATA TATATA
RATA
RATATATA

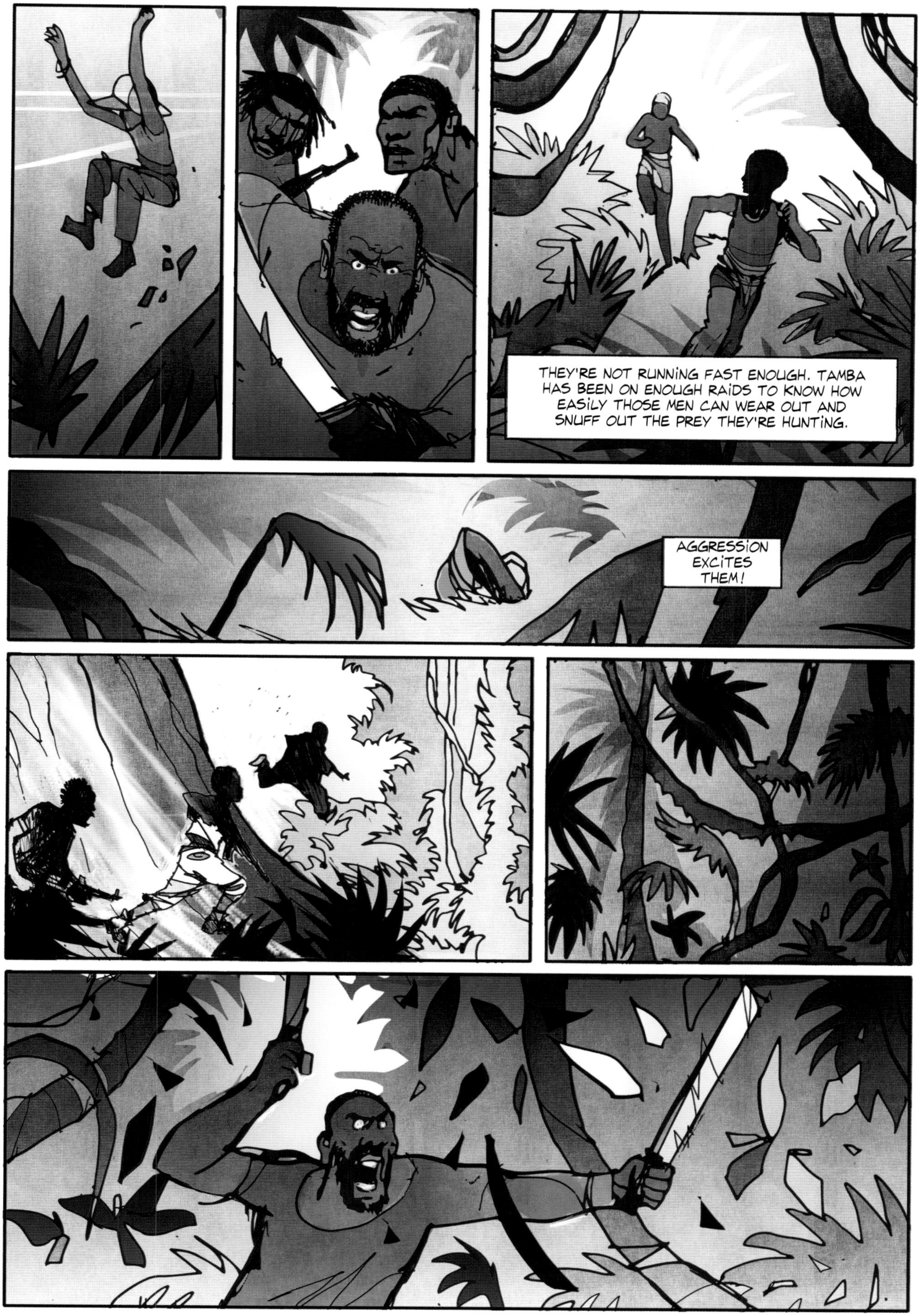
THEY'RE NOT RUNNING FAST ENOUGH. TAMBA HAS BEEN ON ENOUGH RAIDS TO KNOW HOW EASILY THOSE MEN CAN WEAR OUT AND SNUFF OUT THE PREY THEY'RE HUNTING.
AGGRESSION EXCITES THEM!

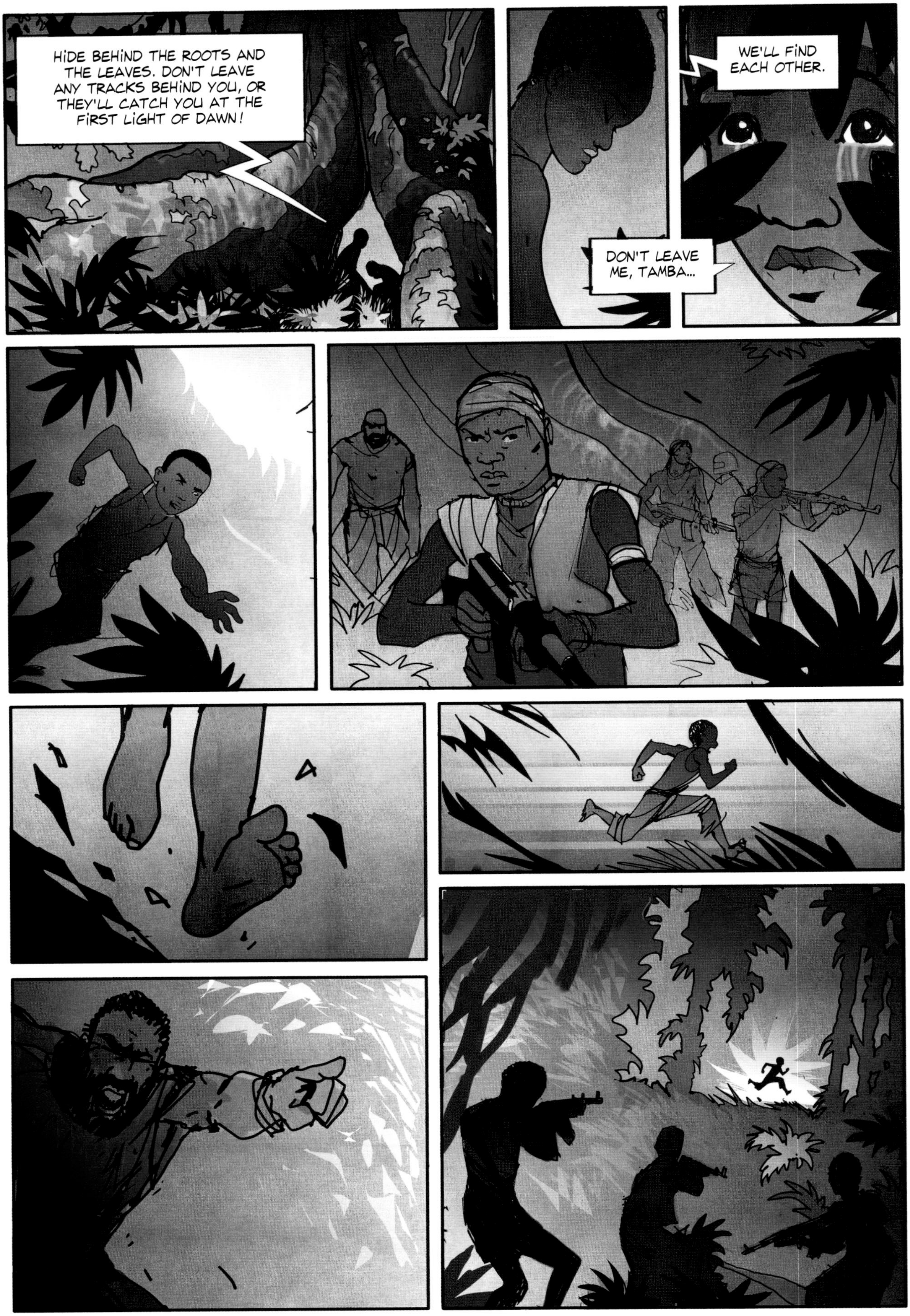
HIDE BEHIND THE ROOTS AND THE LEAVES. DON'T LEAVE ANY TRACKS BEHIND YOU, OR THEY'LL CATCH YOU AT THE FIRST LIGHT OF DAWN!
WE'LL FIND EACH OTHER.
DON'T LEAVE ME, TAMBA...

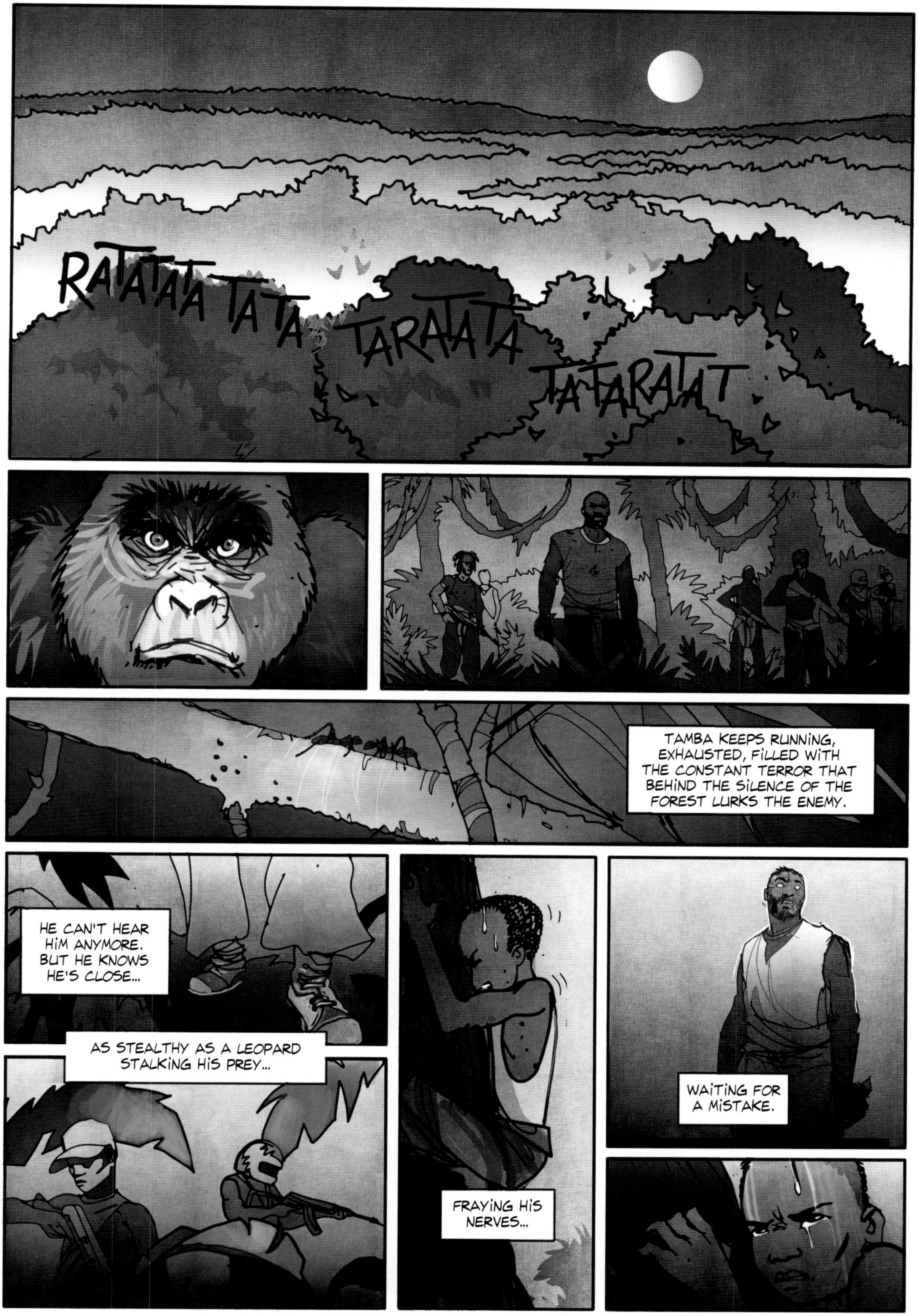
RATATATA TATA TARATATA TATARATAT
TAMBA KEEPS RUNNING, EXHAUSTED, FILLED WITH THE CONSTANT TERROR THAT BEHIND THE SILENCE OF THE FOREST LURKS THE ENEMY.
HE CAN'T HEAR HIM ANYMORE. BUT HE KNOWS HE'S CLOSE...
AS STEALTHY AS A LEOPARD STALKING HIS PREY...
FRAYING HIS NERVES...
WAITING FOR A MISTAKE.

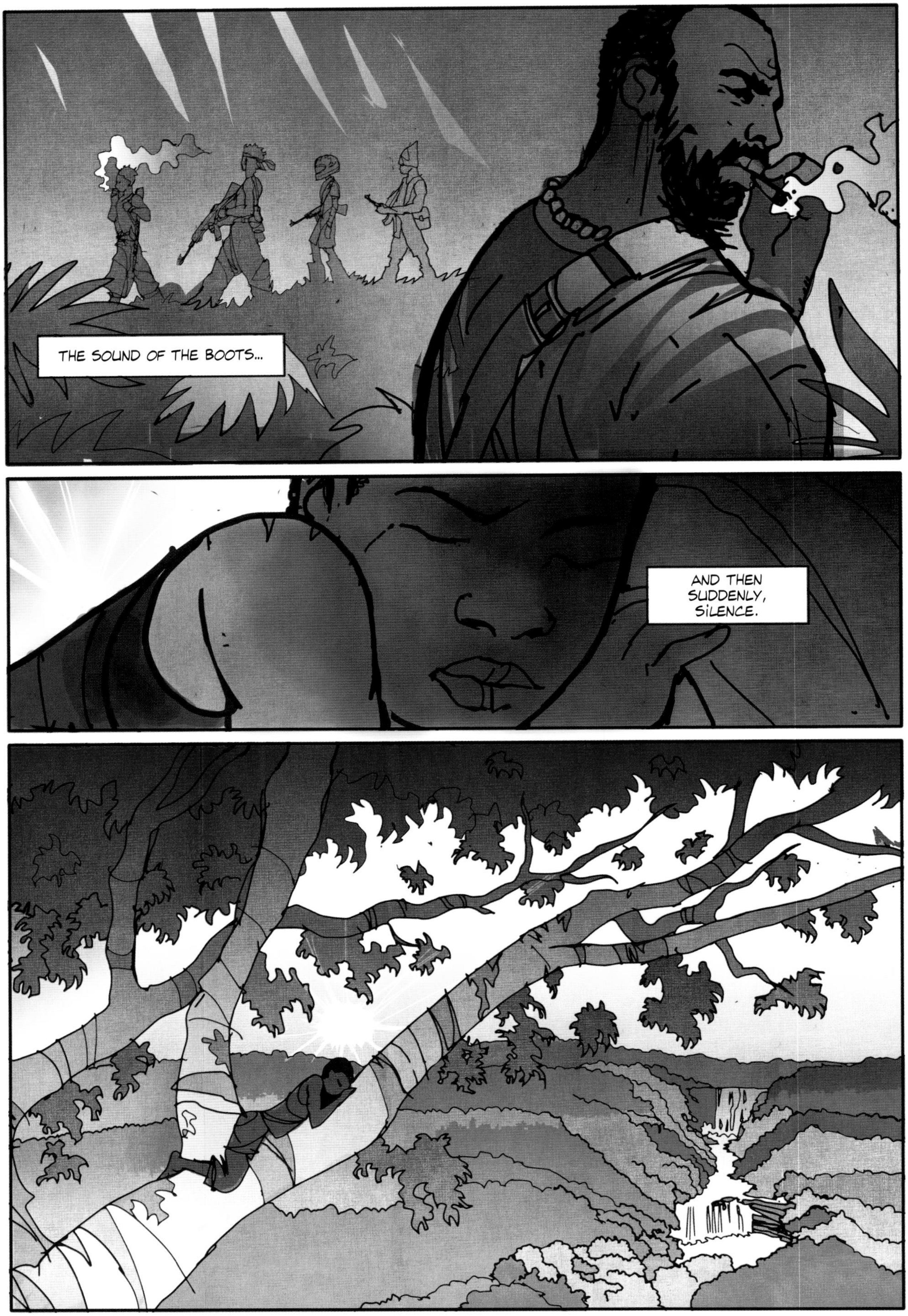
THE SOUND OF THE BOOTS...
AND THEN SUDDENLY, SiLENCE.

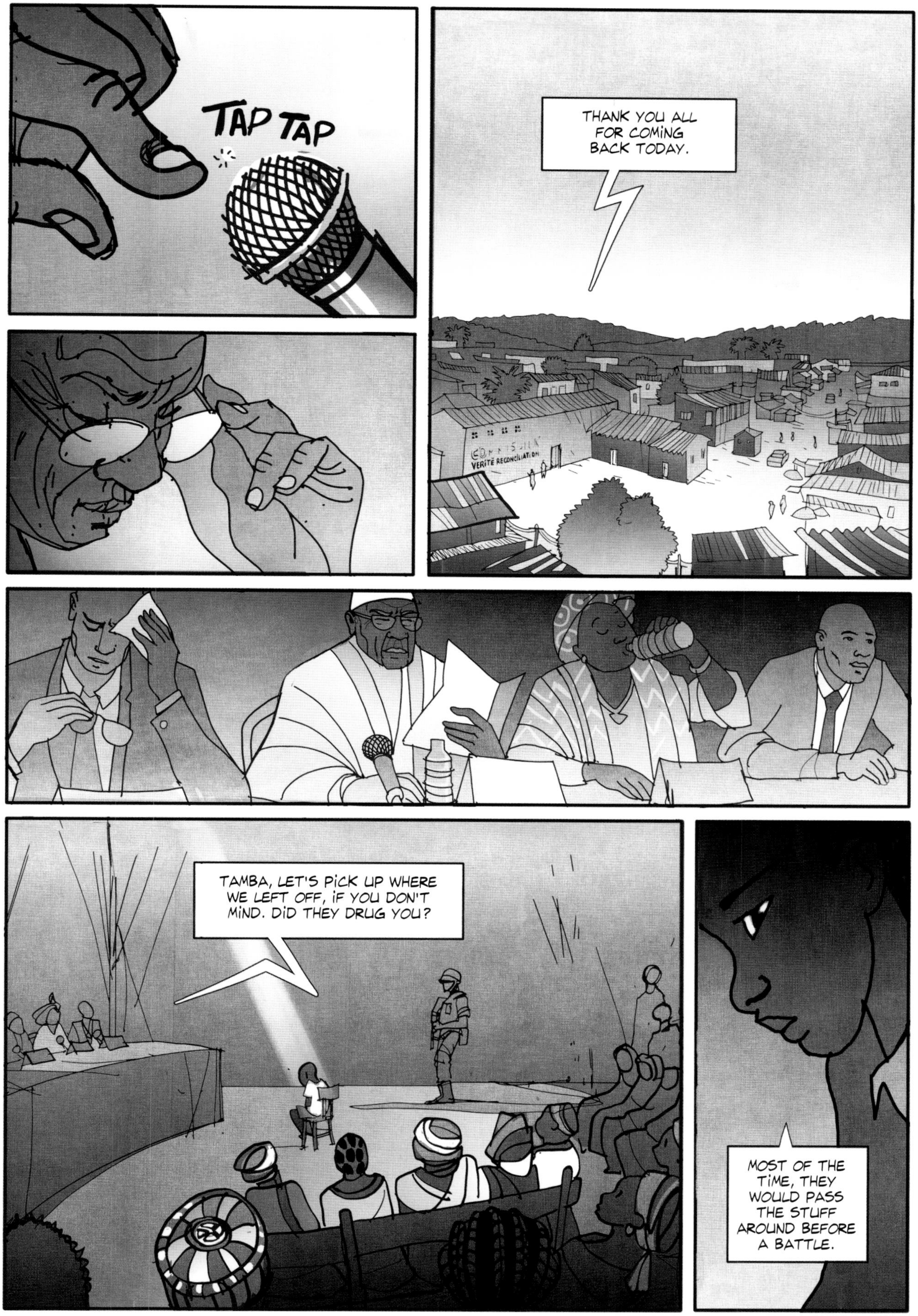
TAP TAP
THANK YOU ALL FOR COMING BACK TODAY.
COMMISSION VERITÉ RECONCILIATION
TAMBA, LET'S PICK UP WHERE WE LEFT OFF, IF YOU DON'T MIND. DID THEY DRUG YOU?
MOST OF THE TIME, THEY WOULD PASS THE STUFF AROUND BEFORE A BATTLE.

PILLS AND SYRINGES OF BUBBLE. IT GAVE US STRENGTH AND COURAGE.

ONE OF THE SOLDIERS WAS THE SELF-APPOINTED NURSE. WE CALLED HIM "HEALER." THAT WAS HIS WAR NAME.

THOSE GOING ON AN EXPEDITION WOULD GET AN INJECTION.

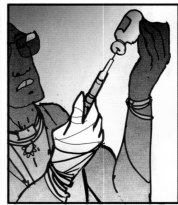

AFTER EVERY THREE SHOTS, HEALER WOULD DIP THE SYRINGE IN A LITTLE BOWL TO STERILIZE IT.

YOU KNOW, WHEN YOU TAKE THAT STUFF, YOU GET THIS INCREDIBLE FEELING OF POWER. YOU FEEL LIKE YOU CAN DO ANYTHING... DESTROY EVERYTHING!

BUT THEN, WHEN THE EFFECT WEARS OFF, AND YOU REALIZE WHAT YOU DID... THE REALITY OF IT... IS UNBEARABLE.

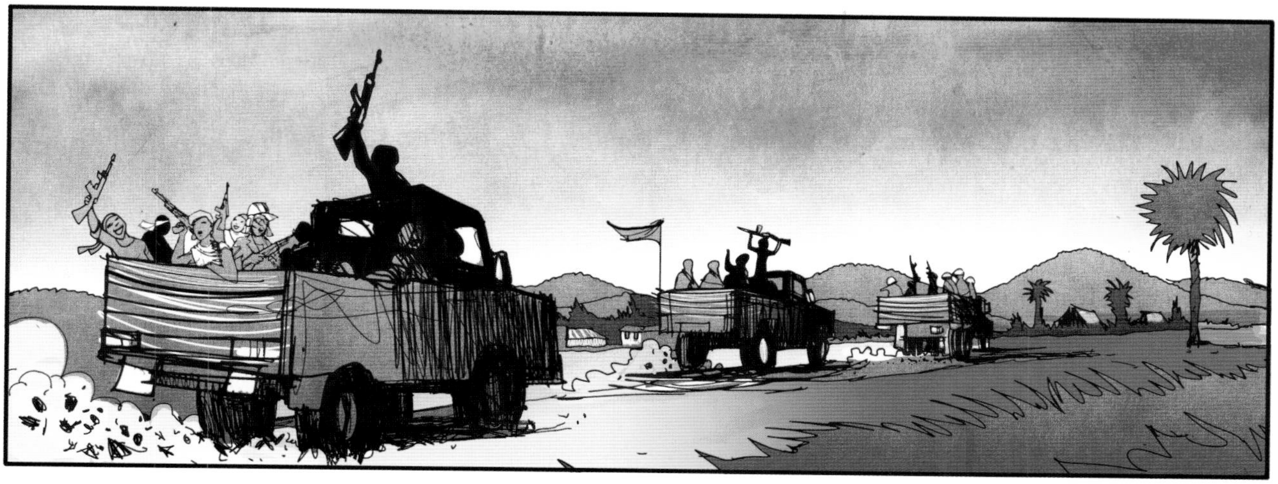

ON EACH EXPEDITION, WE'D GET IN THE BACK IN THE TRUCK AND SING, AND OUR VOICES RANG OUT OVER THE CAMPSITE. AND WE CLAPPED OUR HANDS FOR MOTIVATION.

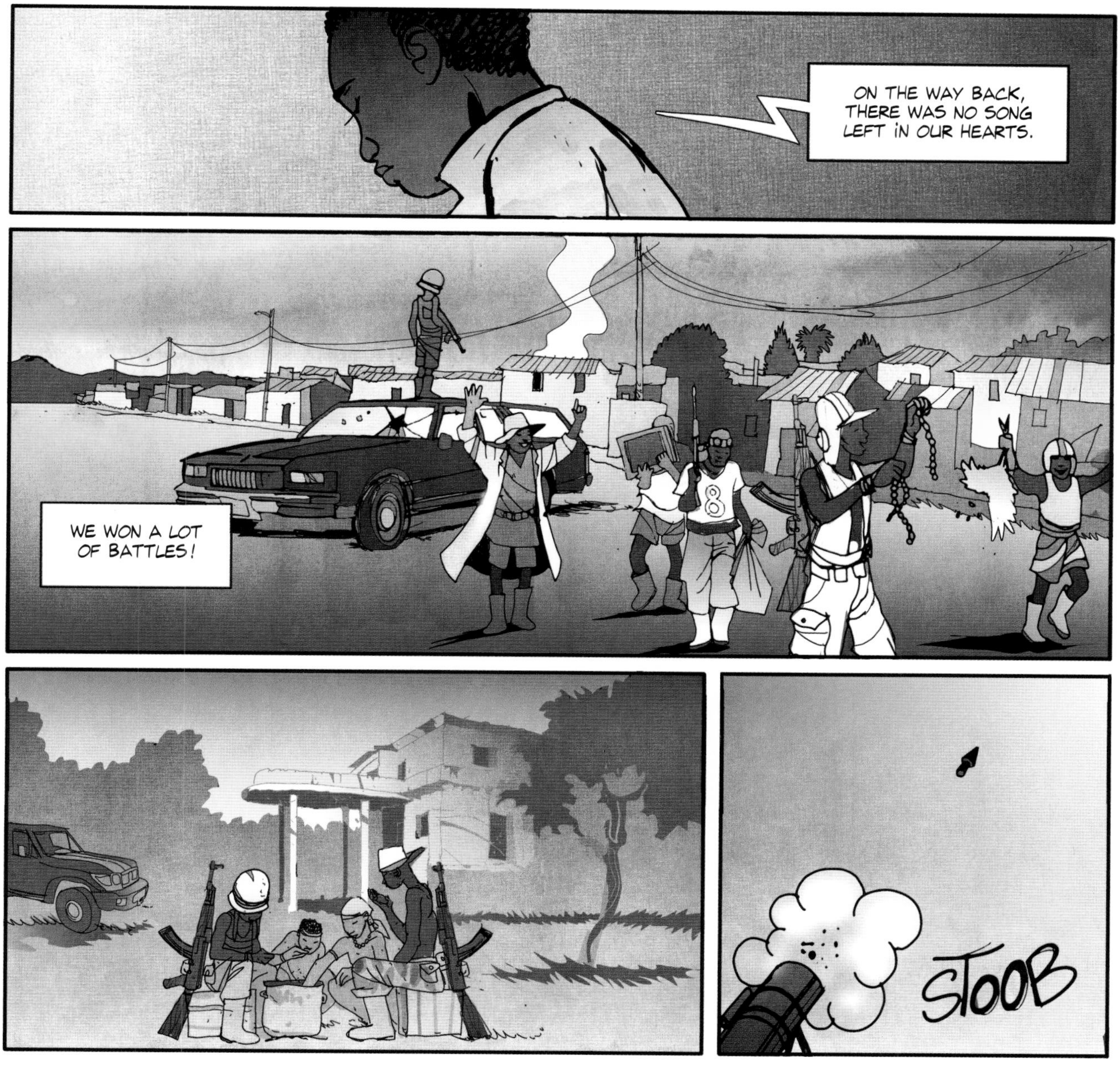
ON THE WAY BACK, THERE WAS NO SONG LEFT IN OUR HEARTS.
WE WON A LOT OF BATTLES!
STOOB

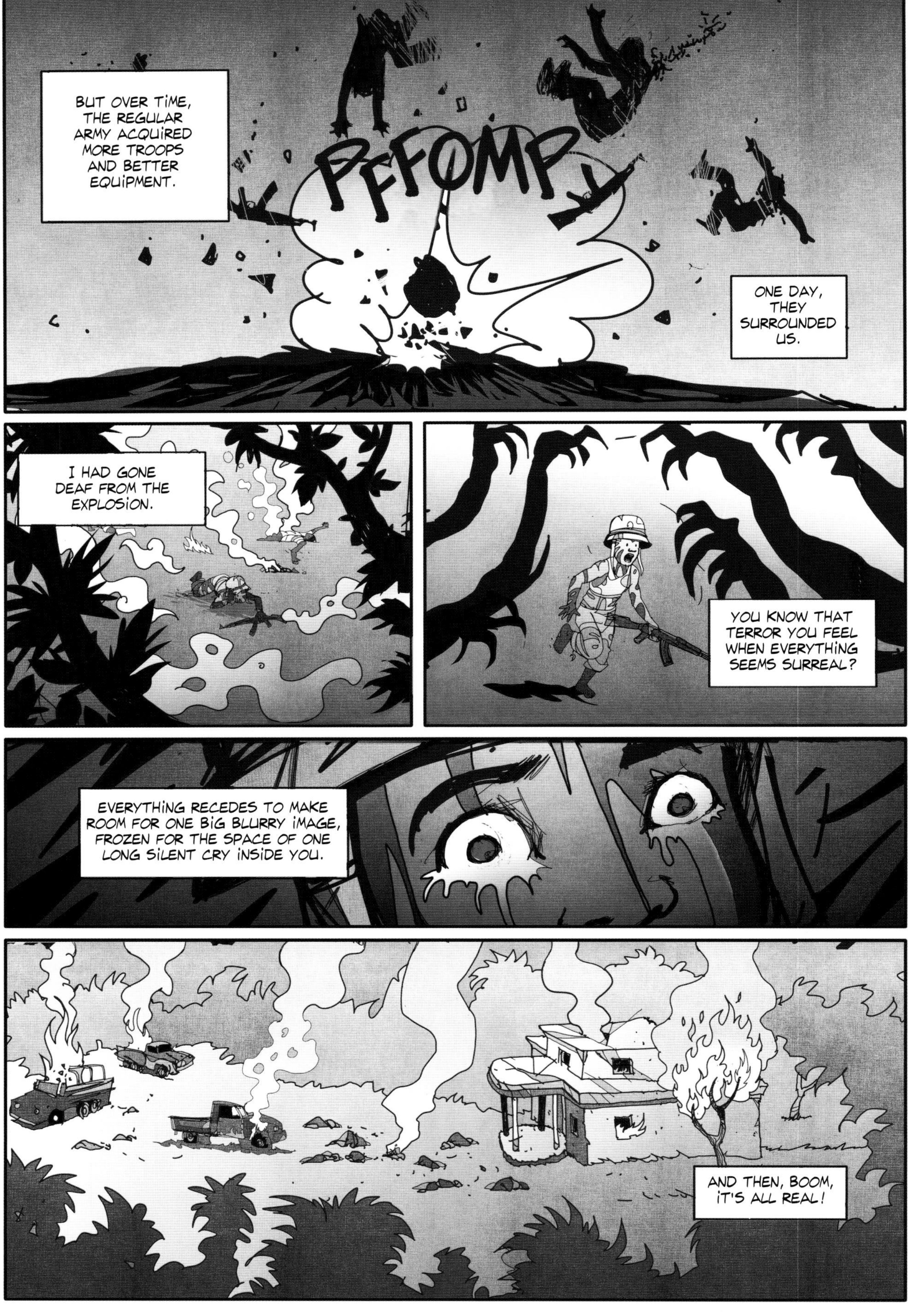
BUT OVER TIME, THE REGULAR ARMY ACQUIRED MORE TROOPS AND BETTER EQUIPMENT.
PFFOMP
ONE DAY, THEY SURROUNDED US.
I HAD GONE DEAF FROM THE EXPLOSION.
YOU KNOW THAT TERROR YOU FEEL WHEN EVERYTHING SEEMS SURREAL?
EVERYTHING RECEDES TO MAKE ROOM FOR ONE BIG BLURRY IMAGE, FROZEN FOR THE SPACE OF ONE LONG SILENT CRY INSIDE YOU.
AND THEN, BOOM, IT'S ALL REAL!

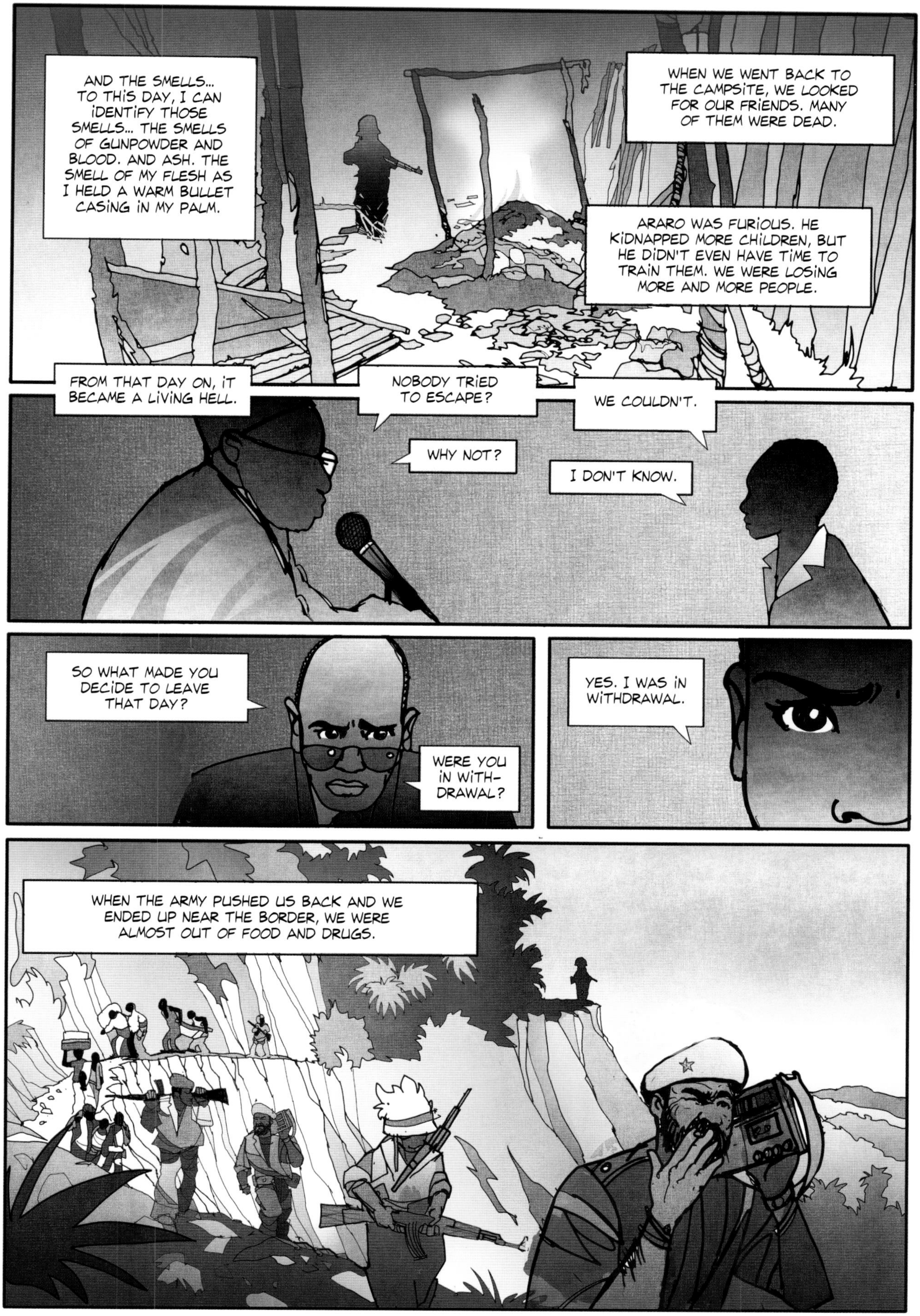
AND THE SMELLS... TO THIS DAY, I CAN IDENTIFY THOSE SMELLS... THE SMELLS OF GUNPOWDER AND BLOOD. AND ASH. THE SMELL OF MY FLESH AS I HELD A WARM BULLET CASING IN MY PALM.
WHEN WE WENT BACK TO THE CAMPSITE, WE LOOKED FOR OUR FRIENDS. MANY OF THEM WERE DEAD.
ARARO WAS FURIOUS. HE KIDNAPPED MORE CHILDREN, BUT HE DIDN'T EVEN HAVE TIME TO TRAIN THEM. WE WERE LOSING MORE AND MORE PEOPLE.
FROM THAT DAY ON, IT BECAME A LIVING HELL.
NOBODY TRIED TO ESCAPE?
WE COULDN'T.
WHY NOT?
I DON'T KNOW.
SO WHAT MADE YOU DECIDE TO LEAVE THAT DAY?
WERE YOU IN WITH-DRAWAL?
YES. I WAS IN WITHDRAWAL.
WHEN THE ARMY PUSHED US BACK AND WE ENDED UP NEAR THE BORDER, WE WERE ALMOST OUT OF FOOD AND DRUGS.

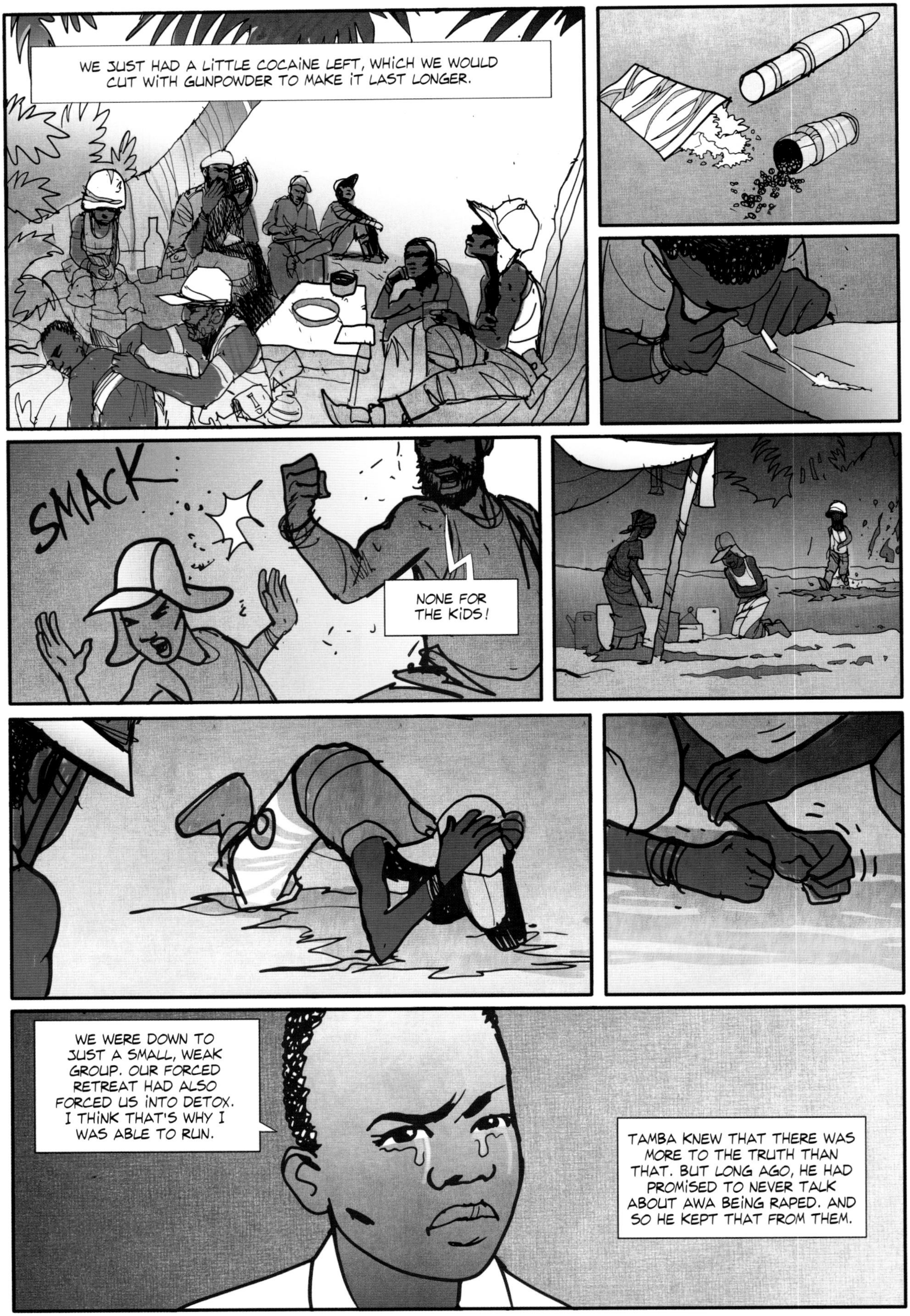
WE JUST HAD A LITTLE COCAINE LEFT, WHICH WE WOULD CUT WITH GUNPOWDER TO MAKE IT LAST LONGER.
SMACK
NONE FOR THE KIDS!
WE WERE DOWN TO JUST A SMALL, WEAK GROUP. OUR FORCED RETREAT HAD ALSO FORCED US INTO DETOX. I THINK THAT'S WHY I WAS ABLE TO RUN.
TAMBA KNEW THAT THERE WAS MORE TO THE TRUTH THAN THAT. BUT LONG AGO, HE HAD PROMISED TO NEVER TALK ABOUT AWA BEING RAPED. AND SO HE KEPT THAT FROM THEM.

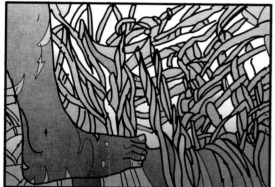

SO AWA WAS RIGHT.

THE CAMP WAS THERE. RIGHT IN FRONT OF HIM.

LIFE. WITHIN REACH.

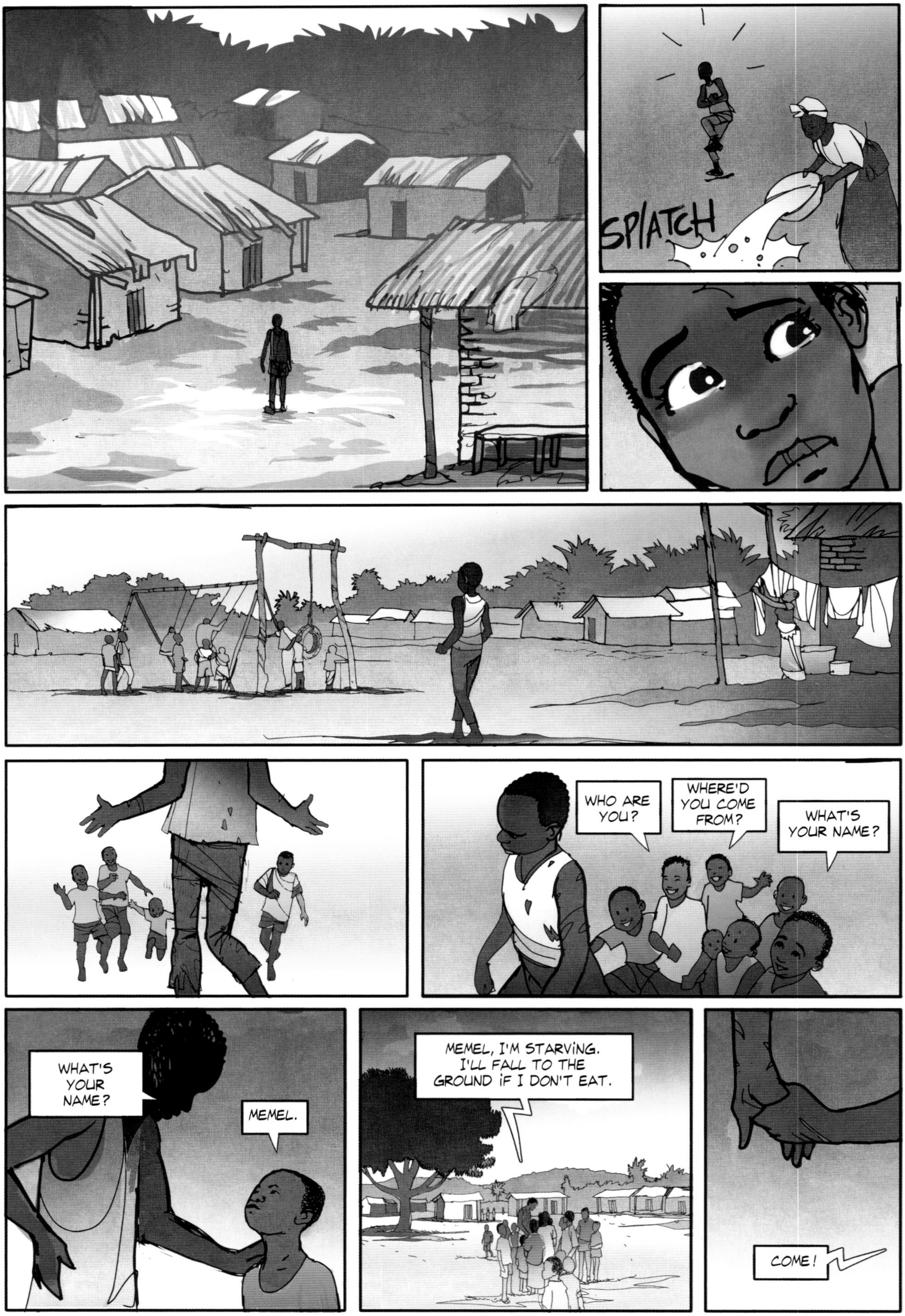
SPlATCH
WHO ARE YOU?
WHERE'D YOU COME FROM?
WHAT'S YOUR NAME?
WHAT'S YOUR NAME?
MEMEL.
MEMEL, I'M STARVING. I'LL FALL TO THE GROUND IF I DON'T EAT.
COME!

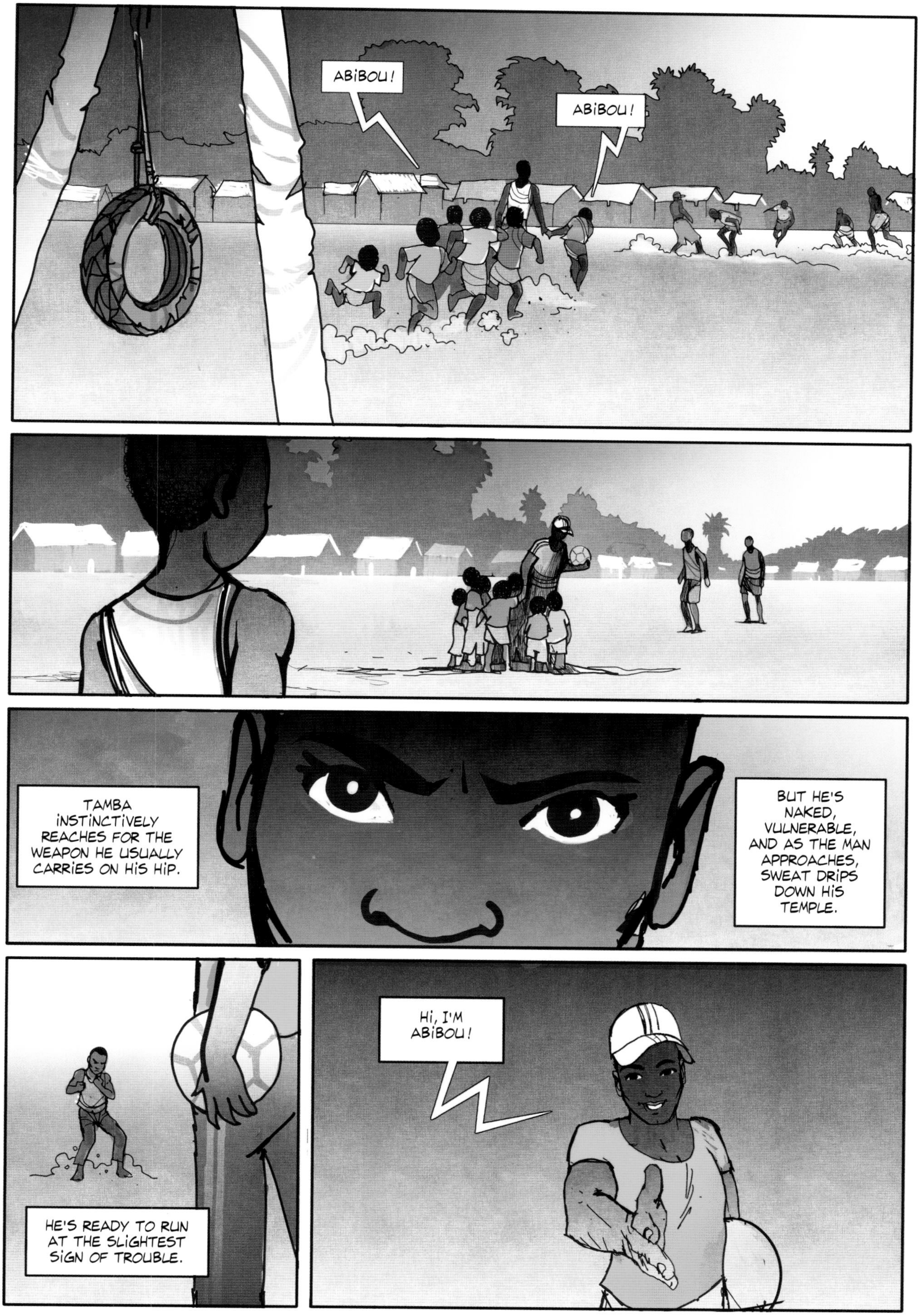
ABiBOU!
ABiBOU!
TAMBA iNSTiNCTiVELY REACHES FOR THE WEAPON HE USUALLY CARRiES ON HiS HiP.
BUT HE'S NAKED, VULNERABLE, AND AS THE MAN APPROACHES, SWEAT DRiPS DOWN HiS TEMPLE.
HE'S READY TO RUN AT THE SLiGHTEST SiGN OF TROUBLE.
Hi, I'M ABiBOU!

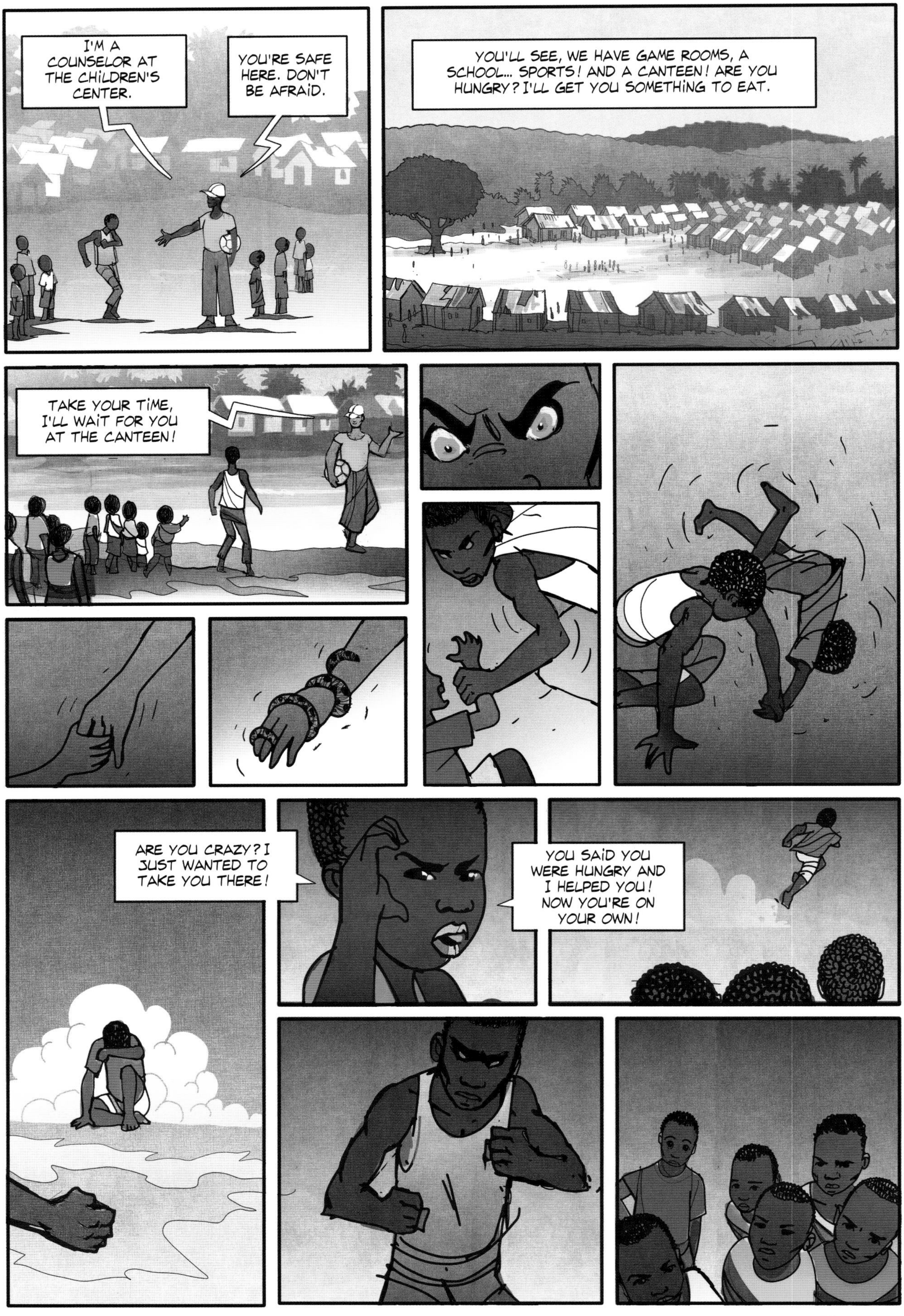
I'M A COUNSELOR AT THE CHILDREN'S CENTER.
YOU'RE SAFE HERE. DON'T BE AFRAID.
YOU'LL SEE, WE HAVE GAME ROOMS, A SCHOOL... SPORTS! AND A CANTEEN! ARE YOU HUNGRY? I'LL GET YOU SOMETHING TO EAT.
TAKE YOUR TIME, I'LL WAIT FOR YOU AT THE CANTEEN!
ARE YOU CRAZY? I JUST WANTED TO TAKE YOU THERE!
YOU SAID YOU WERE HUNGRY AND I HELPED YOU! NOW YOU'RE ON YOUR OWN!

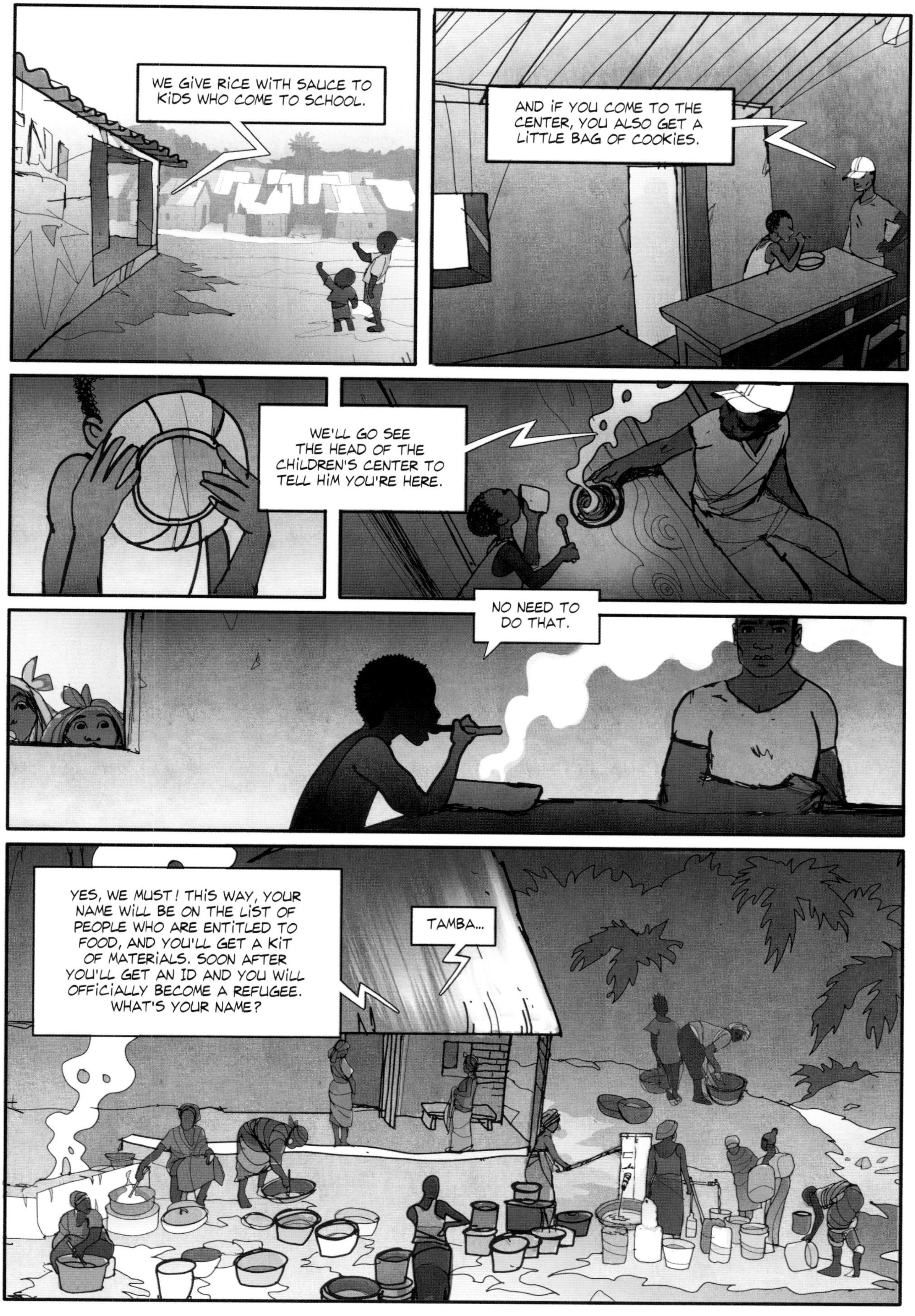
WE GIVE RICE WITH SAUCE TO KIDS WHO COME TO SCHOOL.
AND IF YOU COME TO THE CENTER, YOU ALSO GET A LITTLE BAG OF COOKIES.
WE'LL GO SEE THE HEAD OF THE CHILDREN'S CENTER TO TELL HIM YOU'RE HERE.
NO NEED TO DO THAT.
YES, WE MUST! THIS WAY, YOUR NAME WILL BE ON THE LIST OF PEOPLE WHO ARE ENTITLED TO FOOD, AND YOU'LL GET A KIT OF MATERIALS. SOON AFTER YOU'LL GET AN ID AND YOU WILL OFFICIALLY BECOME A REFUGEE. WHAT'S YOUR NAME?
TAMBA...

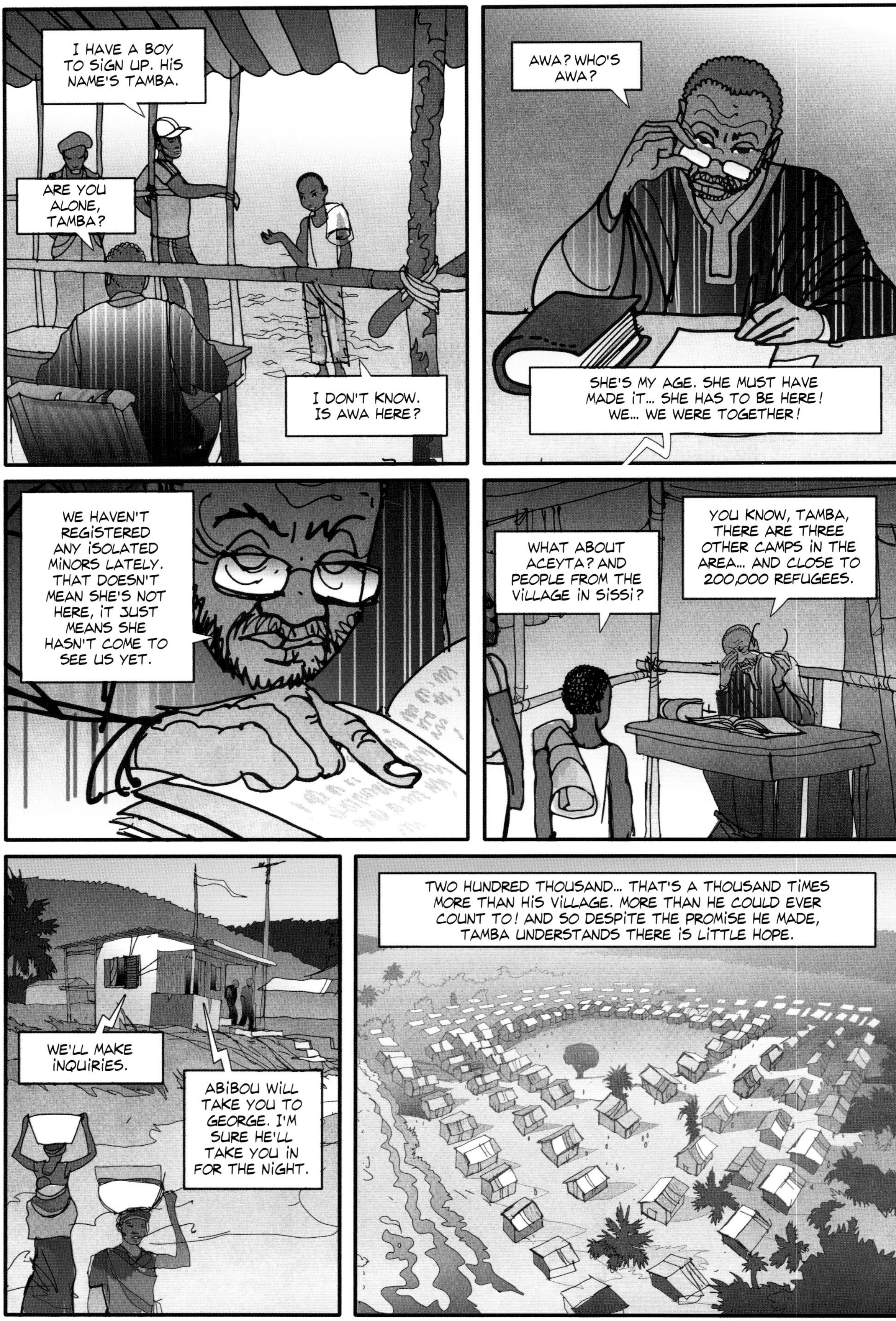
I HAVE A BOY TO SIGN UP. HIS NAME'S TAMBA.
ARE YOU ALONE, TAMBA?
I DON'T KNOW. IS AWA HERE?
AWA? WHO'S AWA?
SHE'S MY AGE. SHE MUST HAVE MADE IT... SHE HAS TO BE HERE! WE... WE WERE TOGETHER!
WE HAVEN'T REGISTERED ANY ISOLATED MINORS LATELY. THAT DOESN'T MEAN SHE'S NOT HERE, IT JUST MEANS SHE HASN'T COME TO SEE US YET.
WHAT ABOUT ACEYTA? AND PEOPLE FROM THE VILLAGE IN SISSI?
YOU KNOW, TAMBA, THERE ARE THREE OTHER CAMPS IN THE AREA... AND CLOSE TO 200,000 REFUGEES.
WE'LL MAKE INQUIRIES.
ABIBOU WILL TAKE YOU TO GEORGE. I'M SURE HE'LL TAKE YOU IN FOR THE NIGHT.
TWO HUNDRED THOUSAND... THAT'S A THOUSAND TIMES MORE THAN HIS VILLAGE. MORE THAN HE COULD EVER COUNT TO! AND SO DESPITE THE PROMISE HE MADE, TAMBA UNDERSTANDS THERE IS LITTLE HOPE.

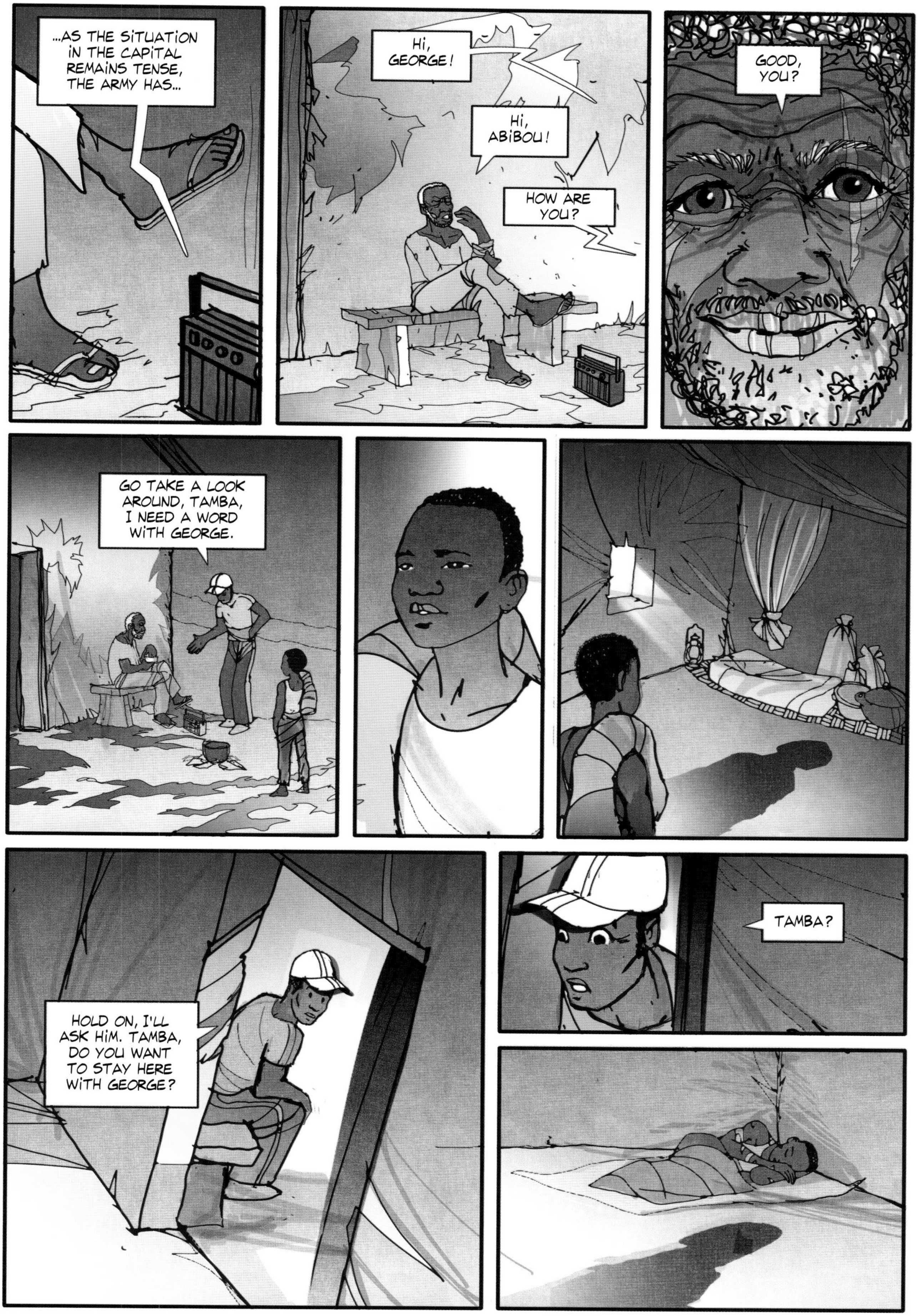
...AS THE SITUATION IN THE CAPITAL REMAINS TENSE, THE ARMY HAS...
HI, GEORGE!
HI, ABIBOU!
HOW ARE YOU?
GOOD, YOU?
GO TAKE A LOOK AROUND, TAMBA, I NEED A WORD WITH GEORGE.
HOLD ON, I'LL ASK HIM. TAMBA, DO YOU WANT TO STAY HERE WITH GEORGE?
TAMBA?

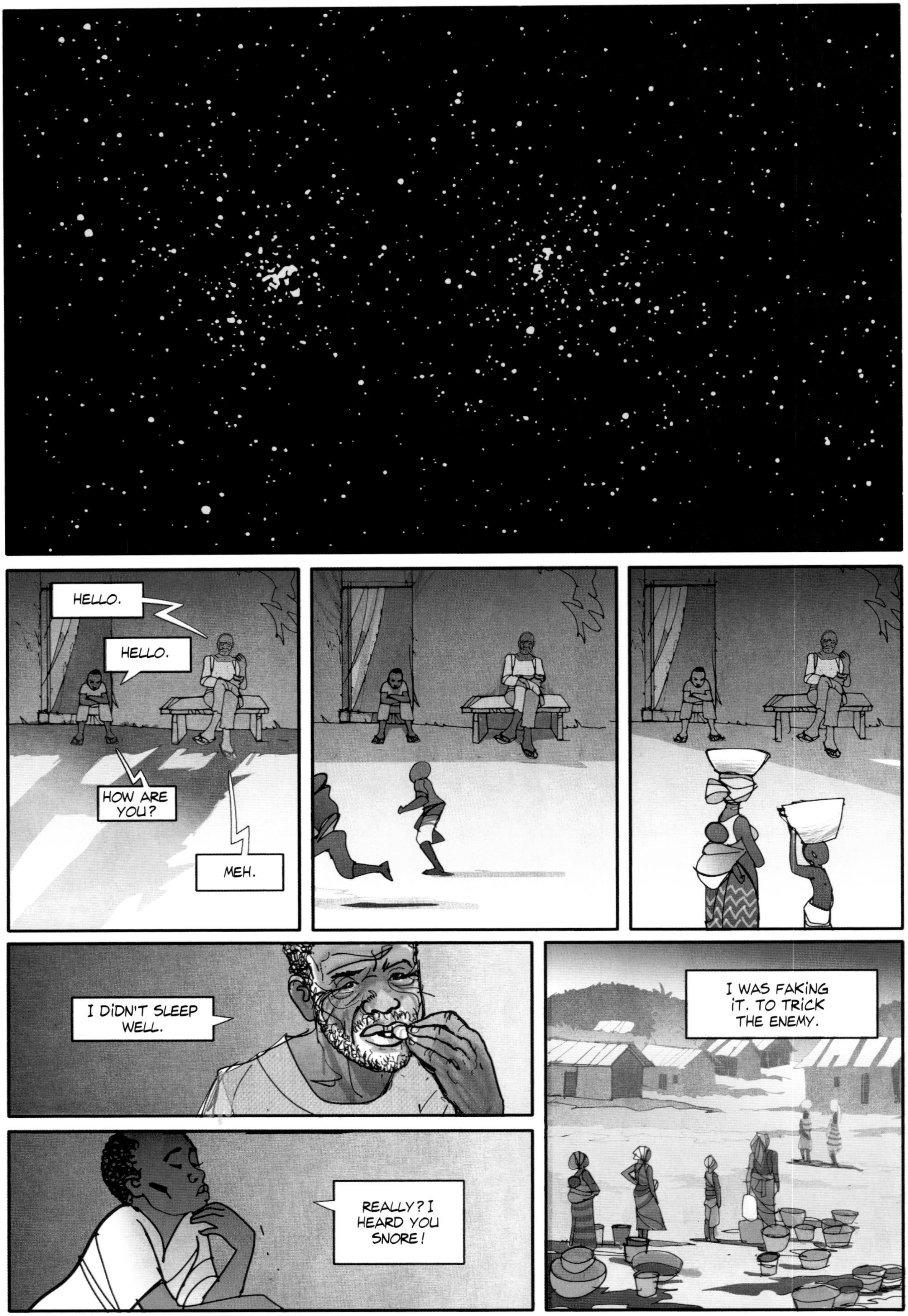
HELLO.
HELLO.
HOW ARE YOU?
MEH.
I DIDN'T SLEEP WELL.
REALLY? I HEARD YOU SNORE!
I WAS FAKING IT. TO TRICK THE ENEMY.

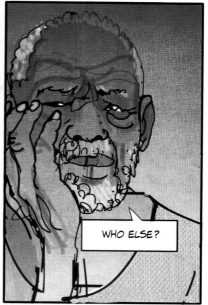

AM I THE ENEMY?

WHO ELSE?

TO TELL YOU THE TRUTH, I'M AFRAID OF YOU.

YOU DON'T THINK I NOTICED? YOU HAVE MUSCLES, SCARS ON YOUR CALVES AND ARMS, AND A BIG PINK MARK ON YOUR HIP. YOU THINK I DON'T KNOW YOU CAME OUT OF THE FOREST, FROM A PLACE WHERE'S THERE'S NOTHING?

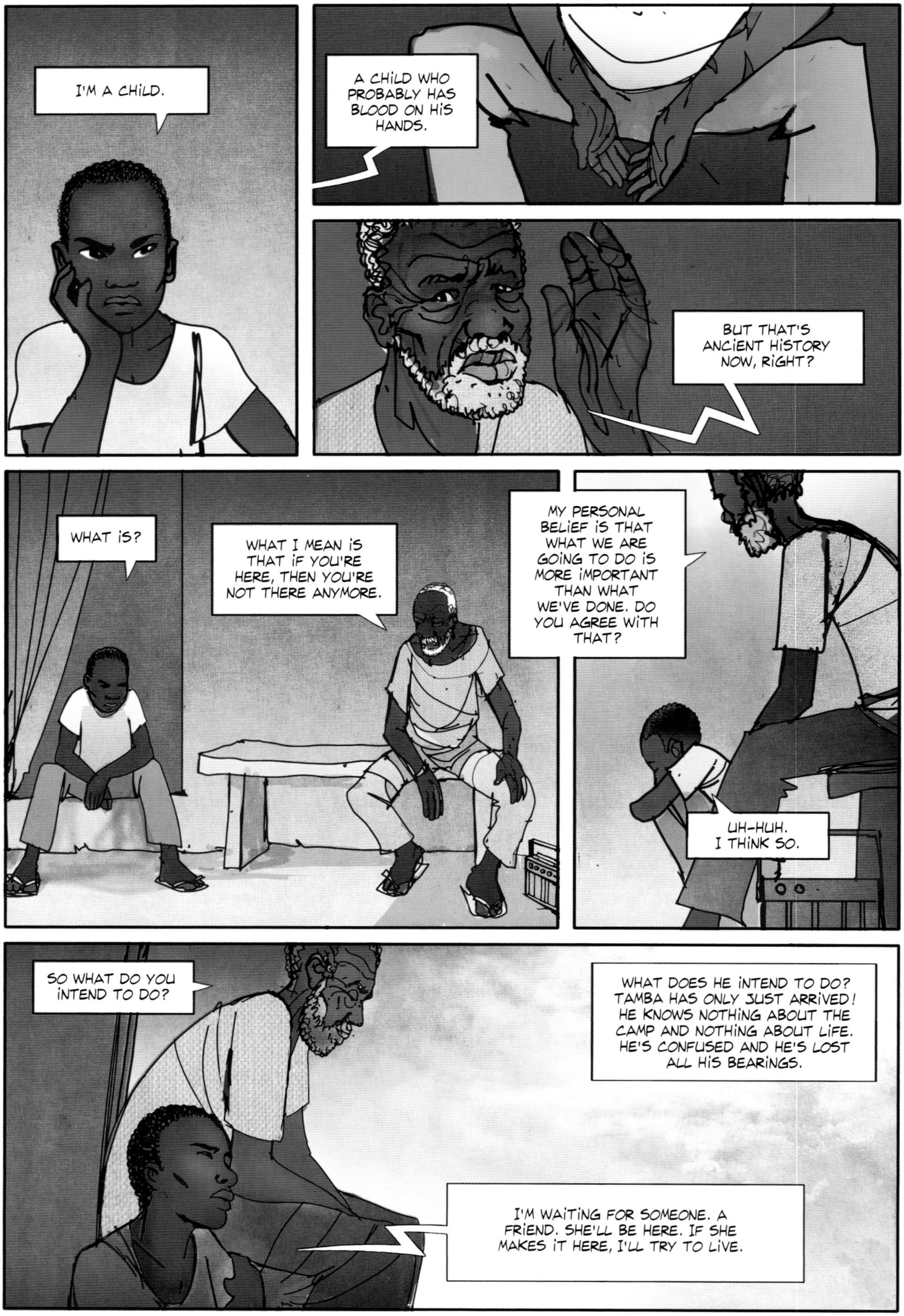
I'M A CHILD.
A CHILD WHO PROBABLY HAS BLOOD ON HIS HANDS.
BUT THAT'S ANCIENT HISTORY NOW, RIGHT?
WHAT IS?
WHAT I MEAN IS THAT IF YOU'RE HERE, THEN YOU'RE NOT THERE ANYMORE.
MY PERSONAL BELIEF IS THAT WHAT WE ARE GOING TO DO IS MORE IMPORTANT THAN WHAT WE'VE DONE. DO YOU AGREE WITH THAT?
UH-HUH. I THINK SO.
SO WHAT DO YOU INTEND TO DO?
WHAT DOES HE INTEND TO DO? TAMBA HAS ONLY JUST ARRIVED! HE KNOWS NOTHING ABOUT THE CAMP AND NOTHING ABOUT LIFE. HE'S CONFUSED AND HE'S LOST ALL HIS BEARINGS.
I'M WAITING FOR SOMEONE. A FRIEND. SHE'LL BE HERE. IF SHE MAKES IT HERE, I'LL TRY TO LIVE.

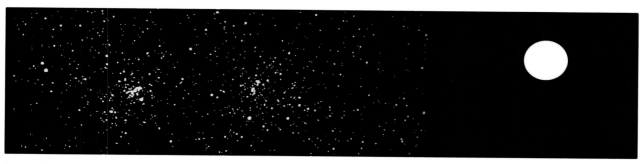

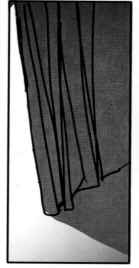

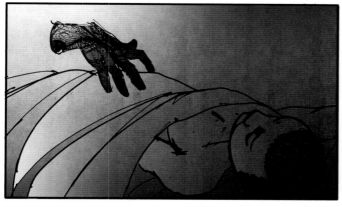
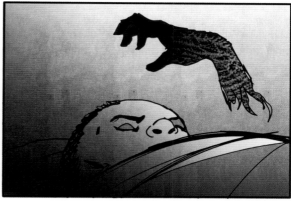

TAMBA!
YOU'RE
CRUSHING ME!

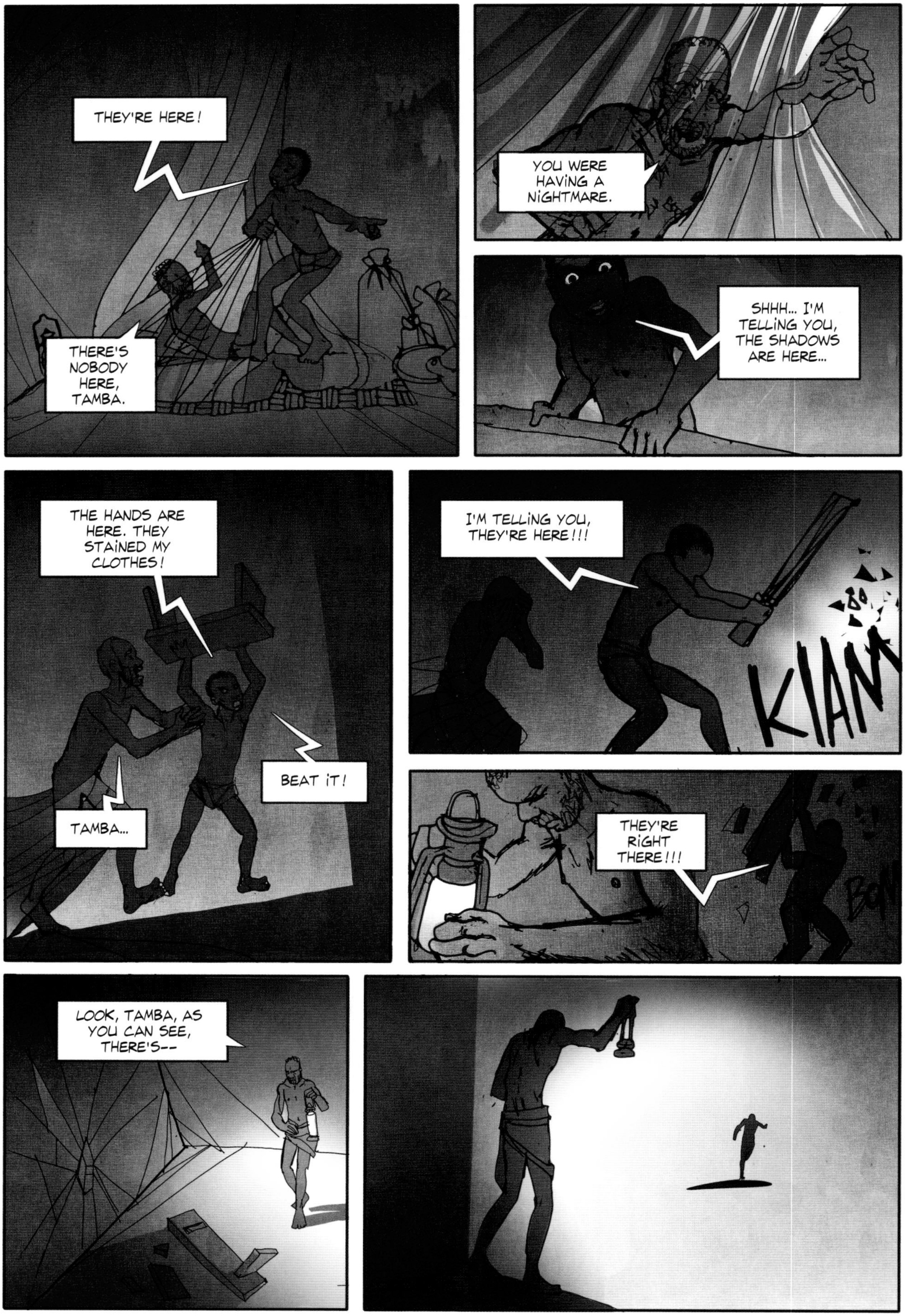
THEY'RE HERE!
THERE'S NOBODY HERE, TAMBA.
YOU WERE HAVING A NIGHTMARE.
SHHH... I'M TELLING YOU, THE SHADOWS ARE HERE...
THE HANDS ARE HERE. THEY STAINED MY CLOTHES!
BEAT IT!
TAMBA...
I'M TELLING YOU, THEY'RE HERE!!!
KLAM
THEY'RE RIGHT THERE!!!
LOOK, TAMBA, AS YOU CAN SEE, THERE'S--

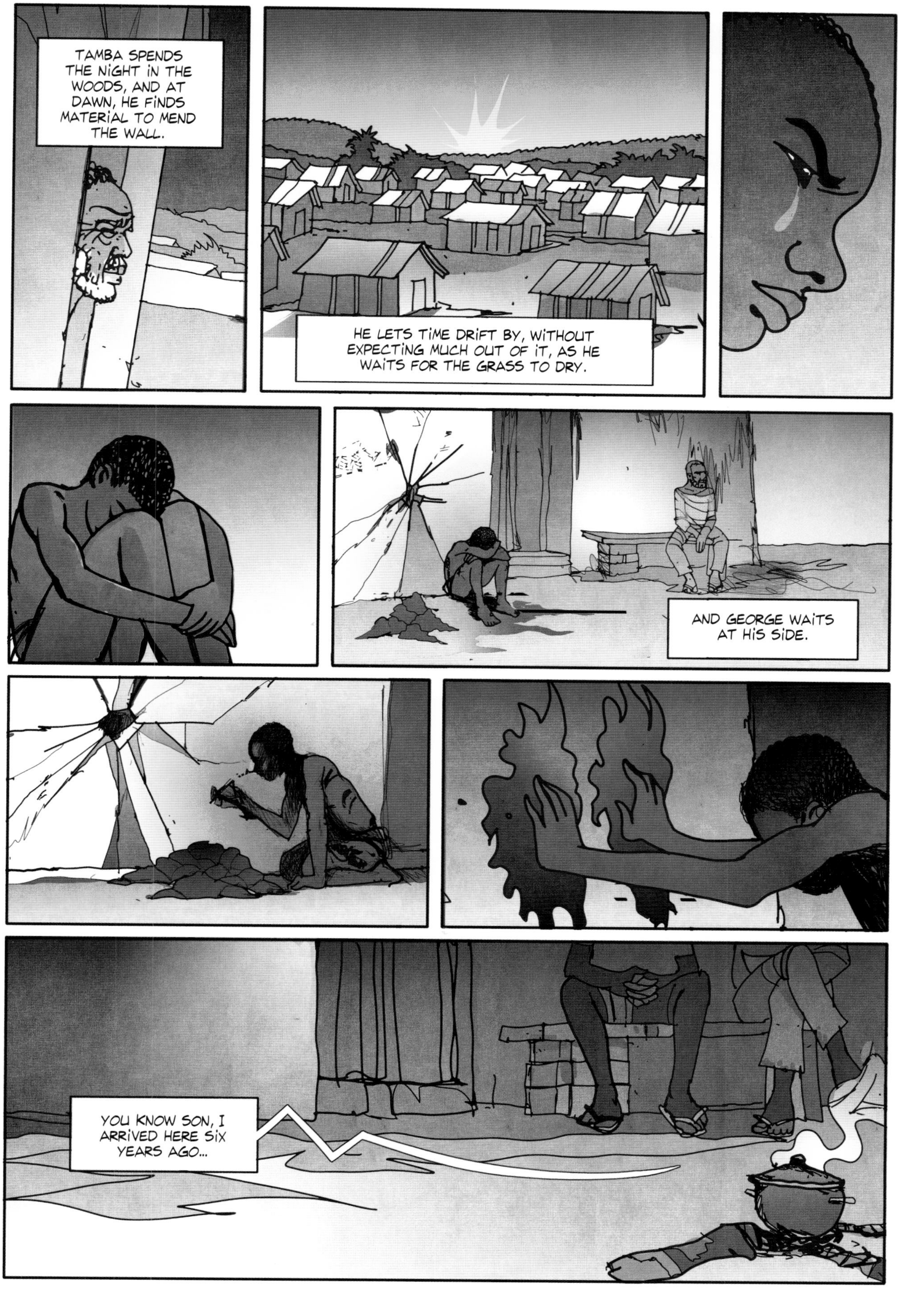

TAMBA SPENDS THE NIGHT IN THE WOODS, AND AT DAWN, HE FINDS MATERIAL TO MEND THE WALL.
HE LETS TIME DRIFT BY, WITHOUT EXPECTING MUCH OUT OF IT, AS HE WAITS FOR THE GRASS TO DRY.
AND GEORGE WAITS AT HIS SIDE.
YOU KNOW SON, I ARRIVED HERE SIX YEARS AGO...

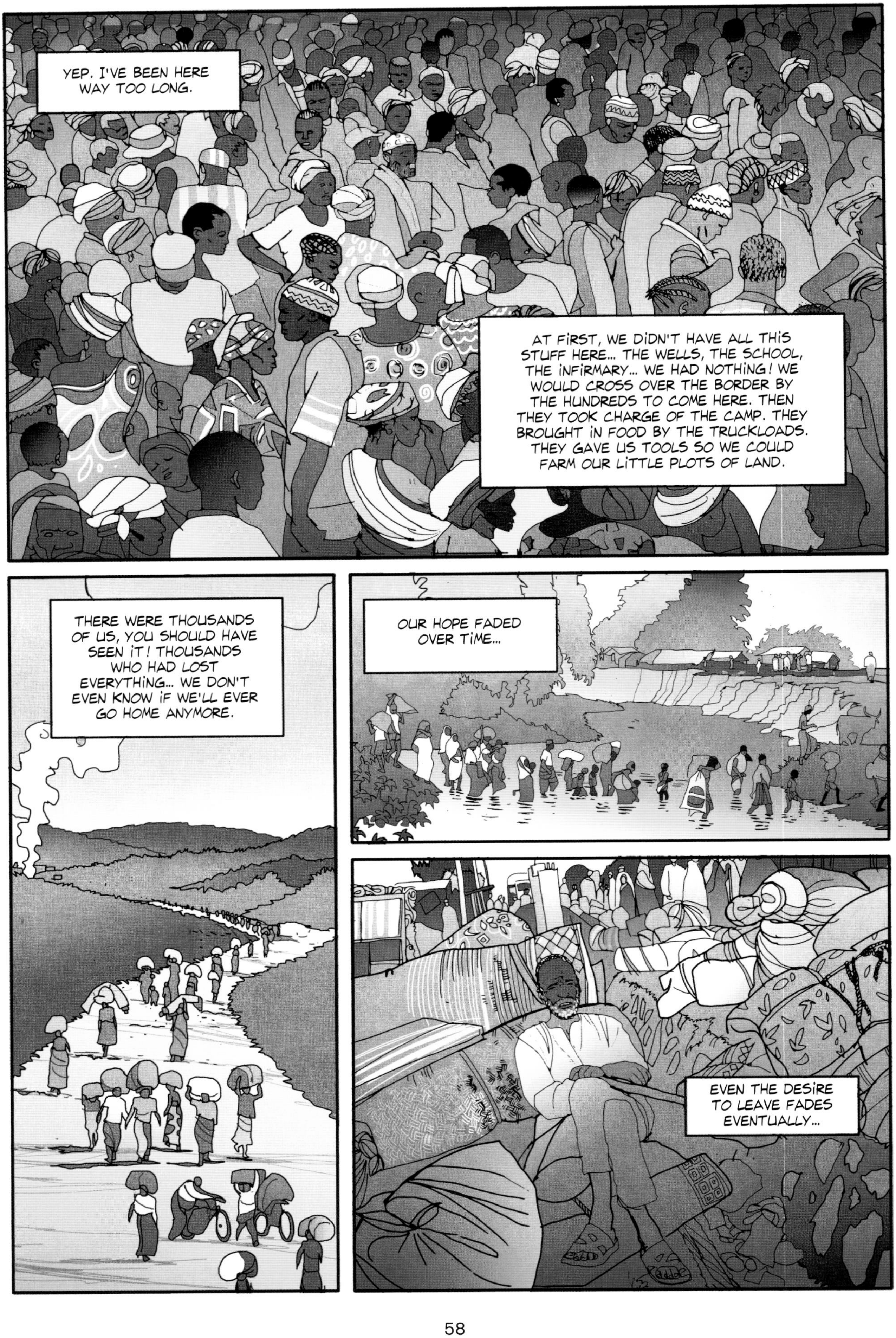
YEP. I'VE BEEN HERE WAY TOO LONG.
AT FIRST, WE DIDN'T HAVE ALL THIS STUFF HERE... THE WELLS, THE SCHOOL, THE INFIRMARY... WE HAD NOTHING! WE WOULD CROSS OVER THE BORDER BY THE HUNDREDS TO COME HERE. THEN THEY TOOK CHARGE OF THE CAMP. THEY BROUGHT IN FOOD BY THE TRUCKLOADS. THEY GAVE US TOOLS SO WE COULD FARM OUR LITTLE PLOTS OF LAND.
THERE WERE THOUSANDS OF US, YOU SHOULD HAVE SEEN IT! THOUSANDS WHO HAD LOST EVERYTHING... WE DON'T EVEN KNOW IF WE'LL EVER GO HOME ANYMORE.
OUR HOPE FADED OVER TIME...
EVEN THE DESIRE TO LEAVE FADES EVENTUALLY...

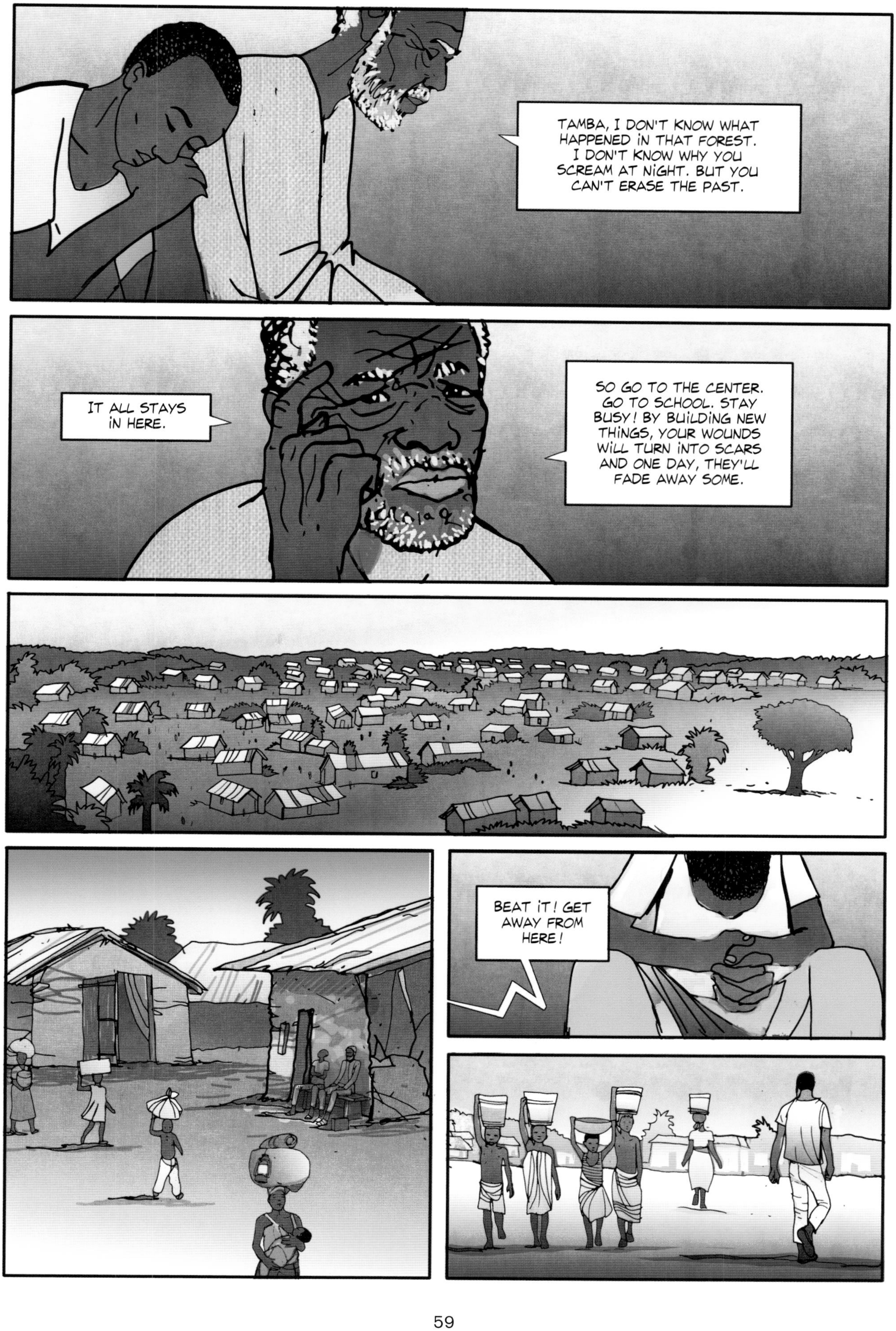
TAMBA, I DON'T KNOW WHAT HAPPENED IN THAT FOREST. I DON'T KNOW WHY YOU SCREAM AT NIGHT. BUT YOU CAN'T ERASE THE PAST.
IT ALL STAYS IN HERE.
SO GO TO THE CENTER. GO TO SCHOOL. STAY BUSY! BY BUILDING NEW THINGS, YOUR WOUNDS WILL TURN INTO SCARS AND ONE DAY, THEY'LL FADE AWAY SOME.
BEAT IT! GET AWAY FROM HERE!

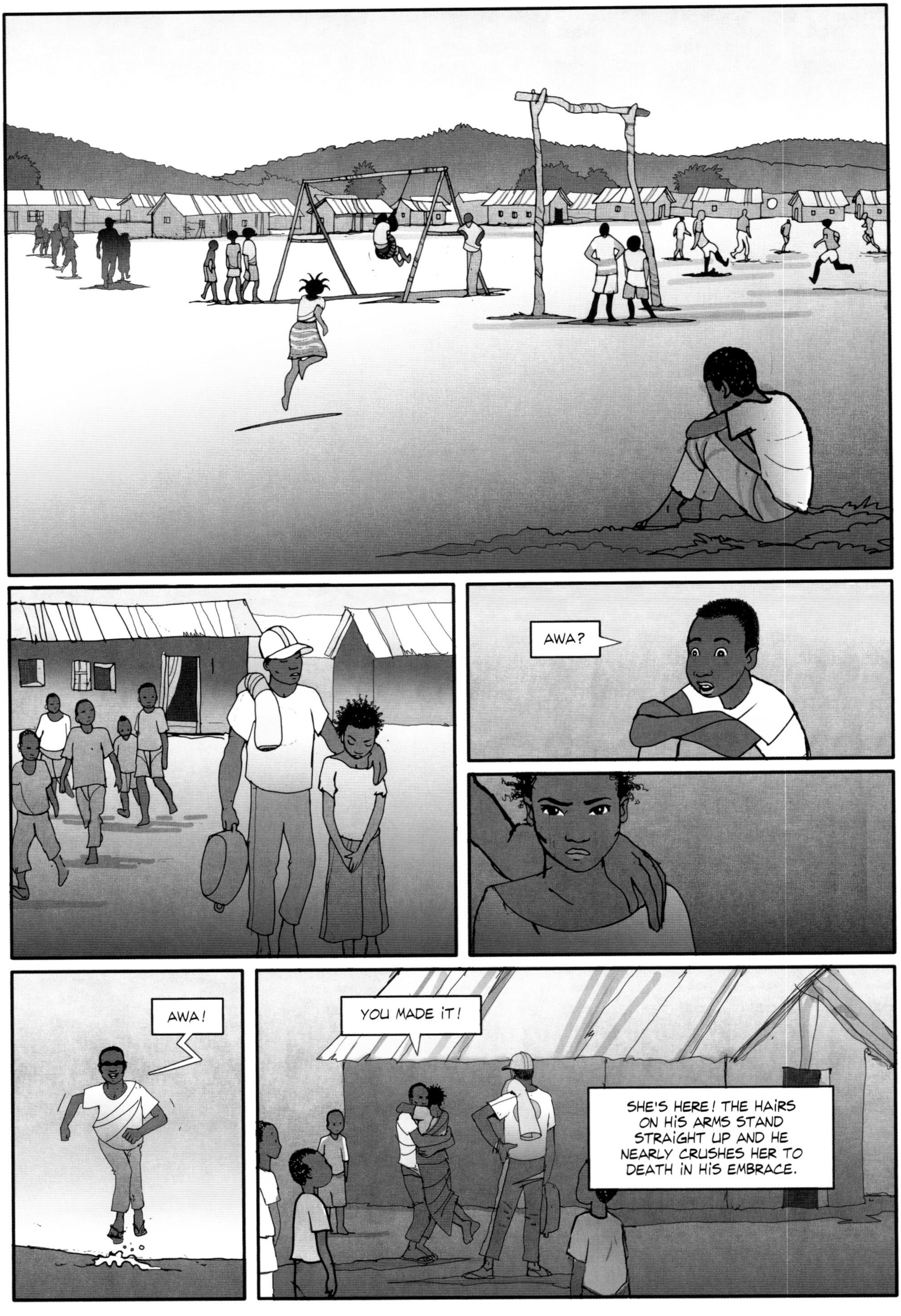
AWA?
AWA!
YOU MADE IT!
SHE'S HERE! THE HAIRS ON HIS ARMS STAND STRAIGHT UP AND HE NEARLY CRUSHES HER TO DEATH IN HIS EMBRACE.

SHE'S HERE. HE HOLDS HER FOR A LONG TIME, BREATHING IN THE SCENT OF HER SKIN AND THE RELIEF OF BEING REUNITED.

AWA STARES SILENTLY AT SOMETHING STRAIGHT AHEAD.

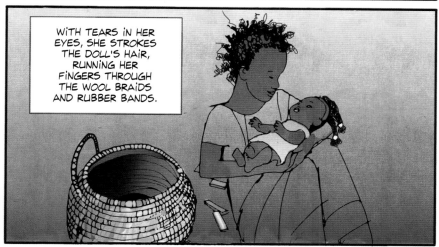

WITH TEARS IN HER EYES, SHE STROKES THE DOLL'S HAIR, RUNNING HER FINGERS THROUGH THE WOOL BRAIDS AND RUBBER BANDS.

TAMBA JUST STANDS THERE, UNABLE TO BE WITH HER THEN.

AND AWA WEEPS, UNREACHABLE, HOLDING THE DOLL TIGHT AGAINST HER HEART.

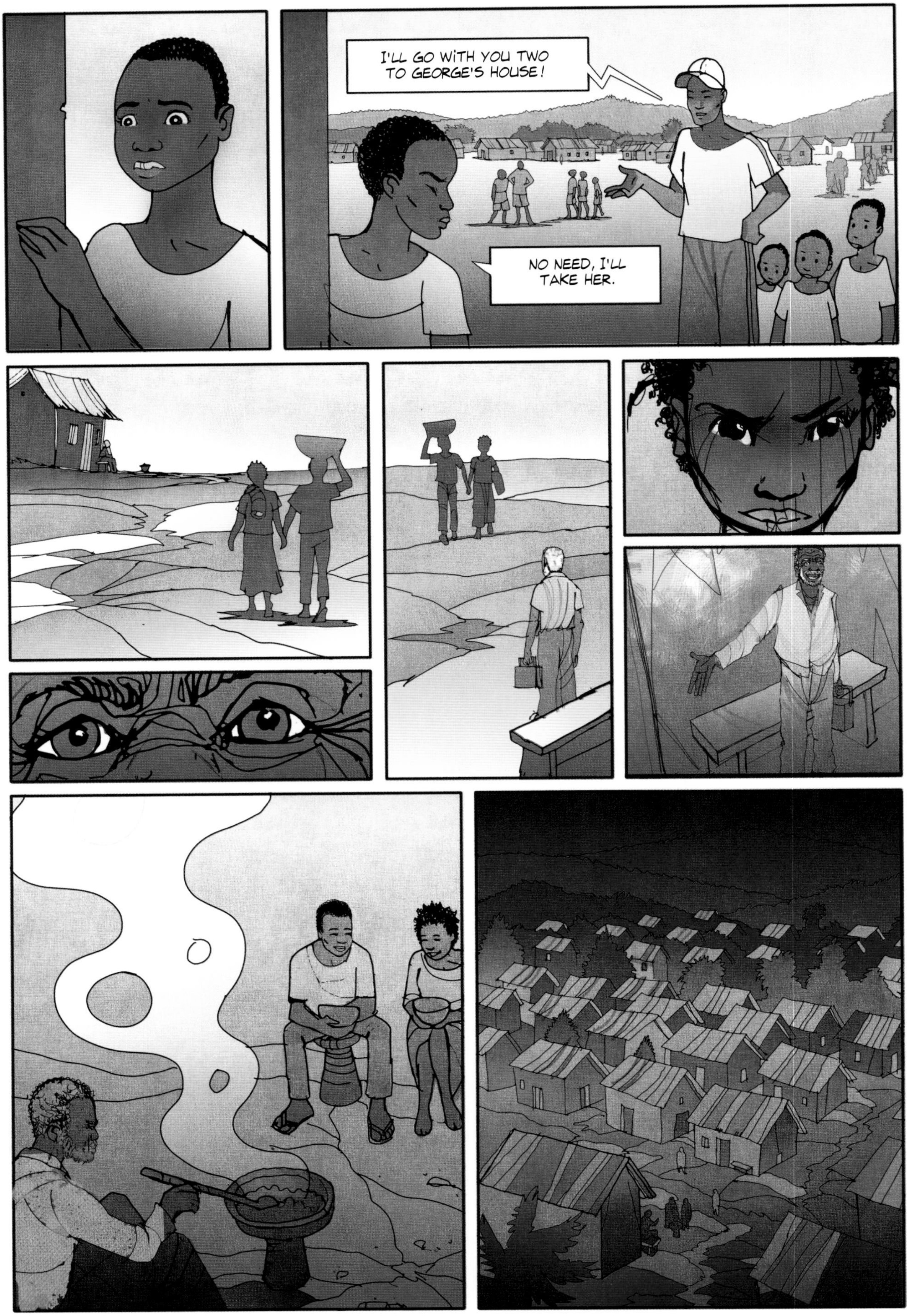
I'LL GO WITH YOU TWO TO GEORGE'S HOUSE!
NO NEED, I'LL TAKE HER.

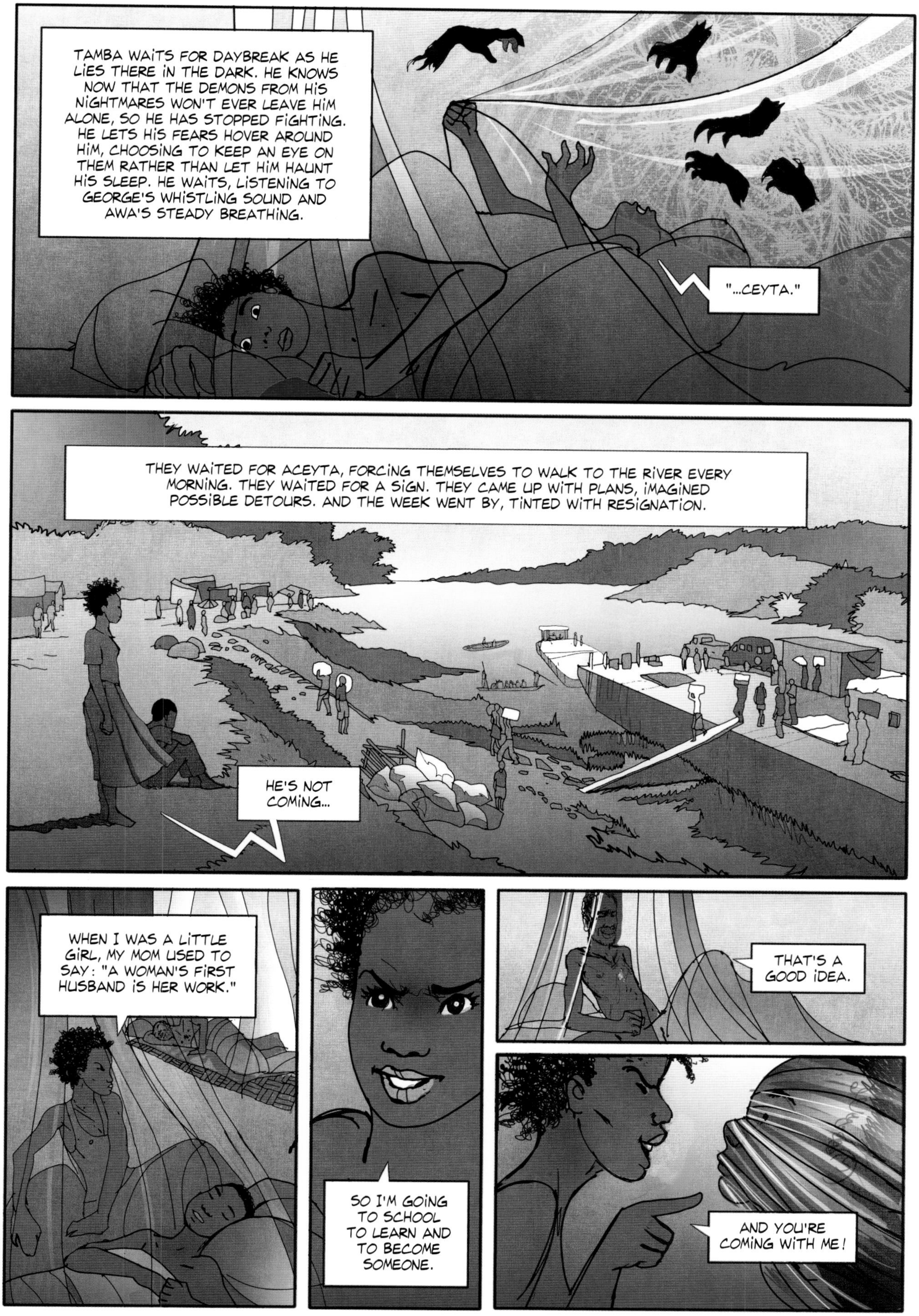

TAMBA WAITS FOR DAYBREAK AS HE LIES THERE IN THE DARK. HE KNOWS NOW THAT THE DEMONS FROM HIS NIGHTMARES WON'T EVER LEAVE HIM ALONE, SO HE HAS STOPPED FIGHTING. HE LETS HIS FEARS HOVER AROUND HIM, CHOOSING TO KEEP AN EYE ON THEM RATHER THAN LET HIM HAUNT HIS SLEEP. HE WAITS, LISTENING TO GEORGE'S WHISTLING SOUND AND AWA'S STEADY BREATHING.
"...CEYTA."
THEY WAITED FOR ACEYTA, FORCING THEMSELVES TO WALK TO THE RIVER EVERY MORNING. THEY WAITED FOR A SIGN. THEY CAME UP WITH PLANS, IMAGINED POSSIBLE DETOURS. AND THE WEEK WENT BY, TINTED WITH RESIGNATION.
HE'S NOT COMING...
WHEN I WAS A LITTLE GIRL, MY MOM USED TO SAY: "A WOMAN'S FIRST HUSBAND IS HER WORK."
SO I'M GOING TO SCHOOL TO LEARN AND TO BECOME SOMEONE.
THAT'S A GOOD IDEA.
AND YOU'RE COMING WITH ME!

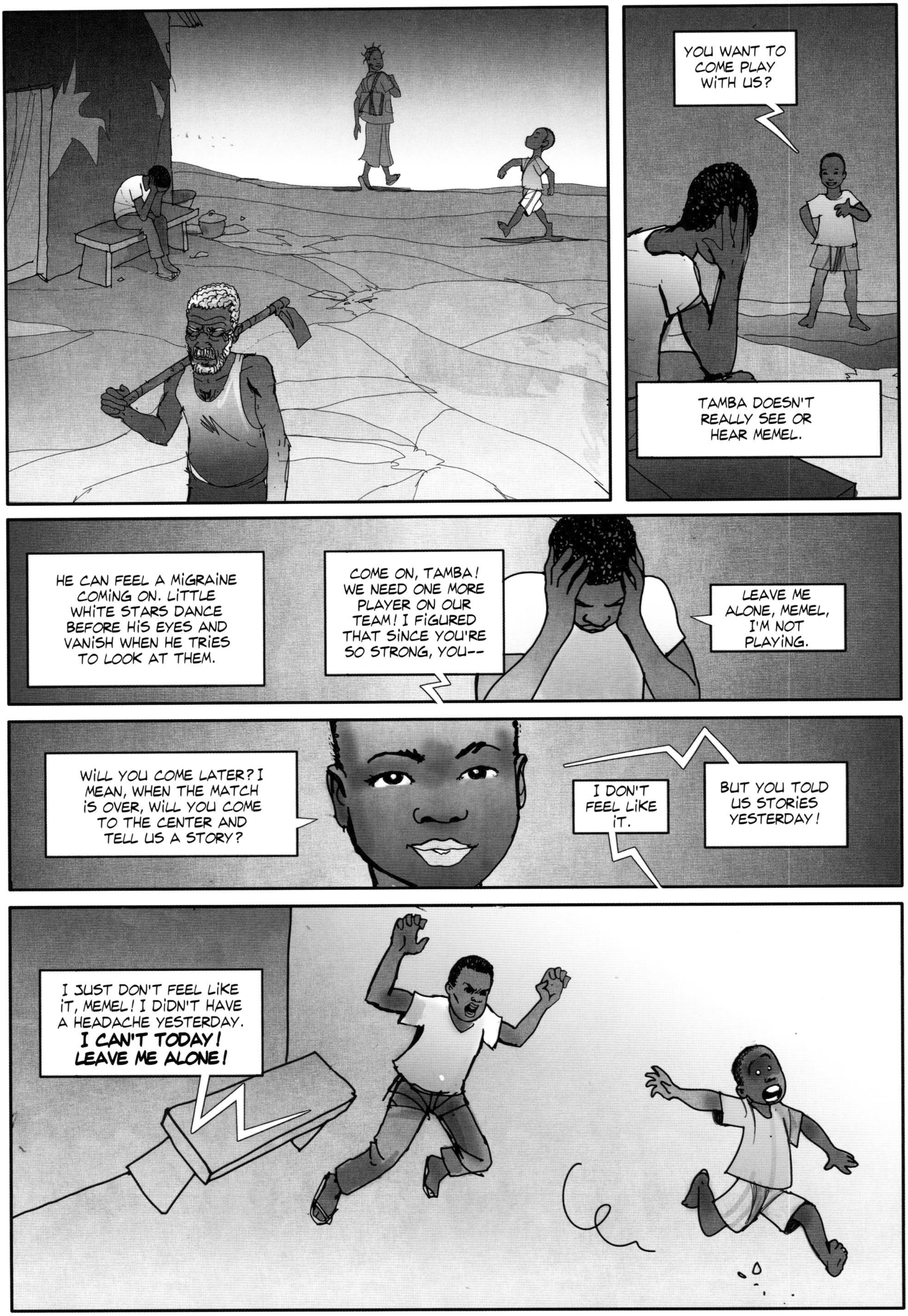
YOU WANT TO COME PLAY WITH US?
TAMBA DOESN'T REALLY SEE OR HEAR MEMEL.
HE CAN FEEL A MIGRAINE COMING ON. LITTLE WHITE STARS DANCE BEFORE HIS EYES AND VANISH WHEN HE TRIES TO LOOK AT THEM.
COME ON, TAMBA! WE NEED ONE MORE PLAYER ON OUR TEAM! I FIGURED THAT SINCE YOU'RE SO STRONG, YOU--
LEAVE ME ALONE, MEMEL, I'M NOT PLAYING.
WILL YOU COME LATER? I MEAN, WHEN THE MATCH IS OVER, WILL YOU COME TO THE CENTER AND TELL US A STORY?
I DON'T FEEL LIKE IT.
BUT YOU TOLD US STORIES YESTERDAY!
I JUST DON'T FEEL LIKE IT, MEMEL! I DIDN'T HAVE A HEADACHE YESTERDAY. **I CAN'T TODAY! LEAVE ME ALONE!**

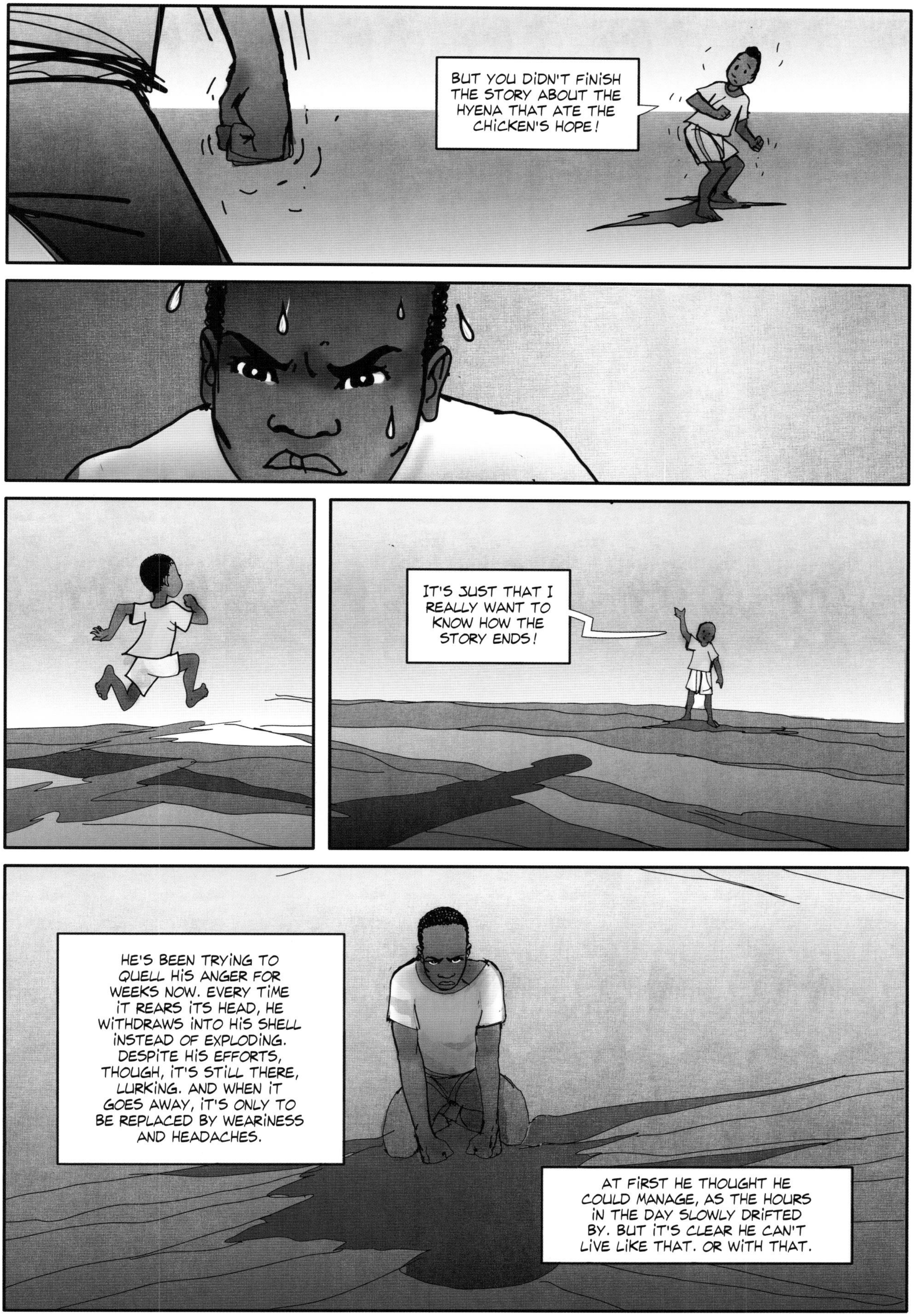
BUT YOU DIDN'T FINISH THE STORY ABOUT THE HYENA THAT ATE THE CHICKEN'S HOPE!
IT'S JUST THAT I REALLY WANT TO KNOW HOW THE STORY ENDS!
HE'S BEEN TRYING TO QUELL HIS ANGER FOR WEEKS NOW. EVERY TIME IT REARS ITS HEAD, HE WITHDRAWS INTO HIS SHELL INSTEAD OF EXPLODING. DESPITE HIS EFFORTS, THOUGH, IT'S STILL THERE, LURKING. AND WHEN IT GOES AWAY, IT'S ONLY TO BE REPLACED BY WEARINESS AND HEADACHES.
AT FIRST HE THOUGHT HE COULD MANAGE, AS THE HOURS IN THE DAY SLOWLY DRIFTED BY. BUT IT'S CLEAR HE CAN'T LIVE LIKE THAT. OR WITH THAT.

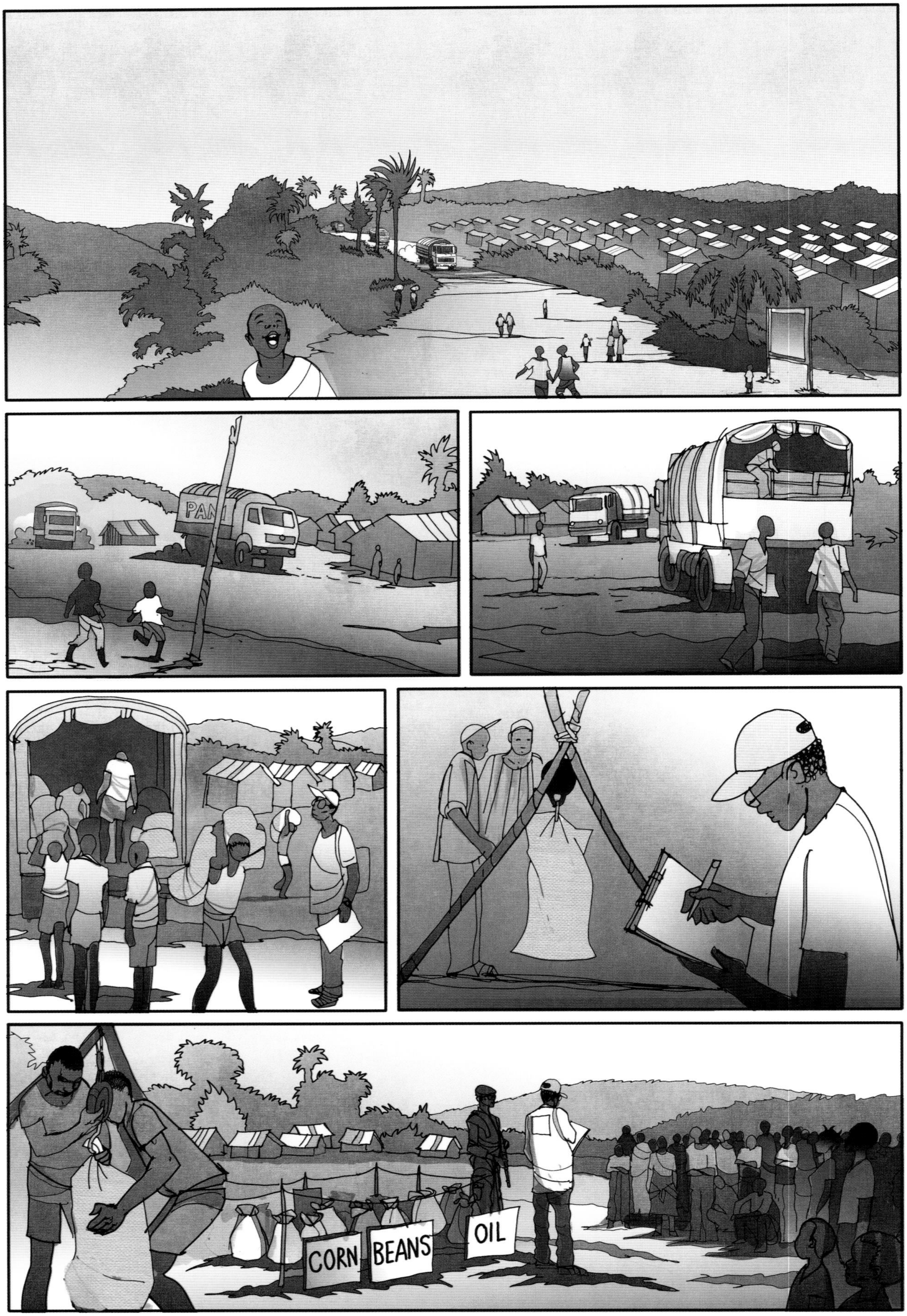
PAM
CORN
BEANS
OIL

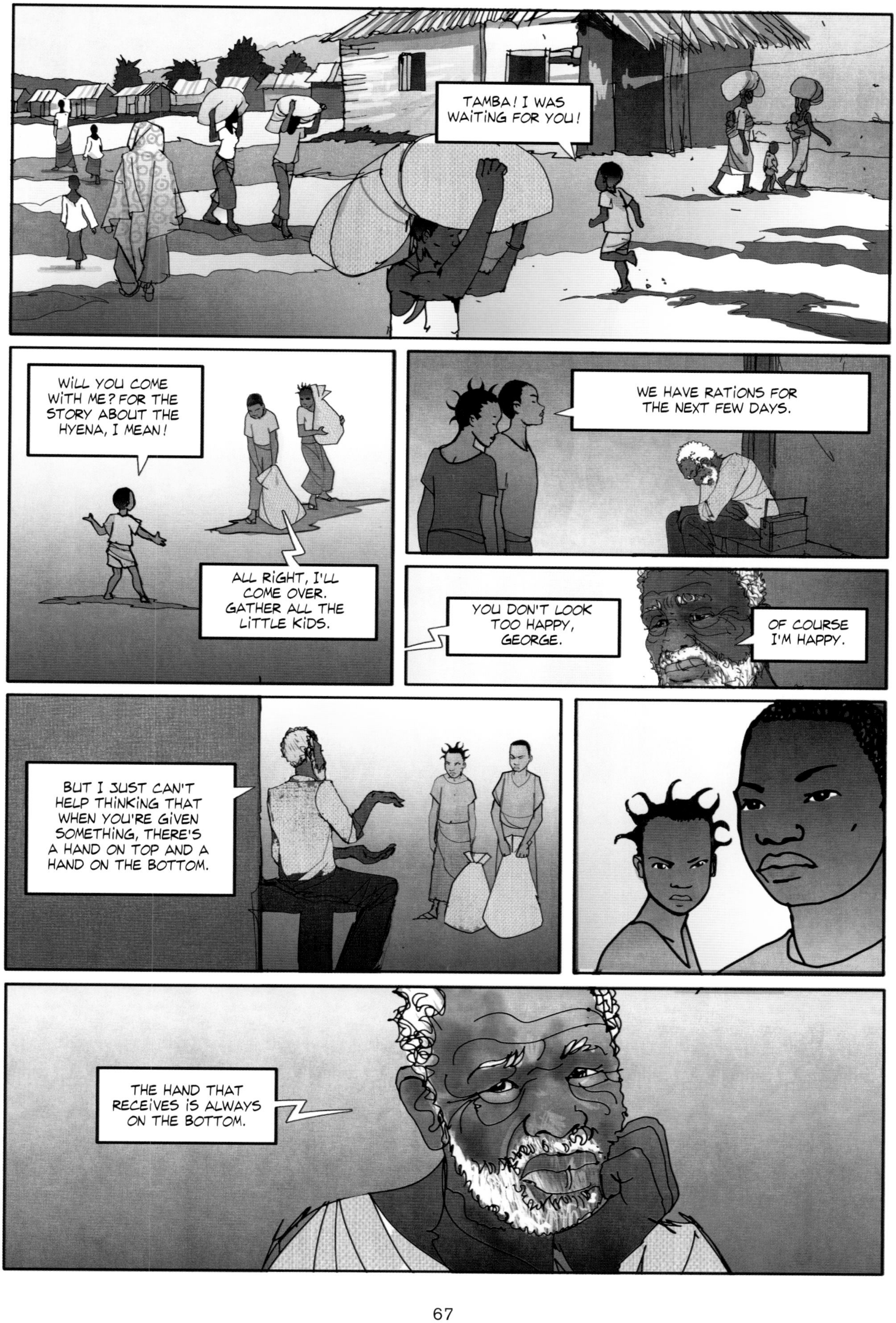
TAMBA! I WAS WAITING FOR YOU!
WILL YOU COME WITH ME? FOR THE STORY ABOUT THE HYENA, I MEAN!
ALL RIGHT, I'LL COME OVER. GATHER ALL THE LITTLE KIDS.
WE HAVE RATIONS FOR THE NEXT FEW DAYS.
YOU DON'T LOOK TOO HAPPY, GEORGE.
OF COURSE I'M HAPPY.
BUT I JUST CAN'T HELP THINKING THAT WHEN YOU'RE GIVEN SOMETHING, THERE'S A HAND ON TOP AND A HAND ON THE BOTTOM.
THE HAND THAT RECEIVES IS ALWAYS ON THE BOTTOM.

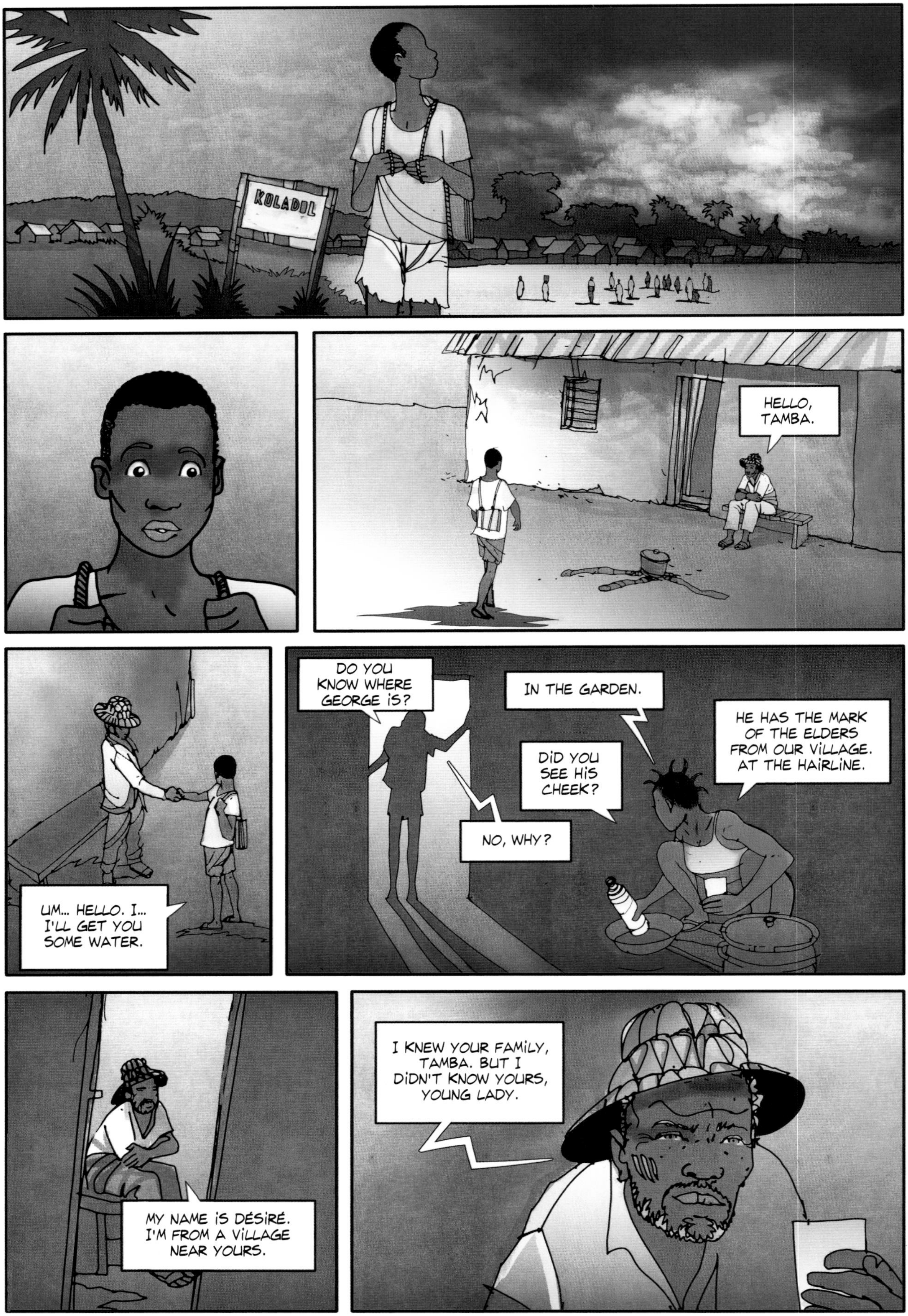
KOLADOL
HELLO, TAMBA.
UM... HELLO. I... I'LL GET YOU SOME WATER.
DO YOU KNOW WHERE GEORGE IS?
IN THE GARDEN.
DID YOU SEE HIS CHEEK?
NO, WHY?
HE HAS THE MARK OF THE ELDERS FROM OUR VILLAGE. AT THE HAIRLINE.
MY NAME IS DÉSIRÉ. I'M FROM A VILLAGE NEAR YOURS.
I KNEW YOUR FAMILY, TAMBA. BUT I DIDN'T KNOW YOURS, YOUNG LADY.

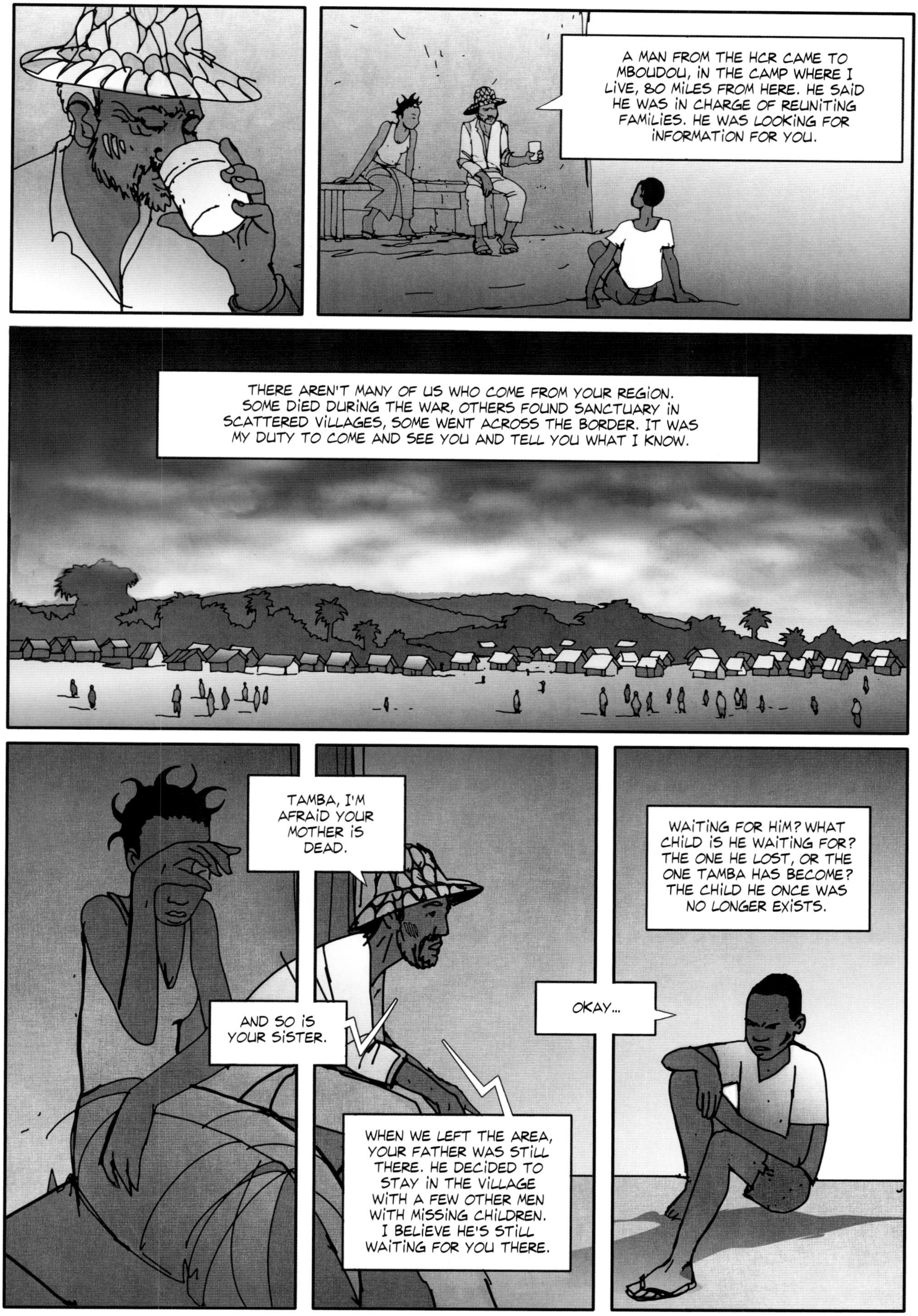
A MAN FROM THE HCR CAME TO MBOUDOU, IN THE CAMP WHERE I LIVE, 80 MILES FROM HERE. HE SAID HE WAS IN CHARGE OF REUNITING FAMILIES. HE WAS LOOKING FOR INFORMATION FOR YOU.
THERE AREN'T MANY OF US WHO COME FROM YOUR REGION. SOME DIED DURING THE WAR, OTHERS FOUND SANCTUARY IN SCATTERED VILLAGES, SOME WENT ACROSS THE BORDER. IT WAS MY DUTY TO COME AND SEE YOU AND TELL YOU WHAT I KNOW.
TAMBA, I'M AFRAID YOUR MOTHER IS DEAD.
AND SO IS YOUR SISTER.
WHEN WE LEFT THE AREA, YOUR FATHER WAS STILL THERE. HE DECIDED TO STAY IN THE VILLAGE WITH A FEW OTHER MEN WITH MISSING CHILDREN. I BELIEVE HE'S STILL WAITING FOR YOU THERE.
WAITING FOR HIM? WHAT CHILD IS HE WAITING FOR? THE ONE HE LOST, OR THE ONE TAMBA HAS BECOME? THE CHILD HE ONCE WAS NO LONGER EXISTS.
OKAY...

I'M SORRY I HAVE NO NEWS FOR YOU, YOUNG LADY.

I BELIEVE IT'S ALWAYS BEST TO KNOW THE TRUTH. IF YOU WANT, YOU CAN COME WITH ME TO MBOUDOU. WE DON'T HAVE MUCH, BUT WHAT WE DO HAVE, WE WILL SHARE WITH YOU.

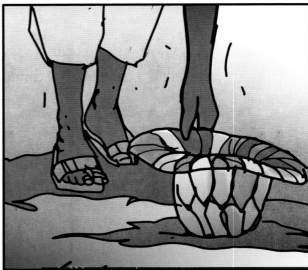

YOU KNOW WHERE TO FIND US.

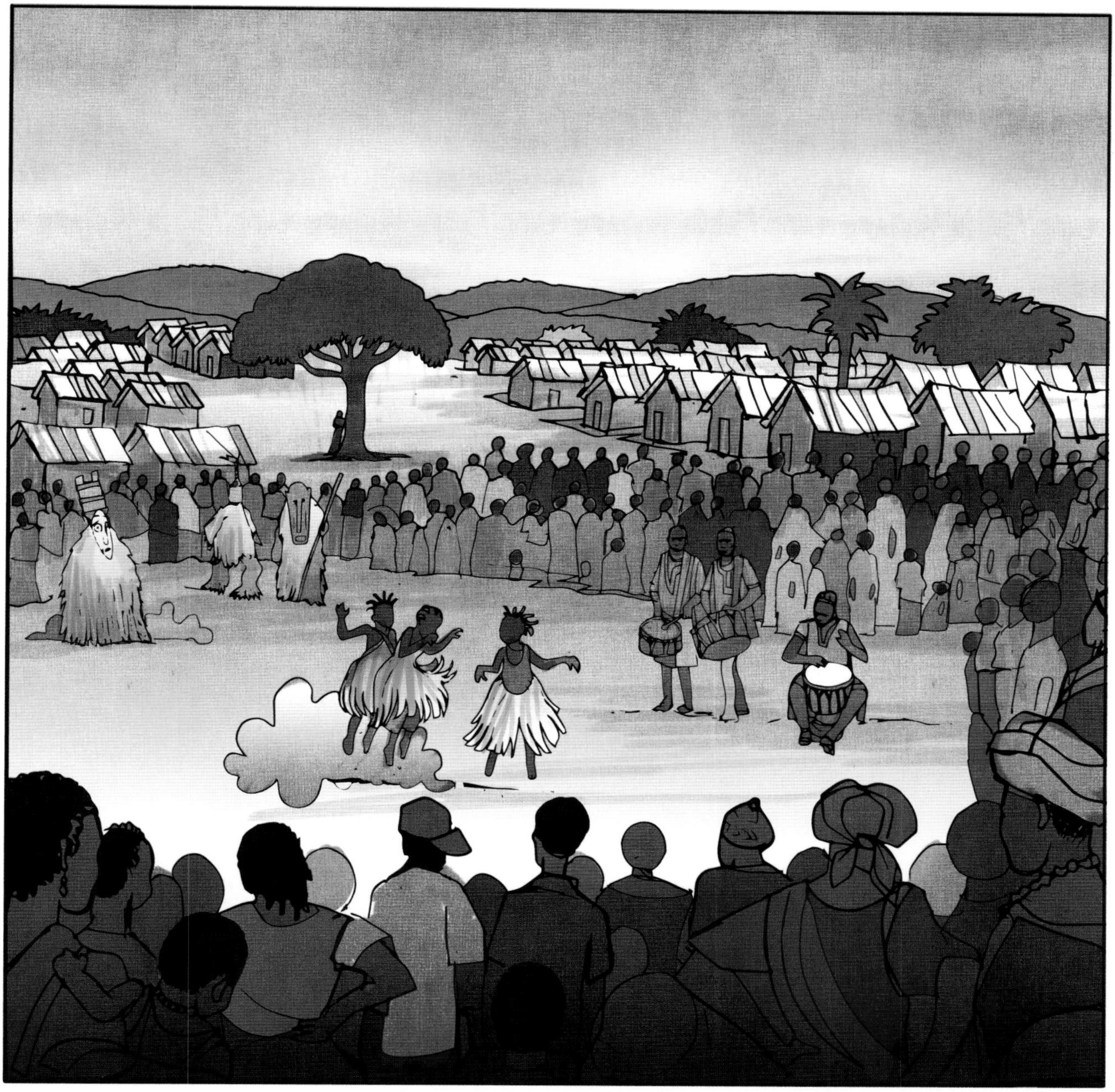

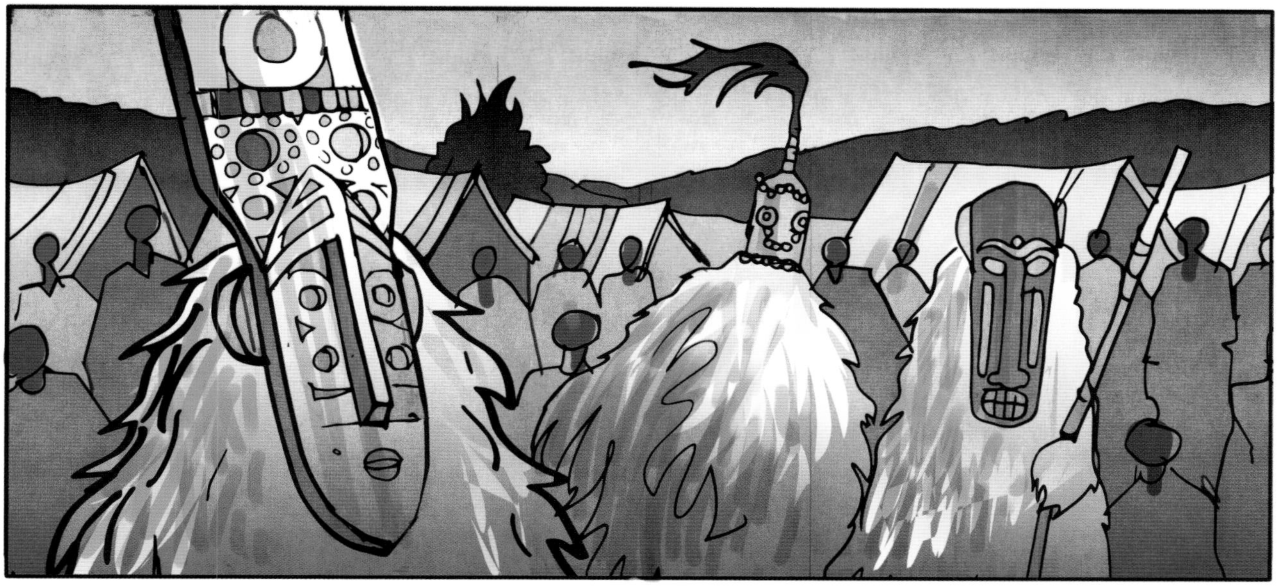

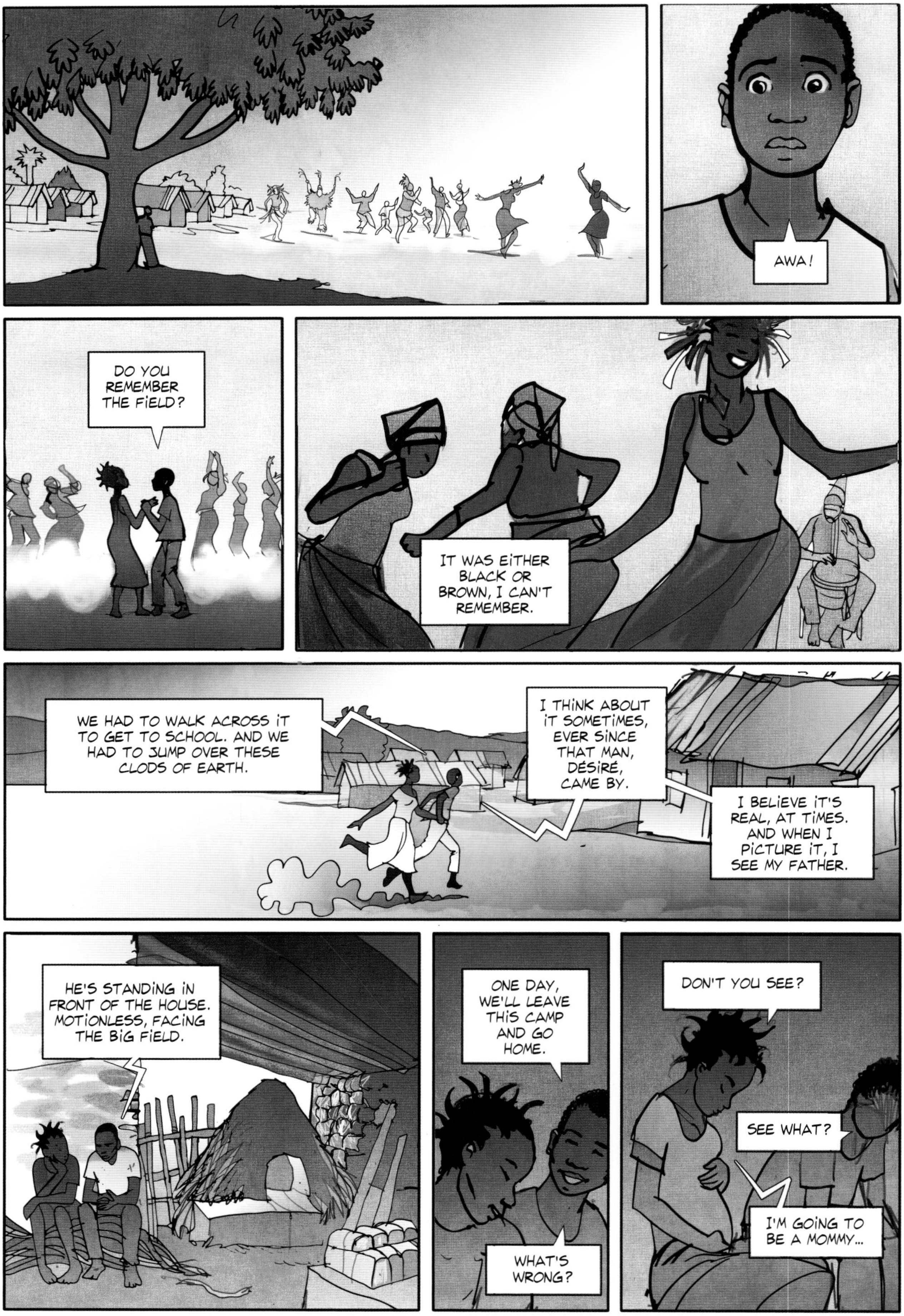
AWA!
DO YOU REMEMBER THE FIELD?
IT WAS EITHER BLACK OR BROWN, I CAN'T REMEMBER.
WE HAD TO WALK ACROSS IT TO GET TO SCHOOL. AND WE HAD TO JUMP OVER THESE CLODS OF EARTH.
I THINK ABOUT IT SOMETIMES, EVER SINCE THAT MAN, DÉSIRÉ, CAME BY.
I BELIEVE IT'S REAL, AT TIMES. AND WHEN I PICTURE IT, I SEE MY FATHER.
HE'S STANDING IN FRONT OF THE HOUSE. MOTIONLESS, FACING THE BIG FIELD.
ONE DAY, WE'LL LEAVE THIS CAMP AND GO HOME.
WHAT'S WRONG?
DON'T YOU SEE?
SEE WHAT?
I'M GOING TO BE A MOMMY...

NO, AWA!

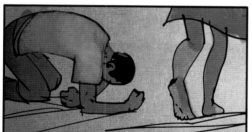

FORGIVE ME... DON'T BE AFRAID OF ME...

I'M NOT AFRAID OF YOU.

AWA, WHEN ALL IS FINISHED, I WILL MARRY YOU.

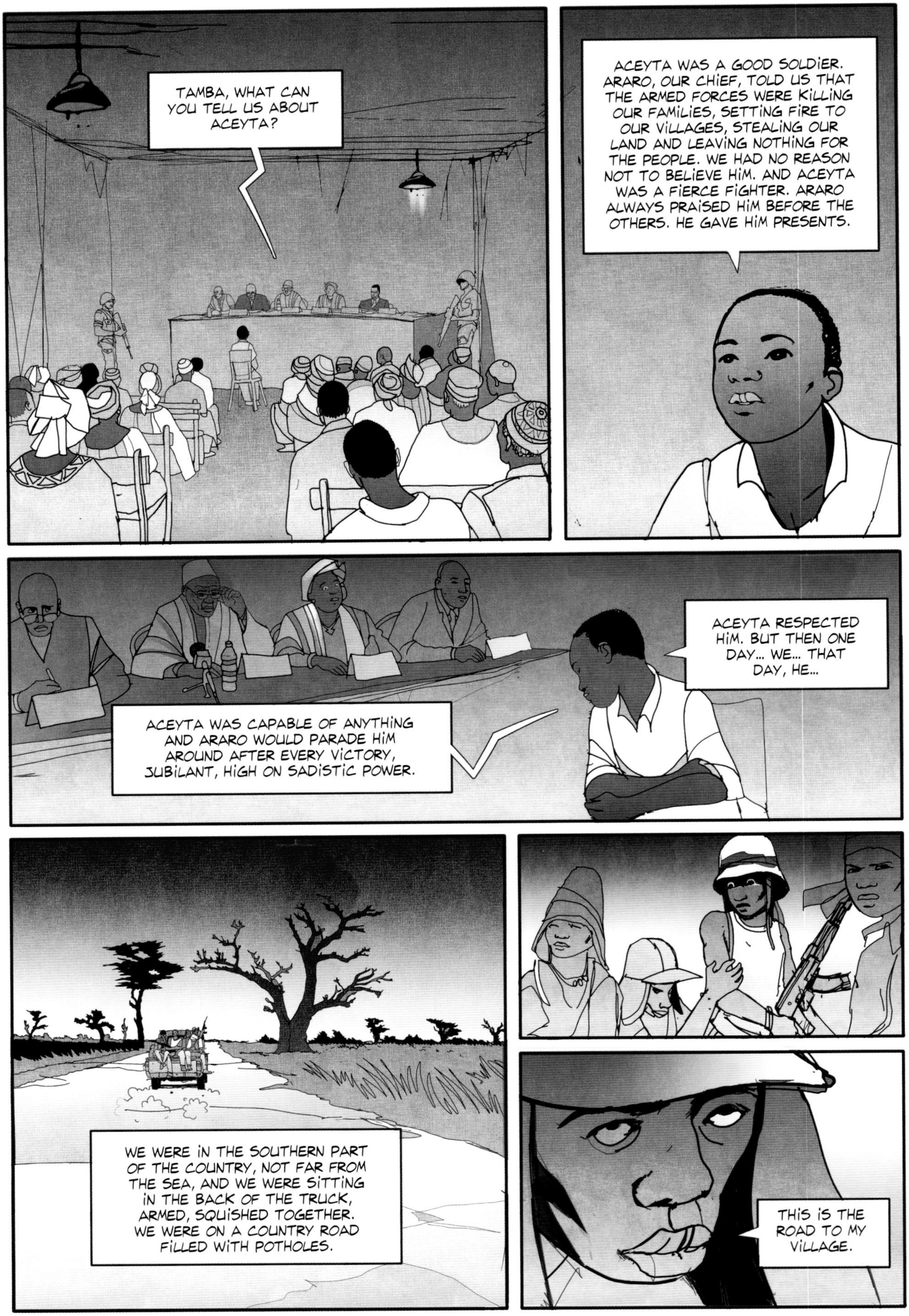
TAMBA, WHAT CAN YOU TELL US ABOUT ACEYTA?
ACEYTA WAS A GOOD SOLDIER. ARARO, OUR CHIEF, TOLD US THAT THE ARMED FORCES WERE KILLING OUR FAMILIES, SETTING FIRE TO OUR VILLAGES, STEALING OUR LAND AND LEAVING NOTHING FOR THE PEOPLE. WE HAD NO REASON NOT TO BELIEVE HIM. AND ACEYTA WAS A FIERCE FIGHTER. ARARO ALWAYS PRAISED HIM BEFORE THE OTHERS. HE GAVE HIM PRESENTS.
ACEYTA RESPECTED HIM. BUT THEN ONE DAY... WE... THAT DAY, HE...
ACEYTA WAS CAPABLE OF ANYTHING AND ARARO WOULD PARADE HIM AROUND AFTER EVERY VICTORY, JUBILANT, HIGH ON SADISTIC POWER.
WE WERE IN THE SOUTHERN PART OF THE COUNTRY, NOT FAR FROM THE SEA, AND WE WERE SITTING IN THE BACK OF THE TRUCK, ARMED, SQUISHED TOGETHER. WE WERE ON A COUNTRY ROAD FILLED WITH POTHOLES.
THIS IS THE ROAD TO MY VILLAGE.

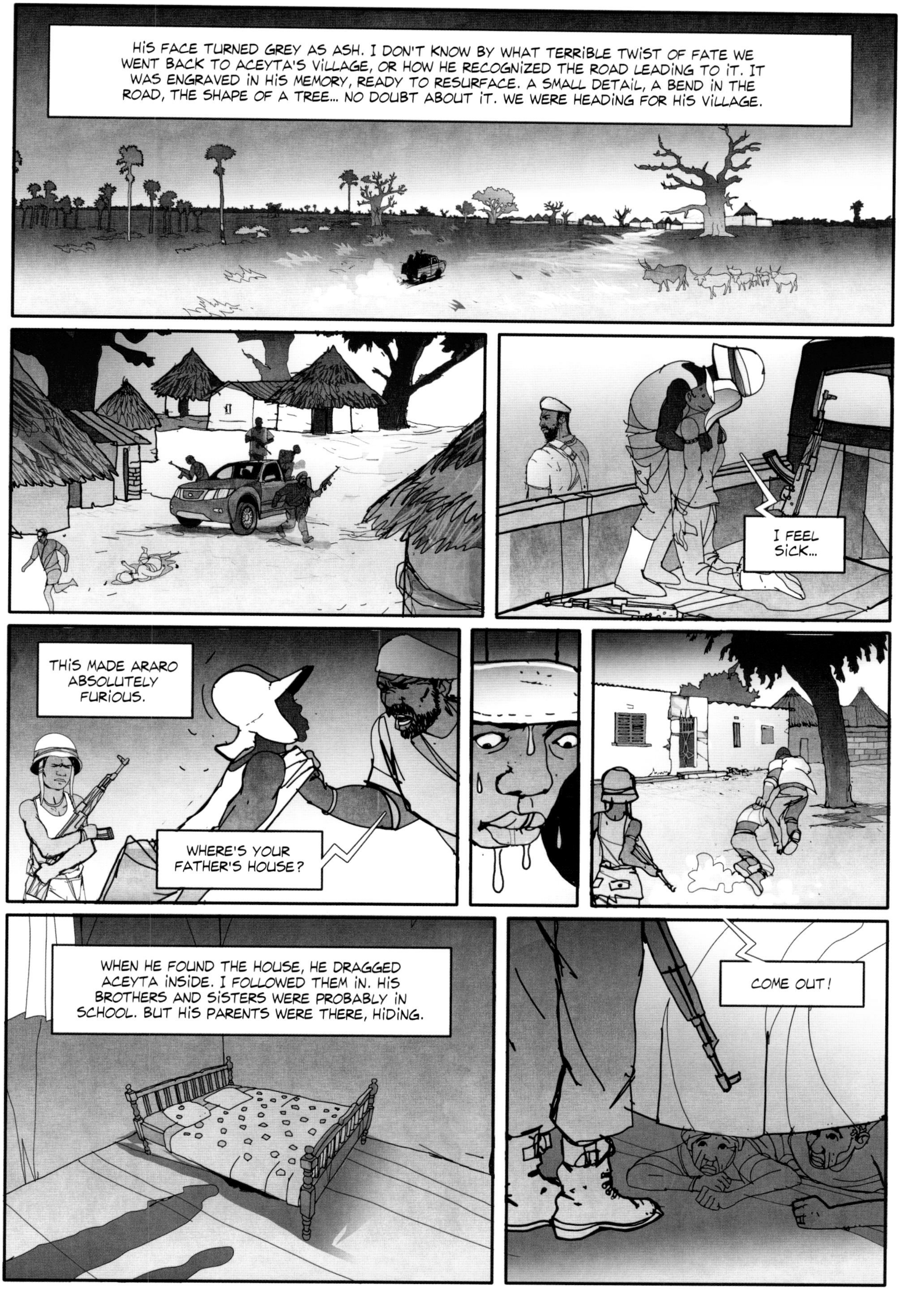
HIS FACE TURNED GREY AS ASH. I DON'T KNOW BY WHAT TERRIBLE TWIST OF FATE WE WENT BACK TO ACEYTA'S VILLAGE, OR HOW HE RECOGNIZED THE ROAD LEADING TO IT. IT WAS ENGRAVED IN HIS MEMORY, READY TO RESURFACE. A SMALL DETAIL, A BEND IN THE ROAD, THE SHAPE OF A TREE... NO DOUBT ABOUT IT. WE WERE HEADING FOR HIS VILLAGE.
I FEEL SICK...
THIS MADE ARARO ABSOLUTELY FURIOUS.
WHERE'S YOUR FATHER'S HOUSE?
WHEN HE FOUND THE HOUSE, HE DRAGGED ACEYTA INSIDE. I FOLLOWED THEM IN. HIS BROTHERS AND SISTERS WERE PROBABLY IN SCHOOL. BUT HIS PARENTS WERE THERE, HIDING.
COME OUT!

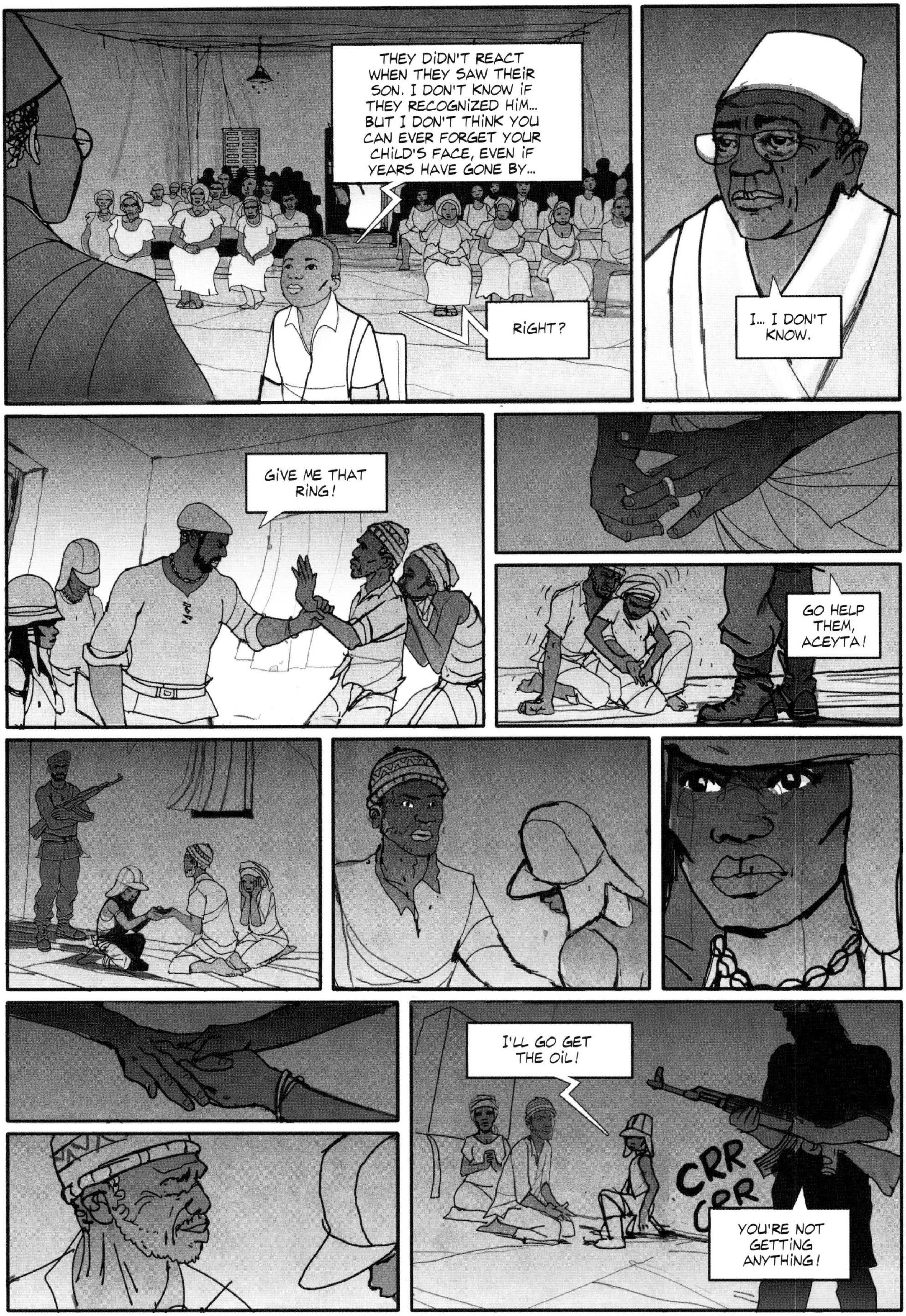
THEY DIDN'T REACT WHEN THEY SAW THEIR SON. I DON'T KNOW IF THEY RECOGNIZED HIM... BUT I DON'T THINK YOU CAN EVER FORGET YOUR CHILD'S FACE, EVEN IF YEARS HAVE GONE BY...
RIGHT?
I... I DON'T KNOW.
GIVE ME THAT RING!
GO HELP THEM, ACEYTA!
I'LL GO GET THE OIL!
CRR CRR
YOU'RE NOT GETTING ANYTHING!

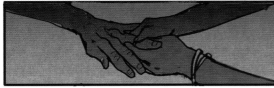

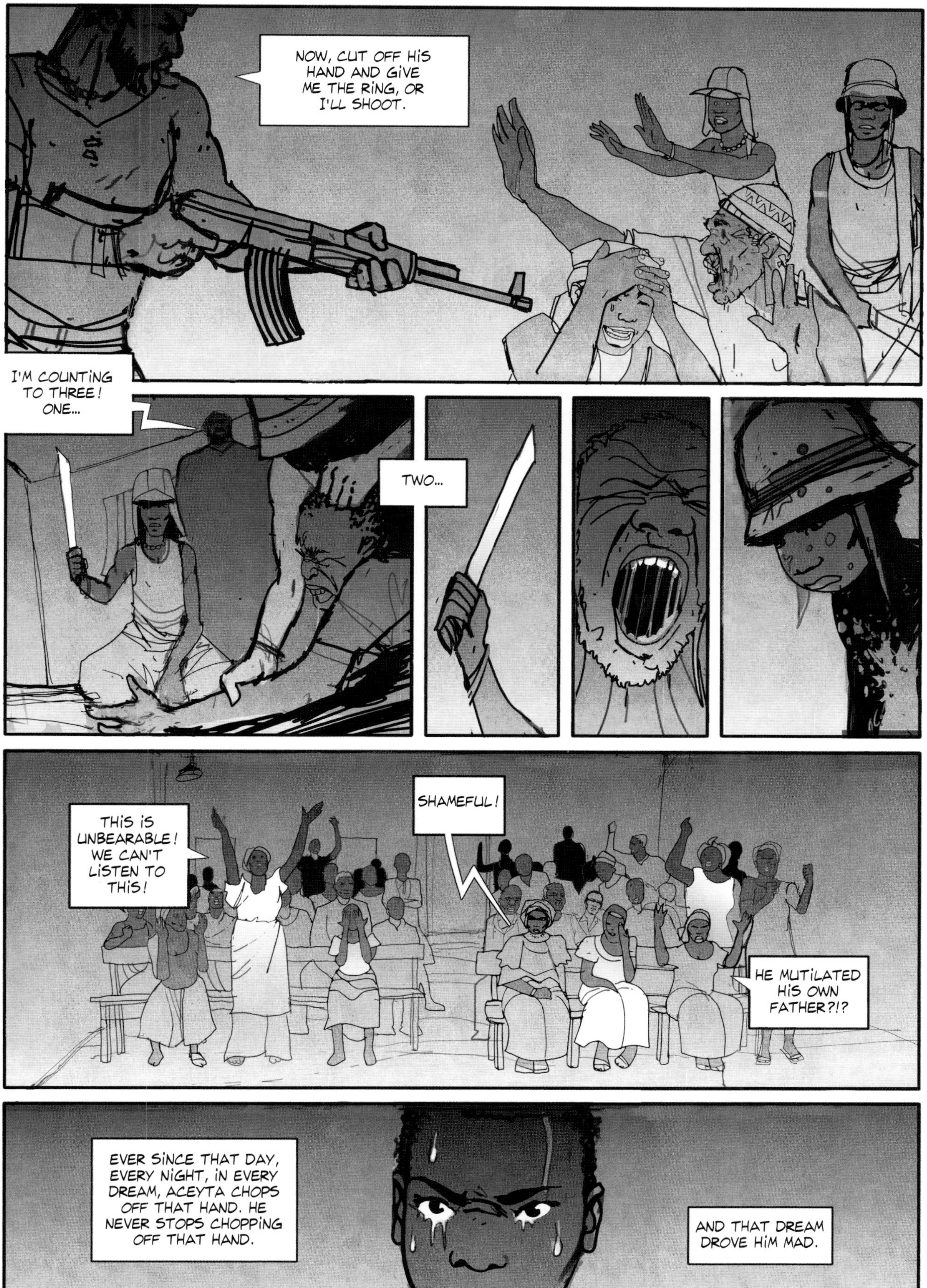
NOW, CUT OFF HIS HAND AND GIVE ME THE RING, OR I'LL SHOOT.
I'M COUNTING TO THREE! ONE...
TWO...
THIS IS UNBEARABLE! WE CAN'T LISTEN TO THIS!
SHAMEFUL!
HE MUTILATED HIS OWN FATHER?!?
EVER SINCE THAT DAY, EVERY NIGHT, IN EVERY DREAM, ACEYTA CHOPS OFF THAT HAND. HE NEVER STOPS CHOPPING OFF THAT HAND.
AND THAT DREAM DROVE HIM MAD.

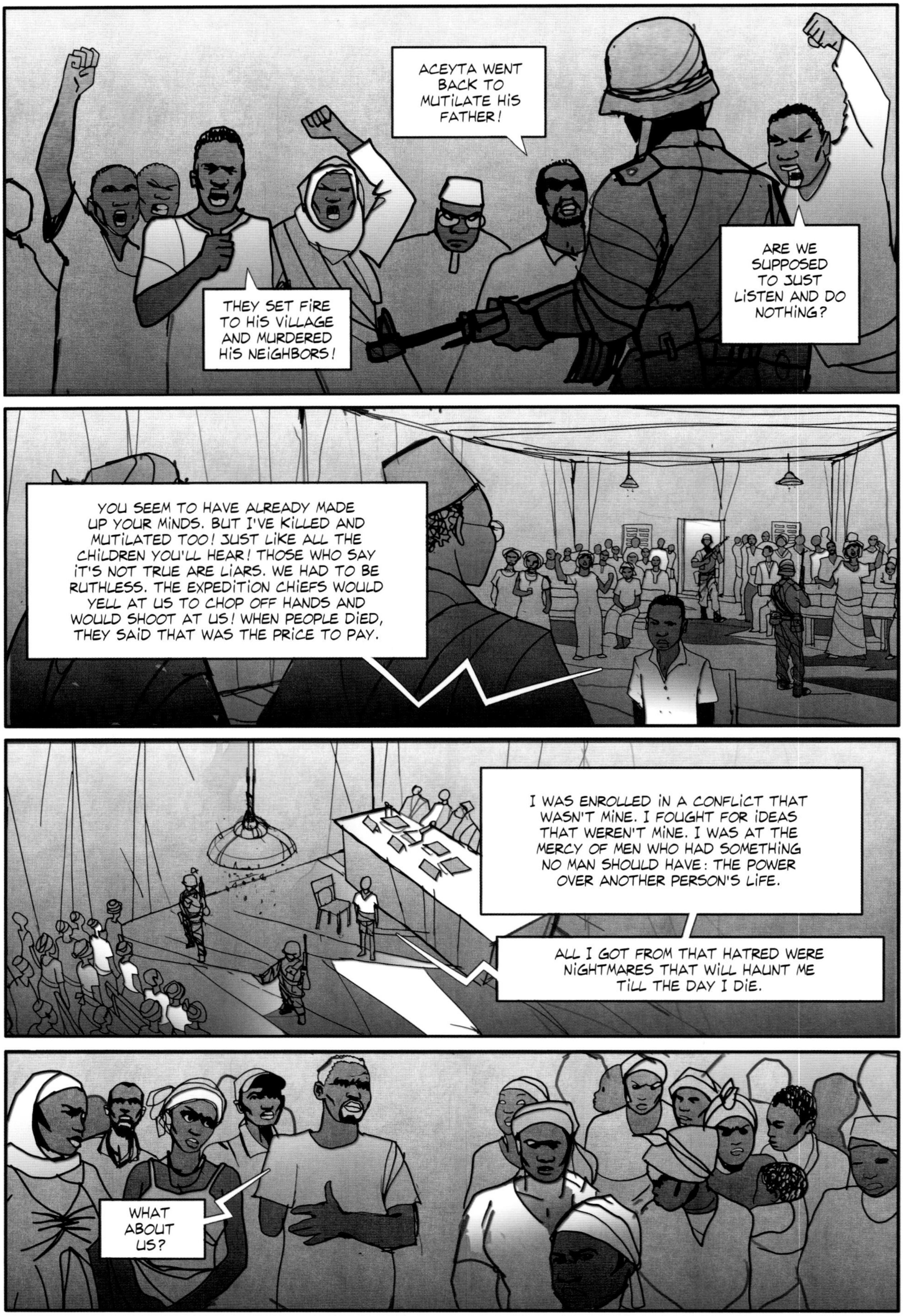
ACEYTA WENT BACK TO MUTILATE HIS FATHER!
THEY SET FIRE TO HIS VILLAGE AND MURDERED HIS NEIGHBORS!
ARE WE SUPPOSED TO JUST LISTEN AND DO NOTHING?
YOU SEEM TO HAVE ALREADY MADE UP YOUR MINDS. BUT I'VE KILLED AND MUTILATED TOO! JUST LIKE ALL THE CHILDREN YOU'LL HEAR! THOSE WHO SAY IT'S NOT TRUE ARE LIARS. WE HAD TO BE RUTHLESS. THE EXPEDITION CHIEFS WOULD YELL AT US TO CHOP OFF HANDS AND WOULD SHOOT AT US! WHEN PEOPLE DIED, THEY SAID THAT WAS THE PRICE TO PAY.
I WAS ENROLLED IN A CONFLICT THAT WASN'T MINE. I FOUGHT FOR IDEAS THAT WEREN'T MINE. I WAS AT THE MERCY OF MEN WHO HAD SOMETHING NO MAN SHOULD HAVE: THE POWER OVER ANOTHER PERSON'S LIFE.
ALL I GOT FROM THAT HATRED WERE NIGHTMARES THAT WILL HAUNT ME TILL THE DAY I DIE.
WHAT ABOUT US?

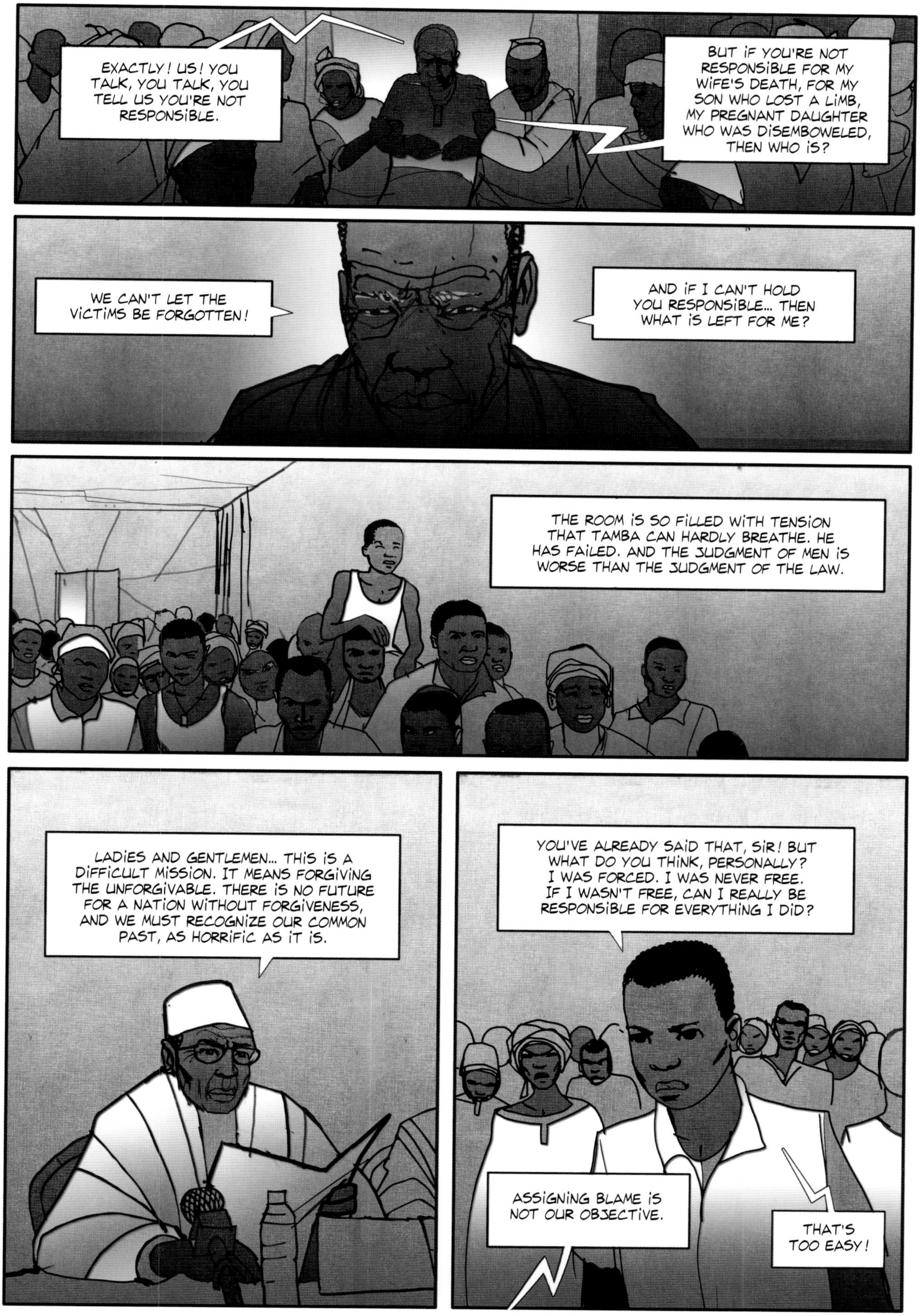
EXACTLY! US! YOU TALK, YOU TALK, YOU TELL US YOU'RE NOT RESPONSIBLE.
BUT IF YOU'RE NOT RESPONSIBLE FOR MY WIFE'S DEATH, FOR MY SON WHO LOST A LIMB, MY PREGNANT DAUGHTER WHO WAS DISEMBOWELED, THEN WHO IS?
WE CAN'T LET THE VICTIMS BE FORGOTTEN!
AND IF I CAN'T HOLD YOU RESPONSIBLE... THEN WHAT IS LEFT FOR ME?
THE ROOM IS SO FILLED WITH TENSION THAT TAMBA CAN HARDLY BREATHE. HE HAS FAILED. AND THE JUDGMENT OF MEN IS WORSE THAN THE JUDGMENT OF THE LAW.
LADIES AND GENTLEMEN... THIS IS A DIFFICULT MISSION. IT MEANS FORGIVING THE UNFORGIVABLE. THERE IS NO FUTURE FOR A NATION WITHOUT FORGIVENESS, AND WE MUST RECOGNIZE OUR COMMON PAST, AS HORRIFIC AS IT IS.
YOU'VE ALREADY SAID THAT, SIR! BUT WHAT DO YOU THINK, PERSONALLY? I WAS FORCED. I WAS NEVER FREE. IF I WASN'T FREE, CAN I REALLY BE RESPONSIBLE FOR EVERYTHING I DID?
ASSIGNING BLAME IS NOT OUR OBJECTIVE.
THAT'S TOO EASY!

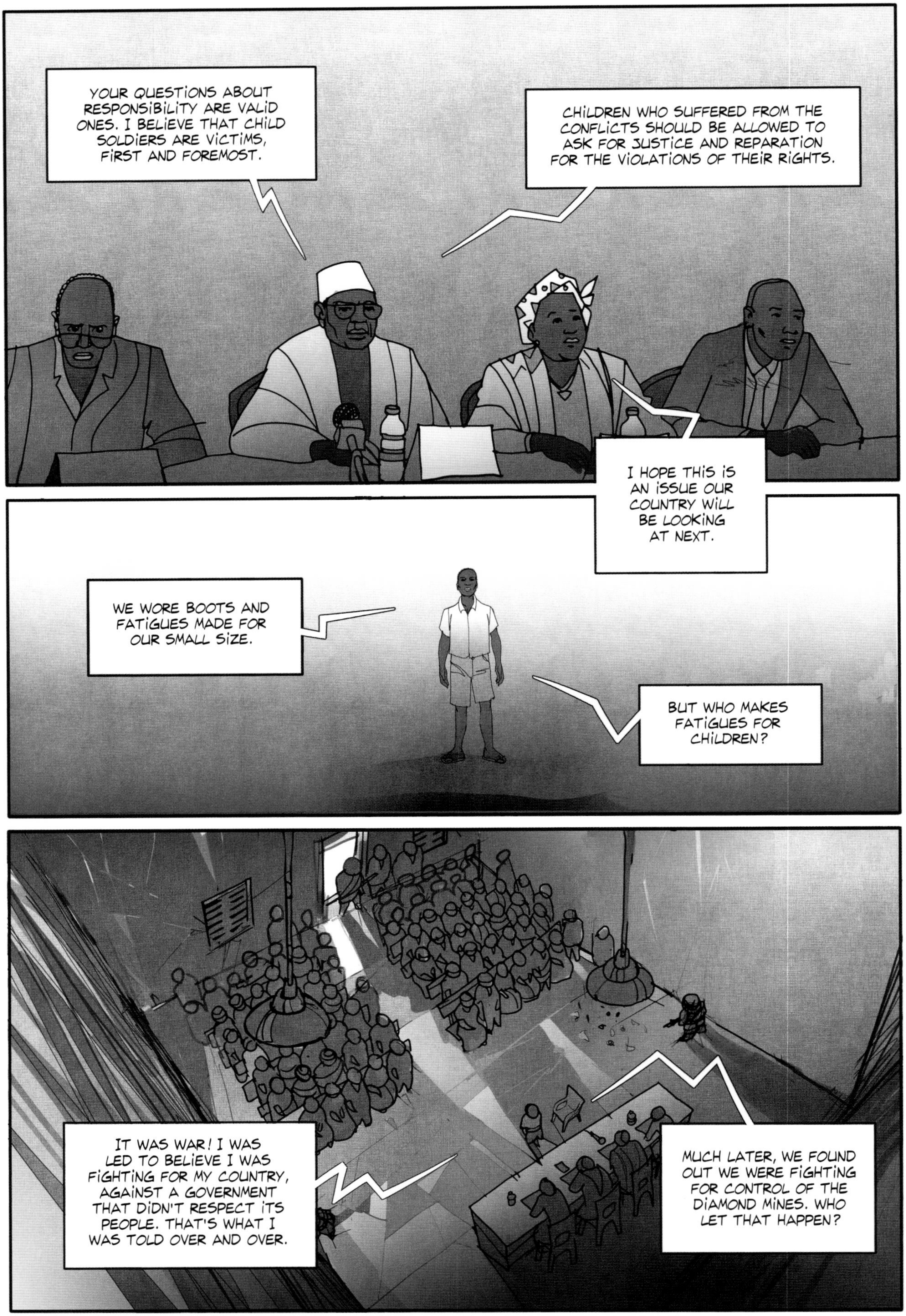
YOUR QUESTIONS ABOUT RESPONSIBILITY ARE VALID ONES. I BELIEVE THAT CHILD SOLDIERS ARE VICTIMS, FIRST AND FOREMOST.
CHILDREN WHO SUFFERED FROM THE CONFLICTS SHOULD BE ALLOWED TO ASK FOR JUSTICE AND REPARATION FOR THE VIOLATIONS OF THEIR RIGHTS.
I HOPE THIS IS AN ISSUE OUR COUNTRY WILL BE LOOKING AT NEXT.
WE WORE BOOTS AND FATIGUES MADE FOR OUR SMALL SIZE.
BUT WHO MAKES FATIGUES FOR CHILDREN?
IT WAS WAR! I WAS LED TO BELIEVE I WAS FIGHTING FOR MY COUNTRY, AGAINST A GOVERNMENT THAT DIDN'T RESPECT ITS PEOPLE. THAT'S WHAT I WAS TOLD OVER AND OVER.
MUCH LATER, WE FOUND OUT WE WERE FIGHTING FOR CONTROL OF THE DIAMOND MINES. WHO LET THAT HAPPEN?

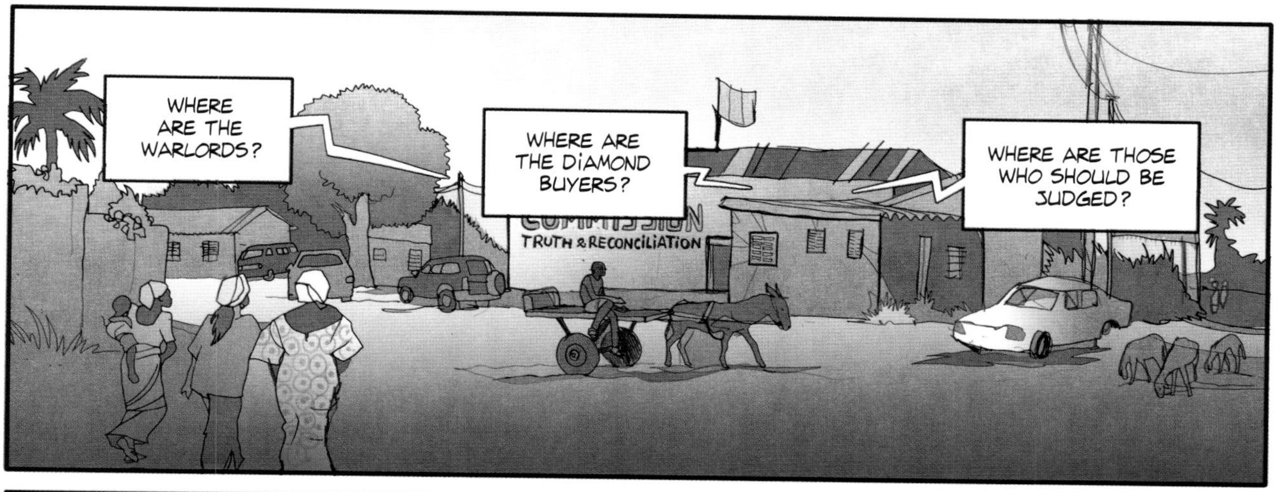
WHERE ARE THE WARLORDS?
WHERE ARE THE DIAMOND BUYERS?
WHERE ARE THOSE WHO SHOULD BE JUDGED?
COMMISSION
TRUTH & RECONCILIATION

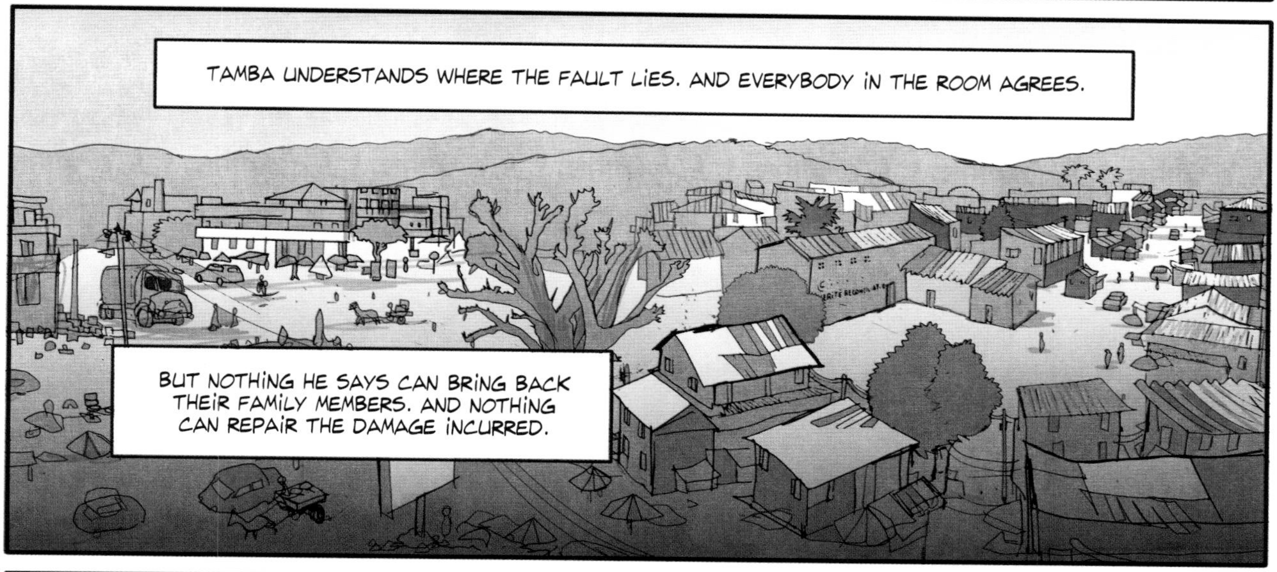
TAMBA UNDERSTANDS WHERE THE FAULT LIES. AND EVERYBODY IN THE ROOM AGREES.
BUT NOTHING HE SAYS CAN BRING BACK THEIR FAMILY MEMBERS. AND NOTHING CAN REPAIR THE DAMAGE INCURRED.

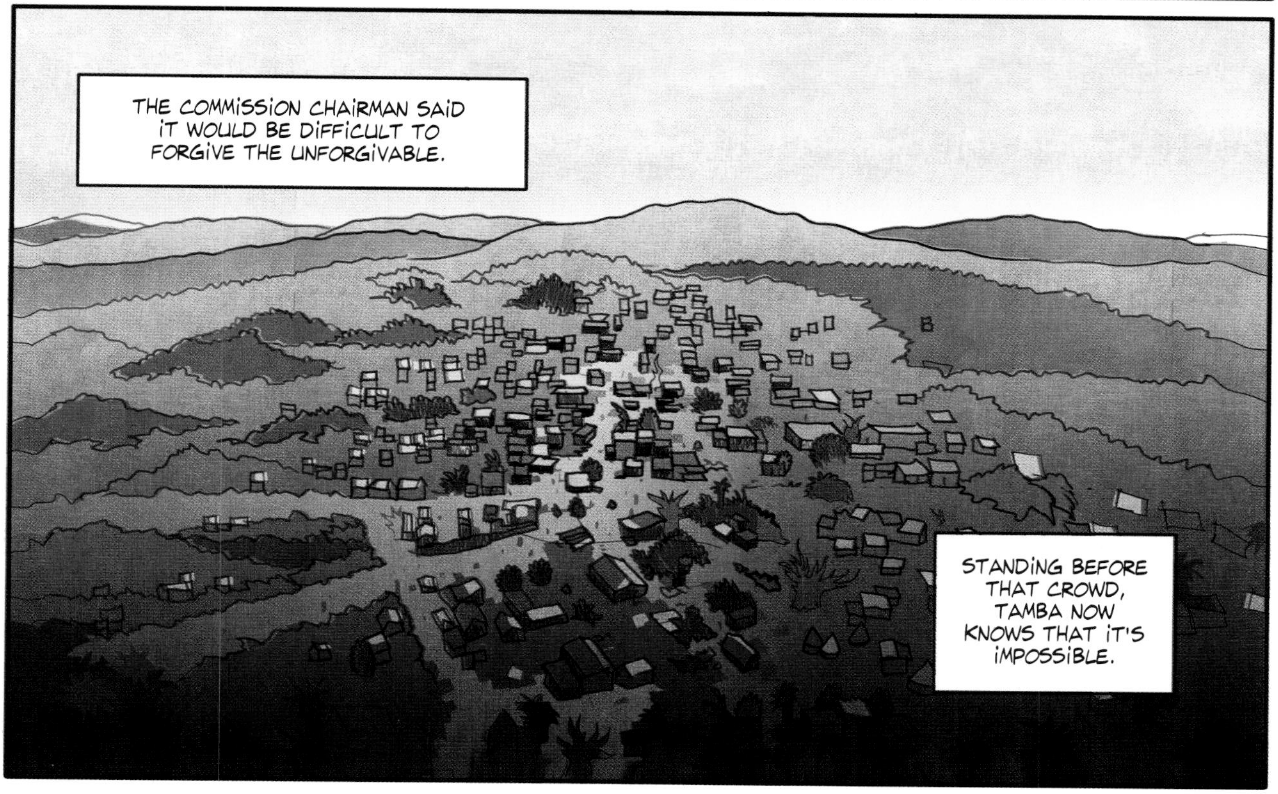
THE COMMISSION CHAIRMAN SAID IT WOULD BE DIFFICULT TO FORGIVE THE UNFORGIVABLE.
STANDING BEFORE THAT CROWD, TAMBA NOW KNOWS THAT IT'S IMPOSSIBLE.

I HAVE NO SOUL LEFT.

I HAVE NO BODY LEFT.

SOMETIMES I PUSH DOWN ON IT WITH MY HANDS. BUT THE CHILD GROWING INSIDE ME IS ALREADY TOO BIG, AND I CAN'T MAKE HIM GO AWAY ANYMORE.

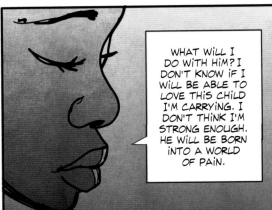

WHAT WILL I DO WITH HIM? I DON'T KNOW IF I WILL BE ABLE TO LOVE THIS CHILD I'M CARRYING. I DON'T THINK I'M STRONG ENOUGH. HE WILL BE BORN INTO A WORLD OF PAIN.

YOU SAY YOU'LL TAKE ME HOME WITH YOU. BUT WHAT WILL THE PEOPLE OF YOUR VILLAGE SAY WHEN THEY SEE ME?

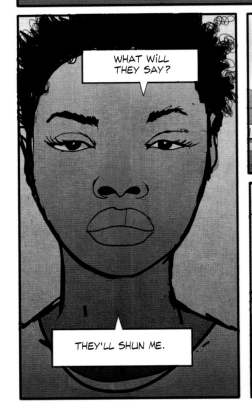

WHAT WILL THEY SAY?

THEY'LL SHUN ME.

I'M JUST A LITTLE GIRL, GEORGE. WHAT AM I SUPPOSED TO DO WITH THIS CHILD?

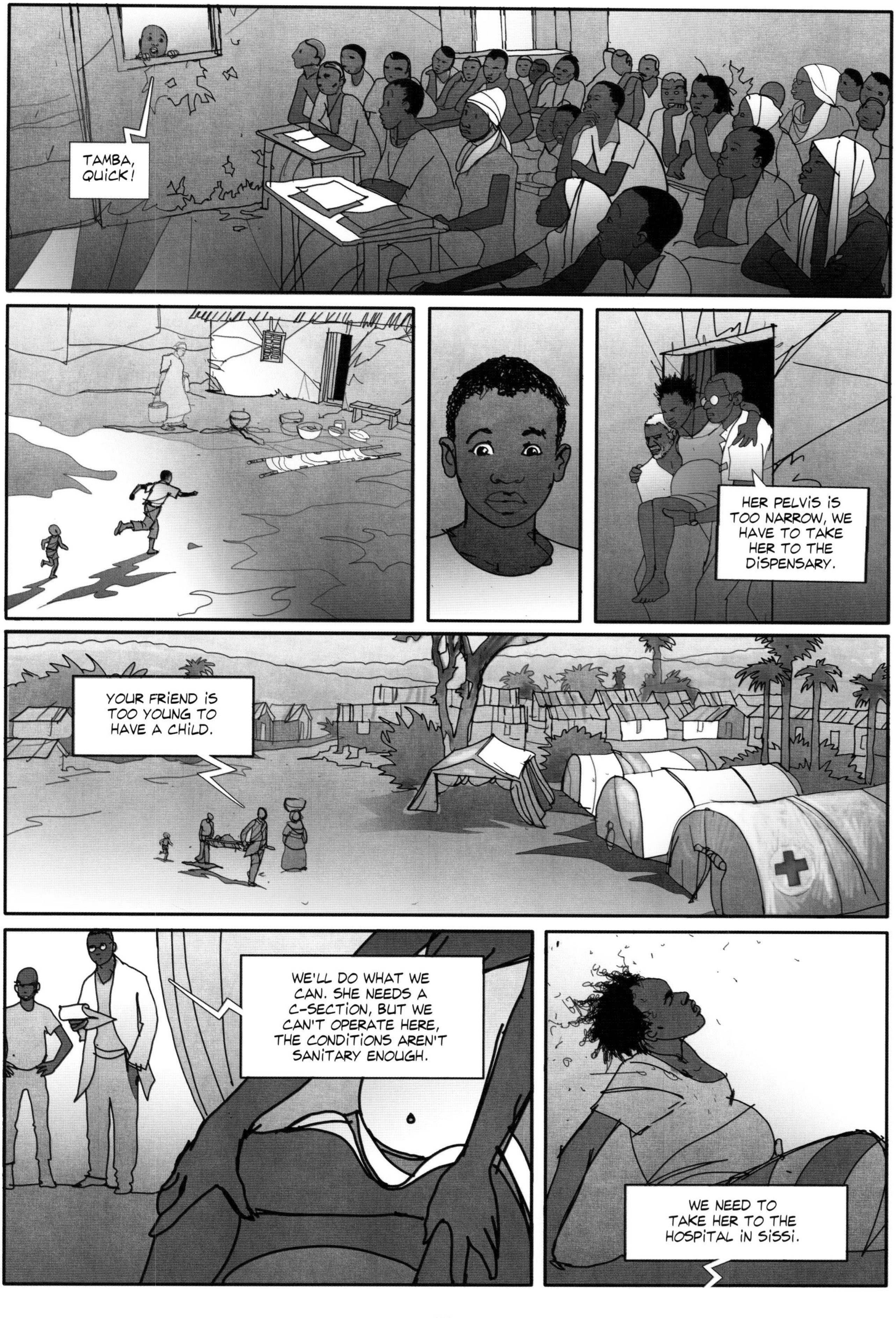
TAMBA, QUICK!
HER PELVIS IS TOO NARROW, WE HAVE TO TAKE HER TO THE DISPENSARY.
YOUR FRIEND IS TOO YOUNG TO HAVE A CHILD.
WE'LL DO WHAT WE CAN. SHE NEEDS A C-SECTION, BUT WE CAN'T OPERATE HERE, THE CONDITIONS AREN'T SANITARY ENOUGH.
WE NEED TO TAKE HER TO THE HOSPITAL IN SISSI.

OKAY. HOW MUCH DOES IT COST?

AT LEAST THIRTY THOUSAND FOR THE RIDE AND SIXTY THOUSAND FOR THE C-SECTION. AND YOU'LL HAVE TO BUY GAS FOR THE GENERATOR. IT'S ALMOST NIGHT, AND THEY WILL NEED LIGHT.

YOU CAN ALSO PRAY THAT EVERYTHING GOES ALL RIGHT. PEOPLE WITH NO MONEY DO THAT AND SOMETIMES IT'S ENOUGH.

HMM...

I'M SORRY.

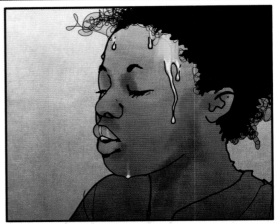

I MADE THIS FOR THE BABY.

COME, NOW. YOU HAVE THINGS TO DO.

WHAT'S THE BABY'S NAME?

I DON'T KNOW.

IT'S BETTER TO HAVE A NAME!

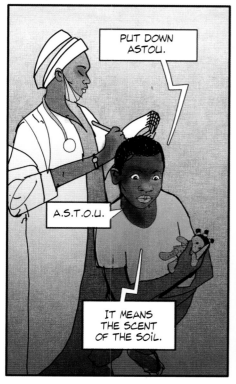

PUT DOWN ASTOU.

A.S.T.O.U.

IT MEANS THE SCENT OF THE SOIL.

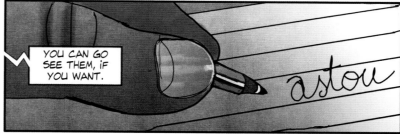

YOU CAN GO SEE THEM, IF YOU WANT.

astou

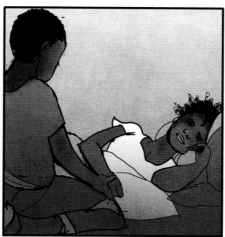

I NAMED HER ASTOU, AND ALL THROUGH HER LIFE WE WILL TELL HER I'M HER FATHER.

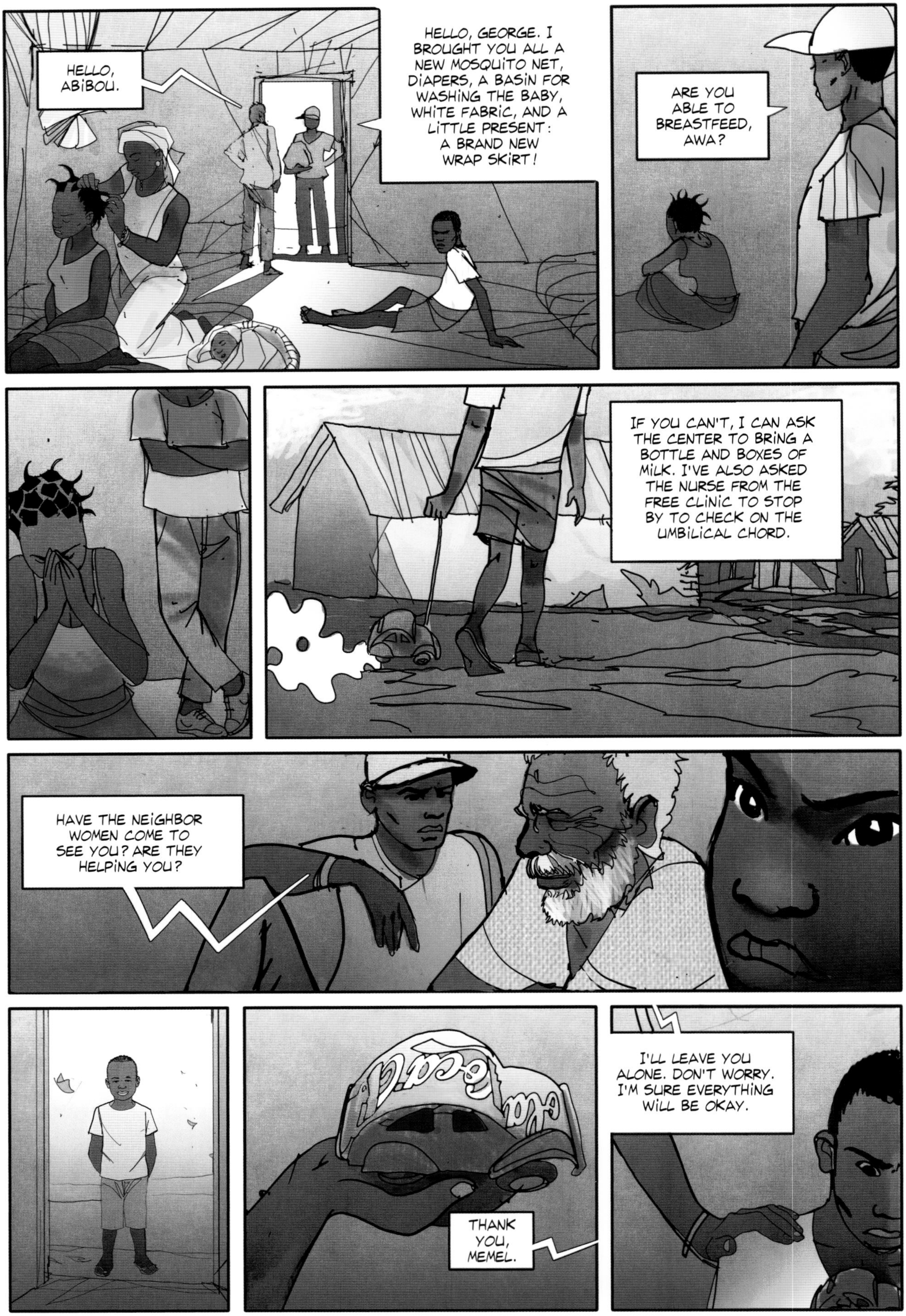
HELLO, ABIBOU.
HELLO, GEORGE. I BROUGHT YOU ALL A NEW MOSQUITO NET, DIAPERS, A BASIN FOR WASHING THE BABY, WHITE FABRIC, AND A LITTLE PRESENT: A BRAND NEW WRAP SKIRT!
ARE YOU ABLE TO BREASTFEED, AWA?
IF YOU CAN'T, I CAN ASK THE CENTER TO BRING A BOTTLE AND BOXES OF MILK. I'VE ALSO ASKED THE NURSE FROM THE FREE CLINIC TO STOP BY TO CHECK ON THE UMBILICAL CHORD.
HAVE THE NEIGHBOR WOMEN COME TO SEE YOU? ARE THEY HELPING YOU?
THANK YOU, MEMEL.
I'LL LEAVE YOU ALONE. DON'T WORRY. I'M SURE EVERYTHING WILL BE OKAY.

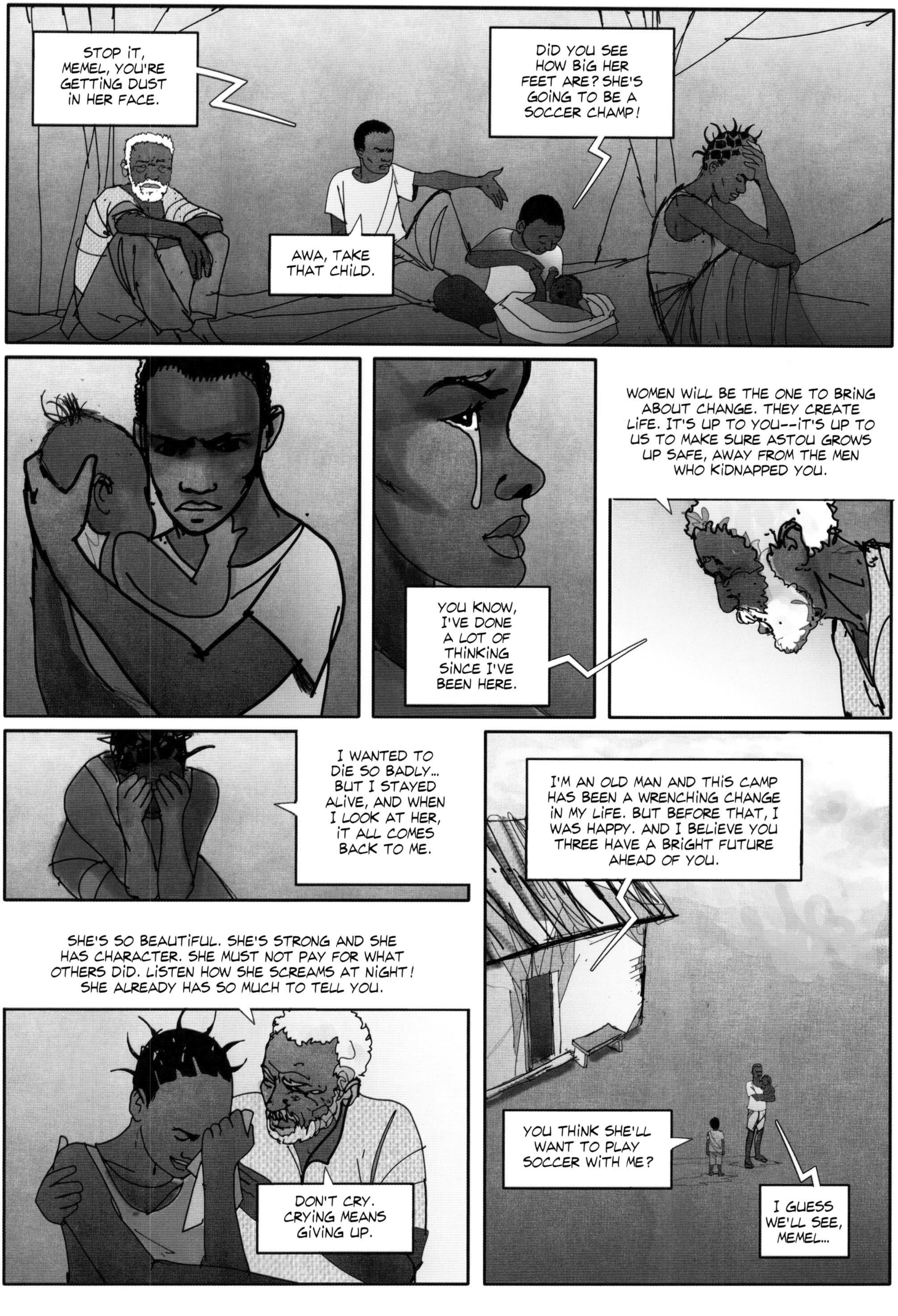
STOP iT, MEMEL, YOU'RE GETTiNG DUST iN HER FACE.
DiD YOU SEE HOW BiG HER FEET ARE? SHE'S GOiNG TO BE A SOCCER CHAMP!
AWA, TAKE THAT CHiLD.
WOMEN WiLL BE THE ONE TO BRiNG ABOUT CHANGE. THEY CREATE LiFE. iT'S UP TO YOU--iT'S UP TO US TO MAKE SURE ASTOU GROWS UP SAFE, AWAY FROM THE MEN WHO KiDNAPPED YOU.
YOU KNOW, I'VE DONE A LOT OF THiNKiNG SiNCE I'VE BEEN HERE.
I WANTED TO DiE SO BADLY... BUT I STAYED ALiVE, AND WHEN I LOOK AT HER, iT ALL COMES BACK TO ME.
SHE'S SO BEAUTiFUL. SHE'S STRONG AND SHE HAS CHARACTER. SHE MUST NOT PAY FOR WHAT OTHERS DiD. LiSTEN HOW SHE SCREAMS AT NiGHT! SHE ALREADY HAS SO MUCH TO TELL YOU.
DON'T CRY. CRYiNG MEANS GiViNG UP.
I'M AN OLD MAN AND THiS CAMP HAS BEEN A WRENCHiNG CHANGE iN MY LiFE. BUT BEFORE THAT, I WAS HAPPY. AND I BELiEVE YOU THREE HAVE A BRiGHT FUTURE AHEAD OF YOU.
YOU THiNK SHE'LL WANT TO PLAY SOCCER WiTH ME?
I GUESS WE'LL SEE, MEMEL...

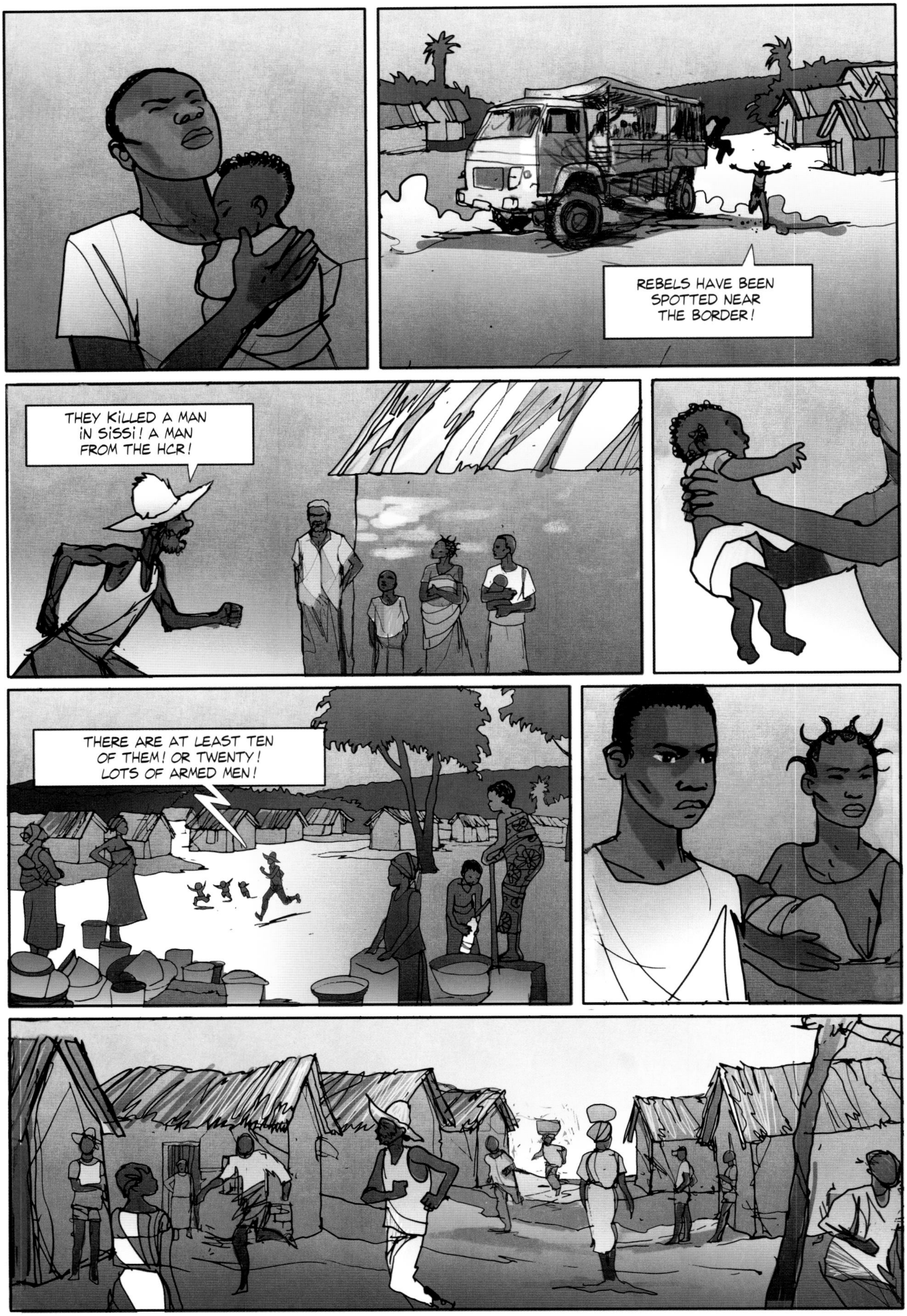
REBELS HAVE BEEN SPOTTED NEAR THE BORDER!
THEY KILLED A MAN IN SISSI! A MAN FROM THE HCR!
THERE ARE AT LEAST TEN OF THEM! OR TWENTY! LOTS OF ARMED MEN!

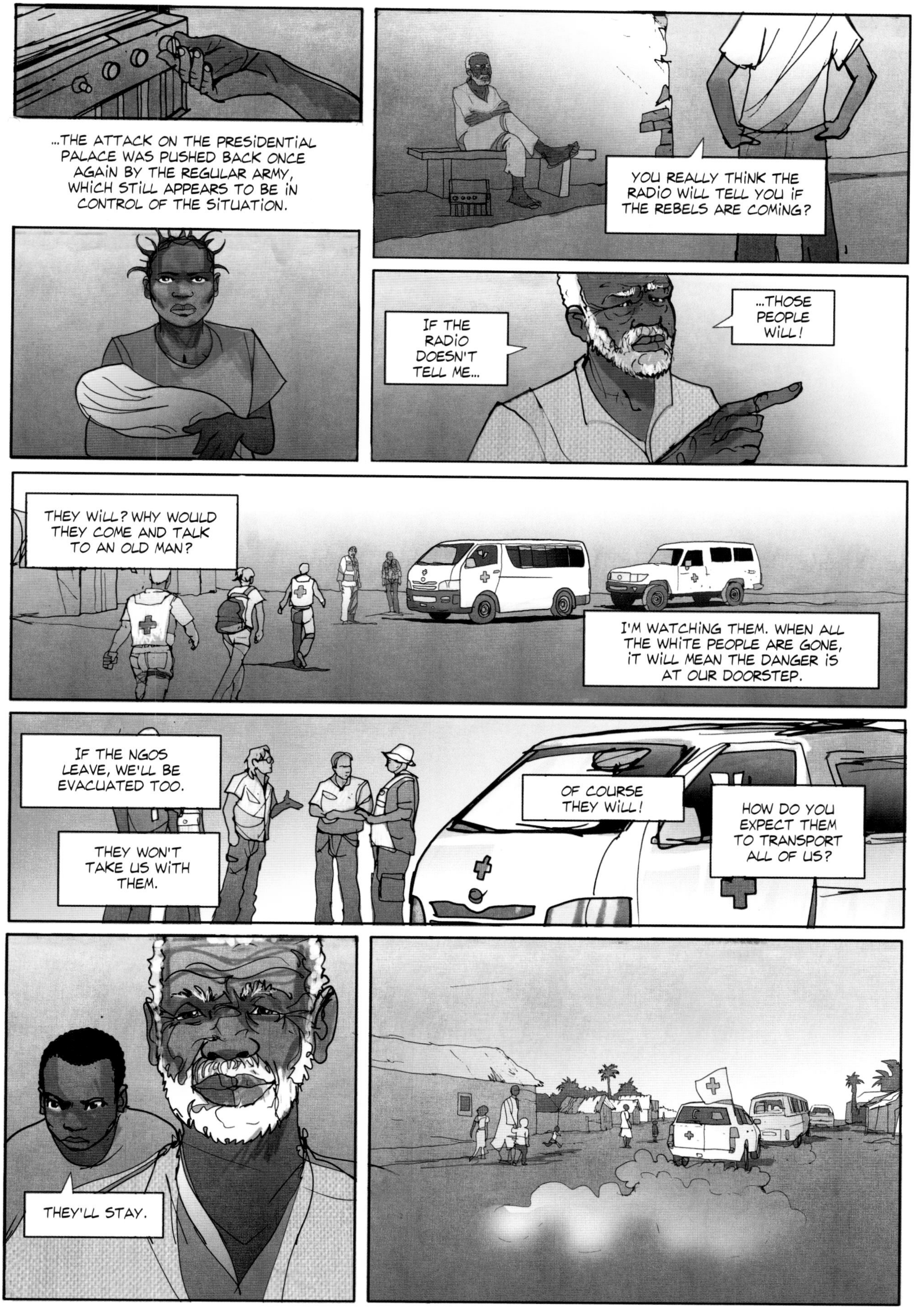
...THE ATTACK ON THE PRESIDENTIAL PALACE WAS PUSHED BACK ONCE AGAIN BY THE REGULAR ARMY, WHICH STILL APPEARS TO BE IN CONTROL OF THE SITUATION.
YOU REALLY THINK THE RADIO WILL TELL YOU IF THE REBELS ARE COMING?
IF THE RADIO DOESN'T TELL ME...
...THOSE PEOPLE WILL!
THEY WILL? WHY WOULD THEY COME AND TALK TO AN OLD MAN?
I'M WATCHING THEM. WHEN ALL THE WHITE PEOPLE ARE GONE, IT WILL MEAN THE DANGER IS AT OUR DOORSTEP.
IF THE NGOS LEAVE, WE'LL BE EVACUATED TOO.
THEY WON'T TAKE US WITH THEM.
OF COURSE THEY WILL!
HOW DO YOU EXPECT THEM TO TRANSPORT ALL OF US?
THEY'LL STAY.

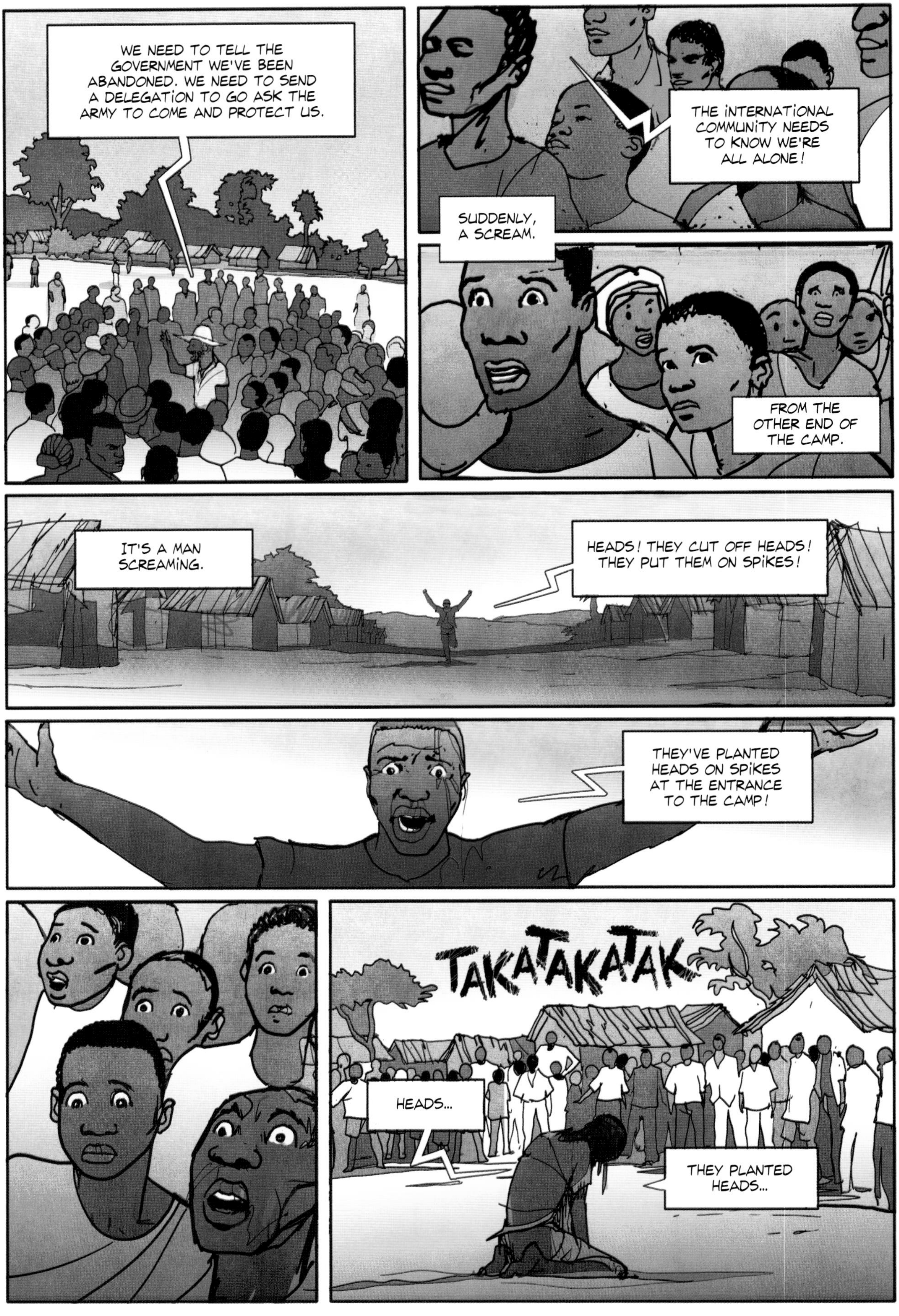
WE NEED TO TELL THE GOVERNMENT WE'VE BEEN ABANDONED. WE NEED TO SEND A DELEGATION TO GO ASK THE ARMY TO COME AND PROTECT US.
THE INTERNATIONAL COMMUNITY NEEDS TO KNOW WE'RE ALL ALONE!
SUDDENLY, A SCREAM.
FROM THE OTHER END OF THE CAMP.
IT'S A MAN SCREAMING.
HEADS! THEY CUT OFF HEADS! THEY PUT THEM ON SPIKES!
THEY'VE PLANTED HEADS ON SPIKES AT THE ENTRANCE TO THE CAMP!
TAKATAKATAK
HEADS...
THEY PLANTED HEADS...

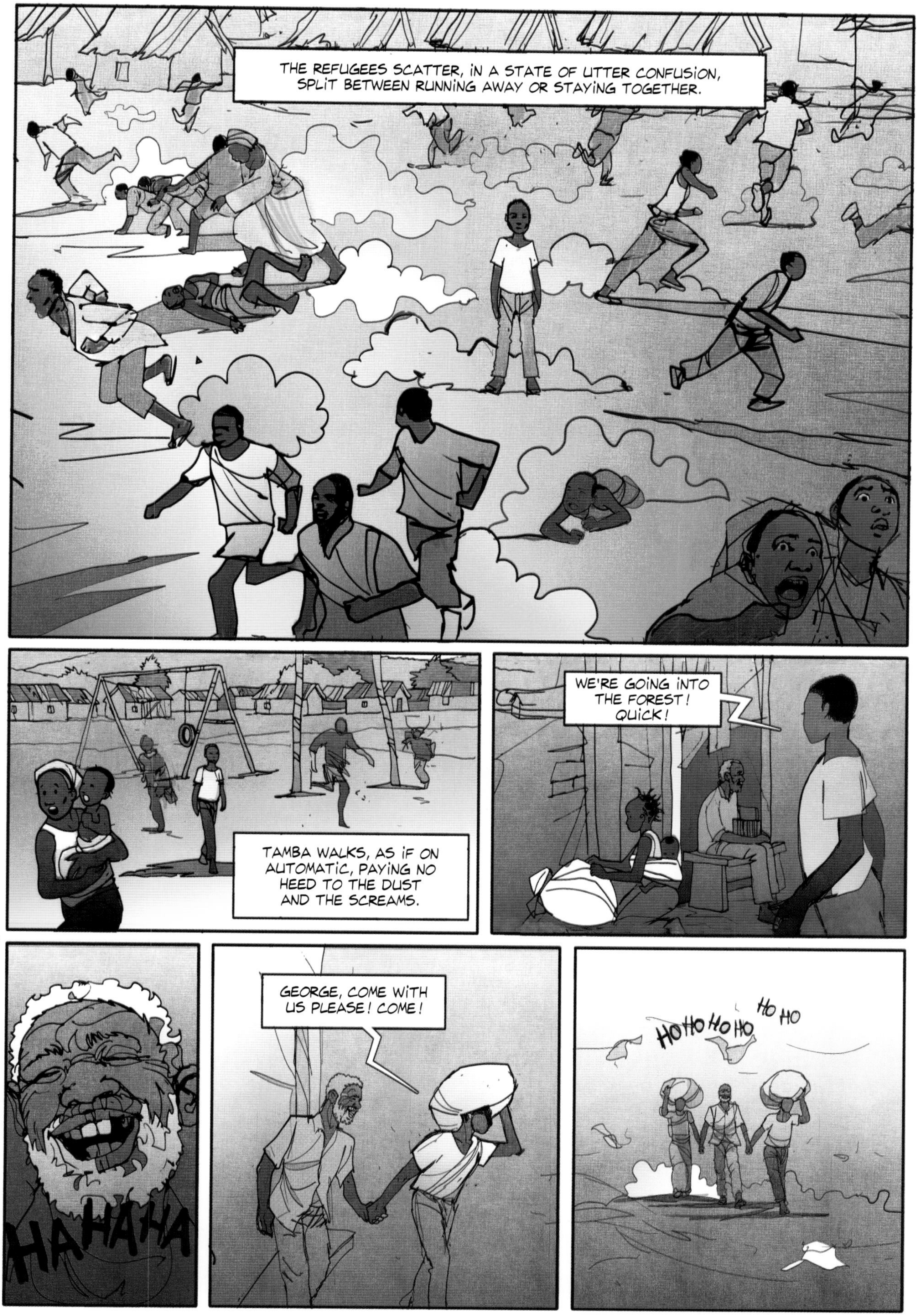
THE REFUGEES SCATTER, IN A STATE OF UTTER CONFUSION, SPLIT BETWEEN RUNNING AWAY OR STAYING TOGETHER.
TAMBA WALKS, AS IF ON AUTOMATIC, PAYING NO HEED TO THE DUST AND THE SCREAMS.
WE'RE GOING INTO THE FOREST! QUICK!
HAHAHA
GEORGE, COME WITH US PLEASE! COME!
HO HO HO HO HO
HO HO

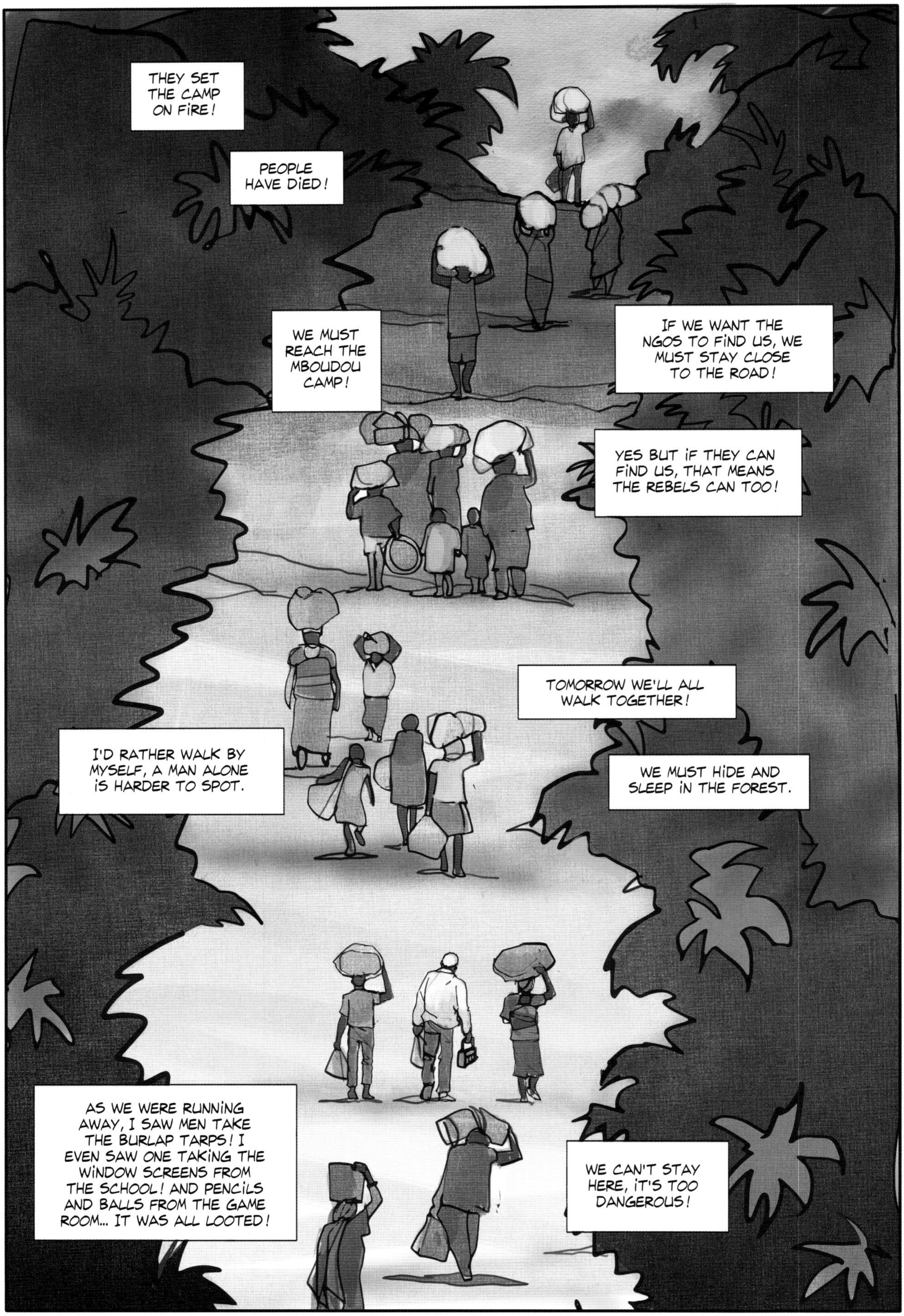
THEY SET THE CAMP ON FIRE!
PEOPLE HAVE DIED!
WE MUST REACH THE MBOUDOU CAMP!
IF WE WANT THE NGOS TO FIND US, WE MUST STAY CLOSE TO THE ROAD!
YES BUT IF THEY CAN FIND US, THAT MEANS THE REBELS CAN TOO!
TOMORROW WE'LL ALL WALK TOGETHER!
I'D RATHER WALK BY MYSELF, A MAN ALONE IS HARDER TO SPOT.
WE MUST HIDE AND SLEEP IN THE FOREST.
AS WE WERE RUNNING AWAY, I SAW MEN TAKE THE BURLAP TARPS! I EVEN SAW ONE TAKING THE WINDOW SCREENS FROM THE SCHOOL! AND PENCILS AND BALLS FROM THE GAME ROOM... IT WAS ALL LOOTED!
WE CAN'T STAY HERE, IT'S TOO DANGEROUS!

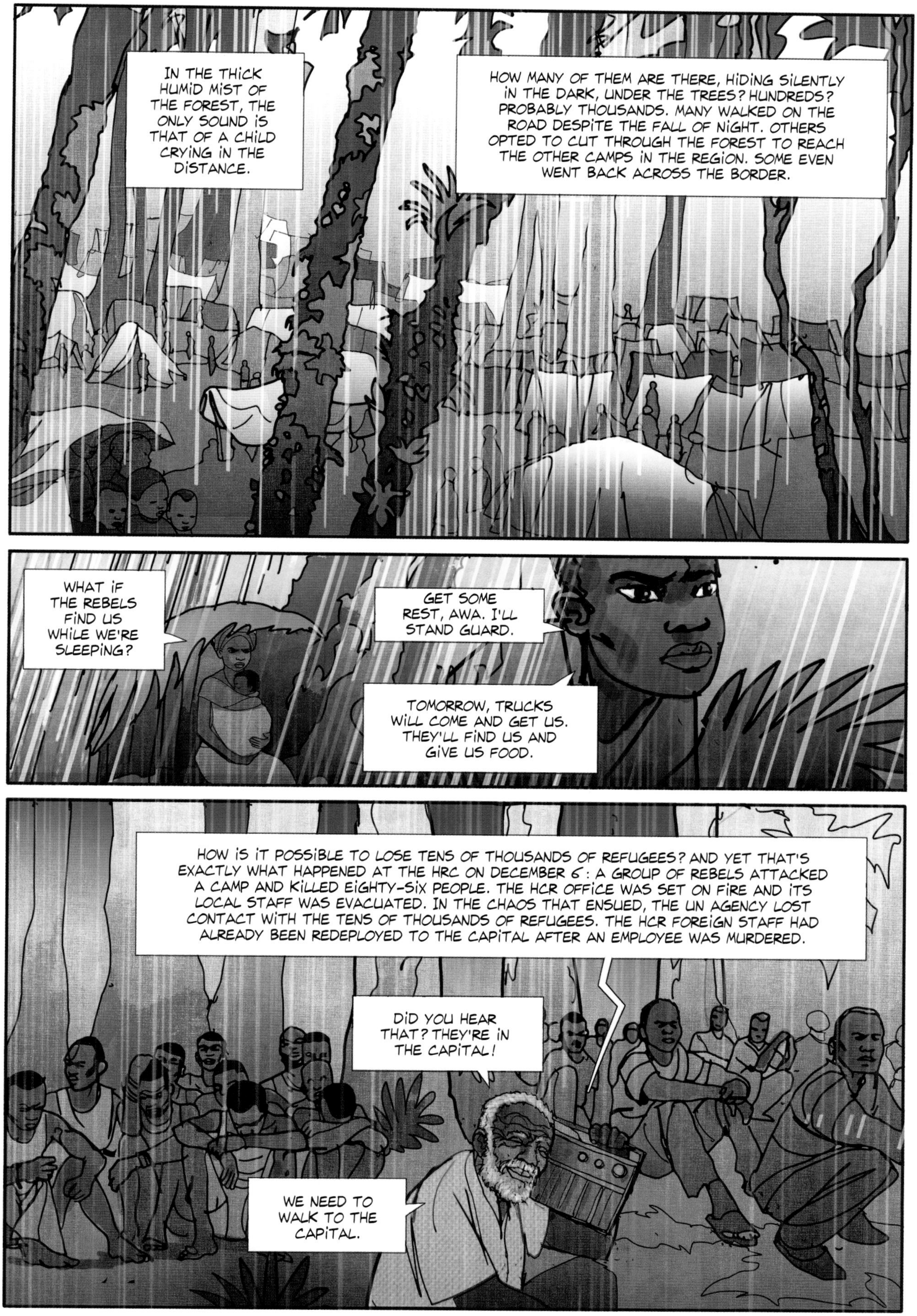
IN THE THICK HUMID MIST OF THE FOREST, THE ONLY SOUND IS THAT OF A CHILD CRYING IN THE DISTANCE.
HOW MANY OF THEM ARE THERE, HIDING SILENTLY IN THE DARK, UNDER THE TREES? HUNDREDS? PROBABLY THOUSANDS. MANY WALKED ON THE ROAD DESPITE THE FALL OF NIGHT. OTHERS OPTED TO CUT THROUGH THE FOREST TO REACH THE OTHER CAMPS IN THE REGION. SOME EVEN WENT BACK ACROSS THE BORDER.
WHAT IF THE REBELS FIND US WHILE WE'RE SLEEPING?
GET SOME REST, AWA. I'LL STAND GUARD.
TOMORROW, TRUCKS WILL COME AND GET US. THEY'LL FIND US AND GIVE US FOOD.
HOW IS IT POSSIBLE TO LOSE TENS OF THOUSANDS OF REFUGEES? AND YET THAT'S EXACTLY WHAT HAPPENED AT THE HRC ON DECEMBER 6 : A GROUP OF REBELS ATTACKED A CAMP AND KILLED EIGHTY-SIX PEOPLE. THE HCR OFFICE WAS SET ON FIRE AND ITS LOCAL STAFF WAS EVACUATED. IN THE CHAOS THAT ENSUED, THE UN AGENCY LOST CONTACT WITH THE TENS OF THOUSANDS OF REFUGEES. THE HCR FOREIGN STAFF HAD ALREADY BEEN REDEPLOYED TO THE CAPITAL AFTER AN EMPLOYEE WAS MURDERED.
DID YOU HEAR THAT? THEY'RE IN THE CAPITAL!
WE NEED TO WALK TO THE CAPITAL.

TAMBA, DO YOU KNOW WHERE ACEYTA IS NOW?

NO.

SO YOU NEVER SAW HIM AGAIN?

JUST ONCE.

WE WERE IN A STATE OF TOTAL PANIC WHEN WE RAN AWAY. SOMETIMES, WE COULD CATCH RADIO FREQUENCIES.

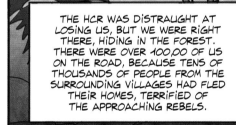

THE HCR WAS DISTRAUGHT AT LOSING US, BUT WE WERE RIGHT THERE, HIDING IN THE FOREST. THERE WERE OVER 100,00 OF US ON THE ROAD, BECAUSE TENS OF THOUSANDS OF PEOPLE FROM THE SURROUNDING VILLAGES HAD FLED THEIR HOMES, TERRIFIED OF THE APPROACHING REBELS.

LUCKILY, THE NGOS ARRIVED EVENTUALLY.

EVERY NIGHT, I ROAMED THE WOODS TO TRADE WHAT I HAD GRABBED FOR THINGS OTHER PEOPLE HAD.

WE WOULD SCRAMBLE AND FIGHT TO GET WHAT THEY BROUGHT. HANDS STRETCHED OUT AND SNATCHED UP WHAT THEY COULD: BLANKETS, TARPS, CANISTERS, CLOTHES, POTS, LAMPS, MOSQUITO NETS, SANITARY NAPKINS... WHEN THE TRUCKS WERE EMPTY, THEY WENT BACK, TAKING THE WEAKEST ALONG WITH THEM.

EVENTUALLY THEY TOOK AWA, ASTOU AND GEORGE. THEY HAD NO ENERGY LEFT. I WALKED ON FOOT. I WALKED FOR SO LONG!

THERE WERE HORRIFIC STORIES CIRCULATING AND SOMETIMES WE WOULD MAKE HUGE DETOURS IN THE FOREST FOR FEAR OF RUNNING INTO AN ARMED GROUP.

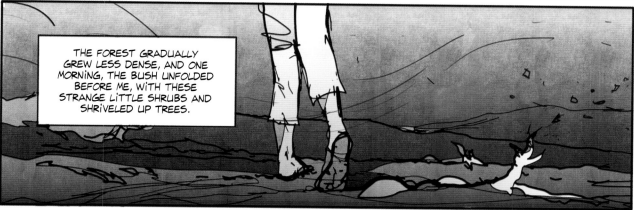

THE FOREST GRADUALLY GREW LESS DENSE, AND ONE MORNING, THE BUSH UNFOLDED BEFORE ME, WITH THESE STRANGE LITTLE SHRUBS AND SHRIVELED UP TREES.

I STARTED WALKING EVEN FASTER, BECAUSE THE VEGETATION WAS TOO SPARSE TO CONCEAL ME. I WAS ALL ALONE, SO I DIDN'T SLEEP MUCH.

THEN THE DIRT PATH WAS REPLACED BY TAR, AND THAT'S WHEN I FELT A BURST OF ENERGY. A ROAD THAT NICE HAD TO MEAN I WASN'T FAR FROM THE CAPITAL.

THAT BLUE RIBBON WAS LIKE THE ROAD TO HOPE. LEADING STRAIGHT AHEAD.

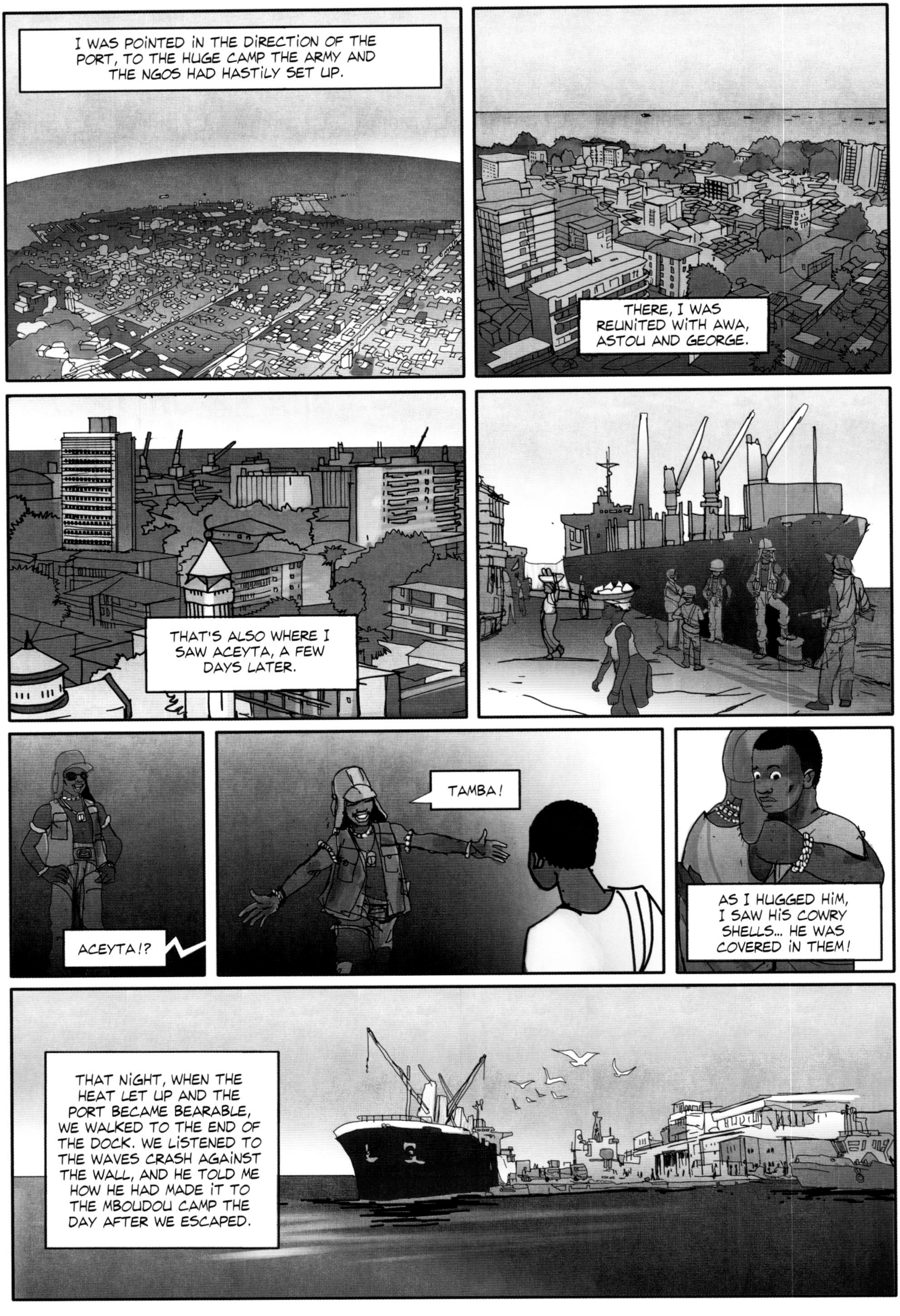
I WAS POINTED IN THE DIRECTION OF THE PORT, TO THE HUGE CAMP THE ARMY AND THE NGOS HAD HASTILY SET UP.
THERE, I WAS REUNITED WITH AWA, ASTOU AND GEORGE.
THAT'S ALSO WHERE I SAW ACEYTA, A FEW DAYS LATER.
ACEYTA!?
TAMBA!
AS I HUGGED HIM, I SAW HIS COWRY SHELLS... HE WAS COVERED IN THEM!
THAT NIGHT, WHEN THE HEAT LET UP AND THE PORT BECAME BEARABLE, WE WALKED TO THE END OF THE DOCK. WE LISTENED TO THE WAVES CRASH AGAINST THE WALL, AND HE TOLD ME HOW HE HAD MADE IT TO THE MBOUDOU CAMP THE DAY AFTER WE ESCAPED.

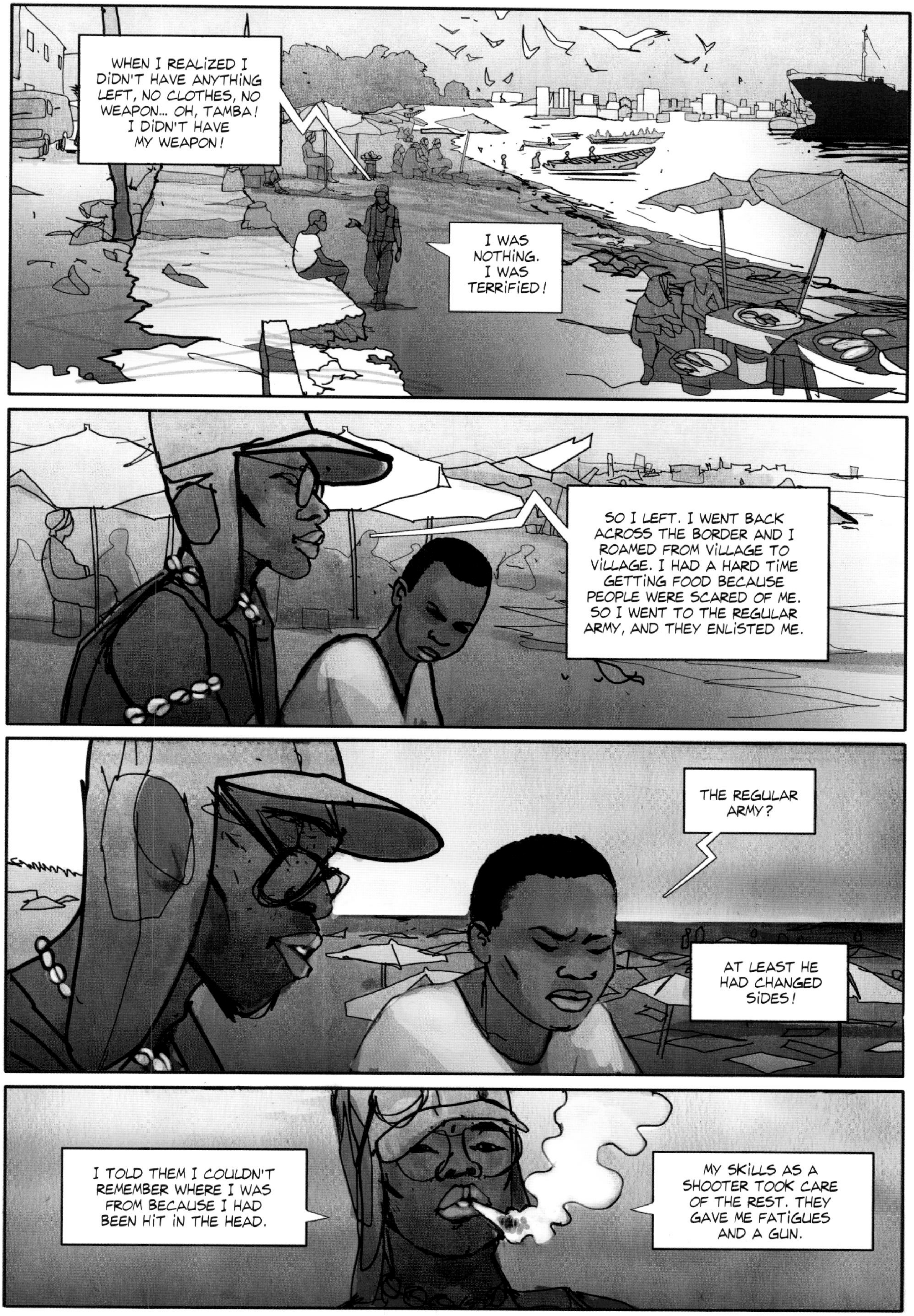
WHEN I REALIZED I DIDN'T HAVE ANYTHING LEFT, NO CLOTHES, NO WEAPON... OH, TAMBA! I DIDN'T HAVE MY WEAPON!
I WAS NOTHING. I WAS TERRIFIED!
SO I LEFT. I WENT BACK ACROSS THE BORDER AND I ROAMED FROM VILLAGE TO VILLAGE. I HAD A HARD TIME GETTING FOOD BECAUSE PEOPLE WERE SCARED OF ME. SO I WENT TO THE REGULAR ARMY, AND THEY ENLISTED ME.
THE REGULAR ARMY?
AT LEAST HE HAD CHANGED SIDES!
I TOLD THEM I COULDN'T REMEMBER WHERE I WAS FROM BECAUSE I HAD BEEN HIT IN THE HEAD.
MY SKILLS AS A SHOOTER TOOK CARE OF THE REST. THEY GAVE ME FATIGUES AND A GUN.

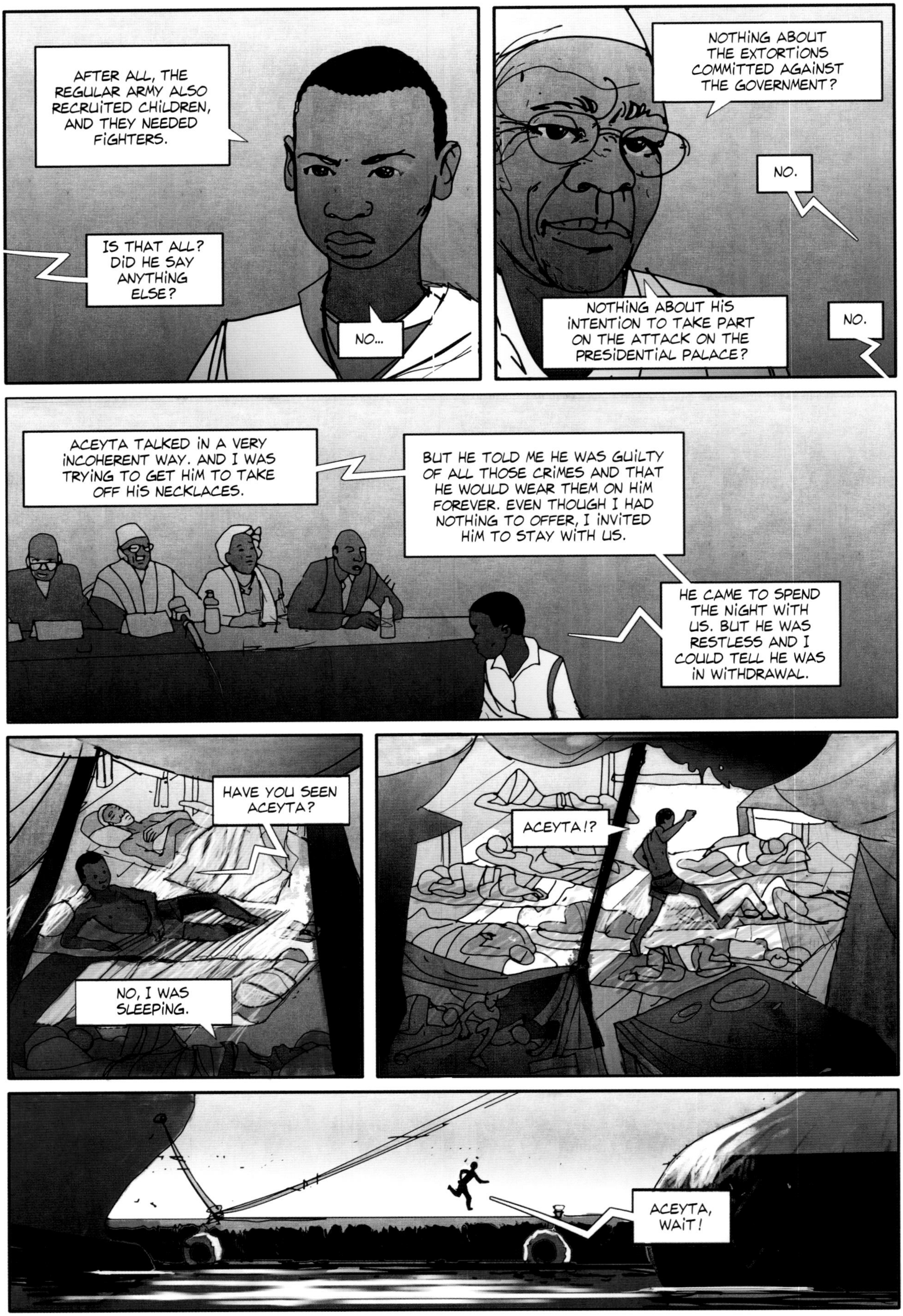
AFTER ALL, THE REGULAR ARMY ALSO RECRUITED CHILDREN, AND THEY NEEDED FIGHTERS.
IS THAT ALL? DID HE SAY ANYTHING ELSE?
NO...
NOTHING ABOUT THE EXTORTIONS COMMITTED AGAINST THE GOVERNMENT?
NO.
NOTHING ABOUT HIS INTENTION TO TAKE PART ON THE ATTACK ON THE PRESIDENTIAL PALACE?
NO.
ACEYTA TALKED IN A VERY INCOHERENT WAY. AND I WAS TRYING TO GET HIM TO TAKE OFF HIS NECKLACES.
BUT HE TOLD ME HE WAS GUILTY OF ALL THOSE CRIMES AND THAT HE WOULD WEAR THEM ON HIM FOREVER. EVEN THOUGH I HAD NOTHING TO OFFER, I INVITED HIM TO STAY WITH US.
HE CAME TO SPEND THE NIGHT WITH US. BUT HE WAS RESTLESS AND I COULD TELL HE WAS IN WITHDRAWAL.
HAVE YOU SEEN ACEYTA?
NO, I WAS SLEEPING.
ACEYTA!?
ACEYTA, WAIT!

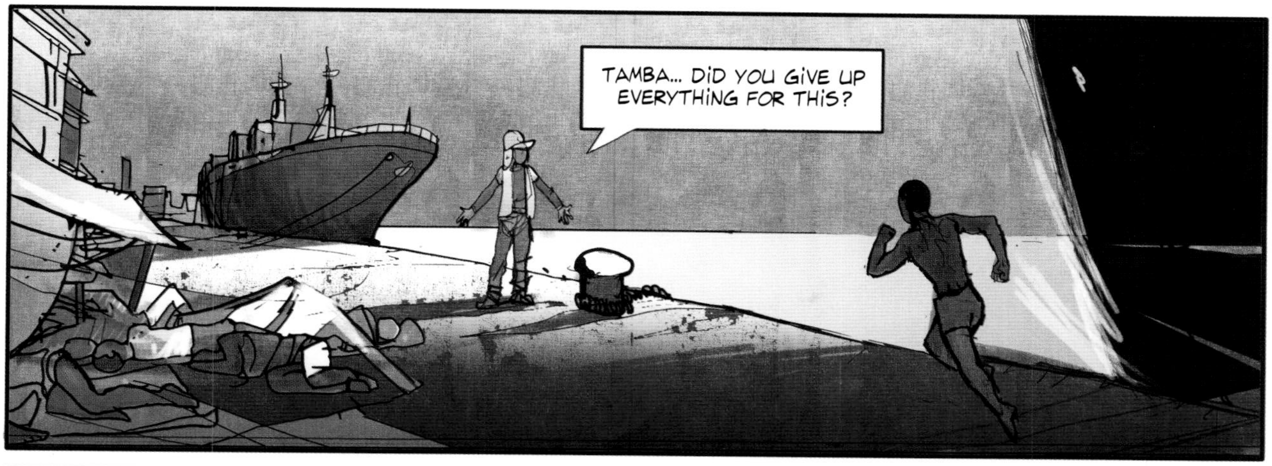
TAMBA... DID YOU GIVE UP EVERYTHING FOR THIS?

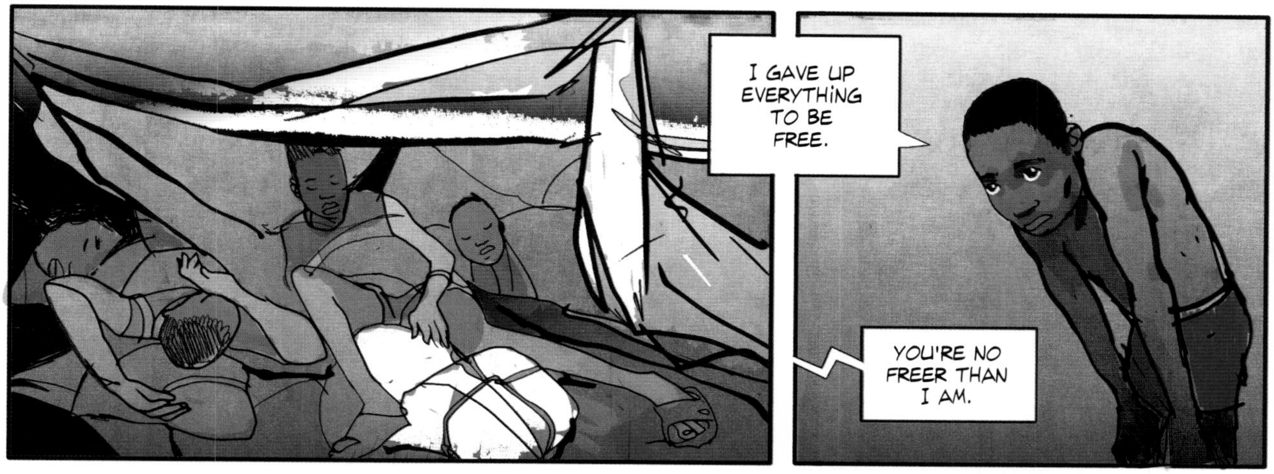
I GAVE UP EVERYTHING TO BE FREE.
YOU'RE NO FREER THAN I AM.

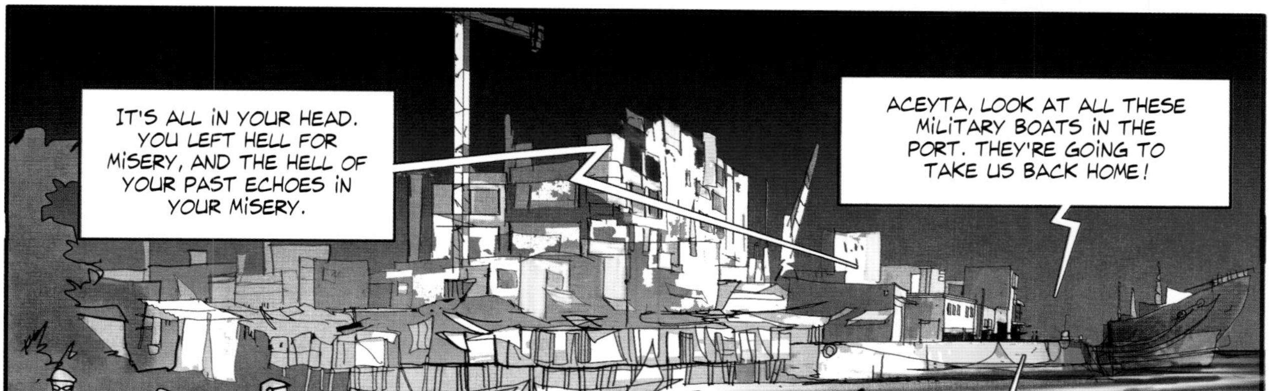
IT'S ALL IN YOUR HEAD. YOU LEFT HELL FOR MISERY, AND THE HELL OF YOUR PAST ECHOES IN YOUR MISERY.
ACEYTA, LOOK AT ALL THESE MILITARY BOATS IN THE PORT. THEY'RE GOING TO TAKE US BACK HOME!
I DON'T CARE.

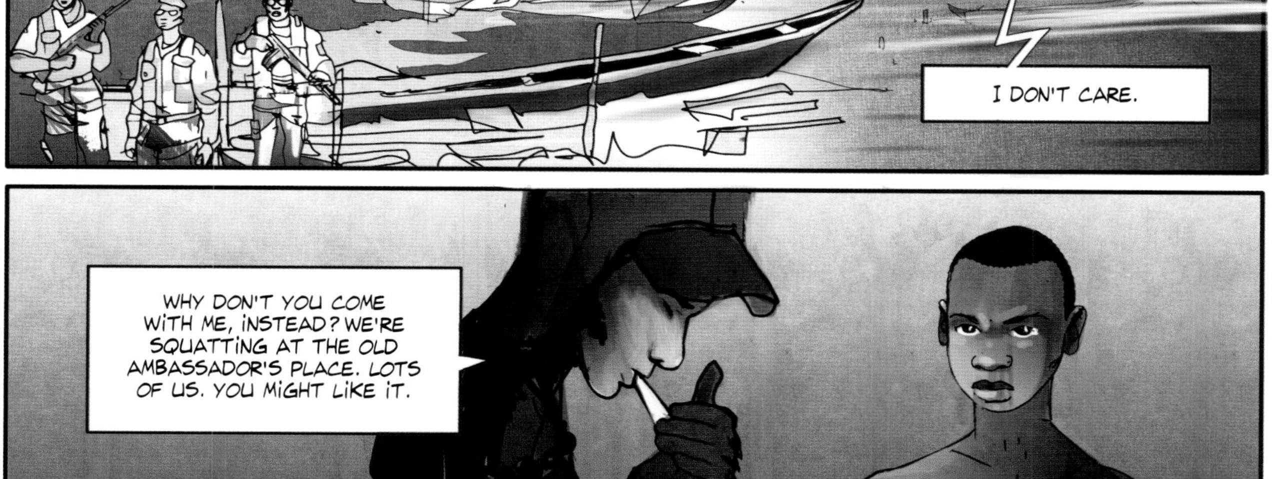
WHY DON'T YOU COME WITH ME, INSTEAD? WE'RE SQUATTING AT THE OLD AMBASSADOR'S PLACE. LOTS OF US. YOU MIGHT LIKE IT.

NO, I'D RATHER WAIT HERE. THE NGOS ARE GETTING ORGANIZED AND TAKING DOWN NAMES FOR THOSE WHO WANT TO LEAVE ON THE BOATS. IT'S JUST A MATTER OF WEEKS. THINGS ARE HAPPENING!

OH, THEY'RE HAPPENING, ALL RIGHT! JUST NOT THE WAY YOU THINK...

SO WHICH SIDE ARE YOU ON, ANYWAY?

I'M NOT ON ANY SIDE. I JUST WANT TO TRY TO GO HOME AND BRING AWA WITH ME.

AWA? OH, RIGHT. I FORGOT, YOU HAVE A FAMILY NOW!

DID YOU KNOW WE WERE FIGHTING FOR DIAMONDS?

I FOUND THAT OUT WHEN I JOINED THE REGULAR ARMY. ALL THAT PILLAGE, ALL THAT HORROR... OVER FREAKING STONES!! THEY'RE KILLING EACH OTHER OVER CONTROL OF THE DIAMOND ZONES.

WHAT ARE YOU TALKING ABOUT?

NOW DO YOU BELIEVE ME?

WHAT IS THAT?

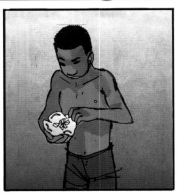

I DIDN'T KNOW...

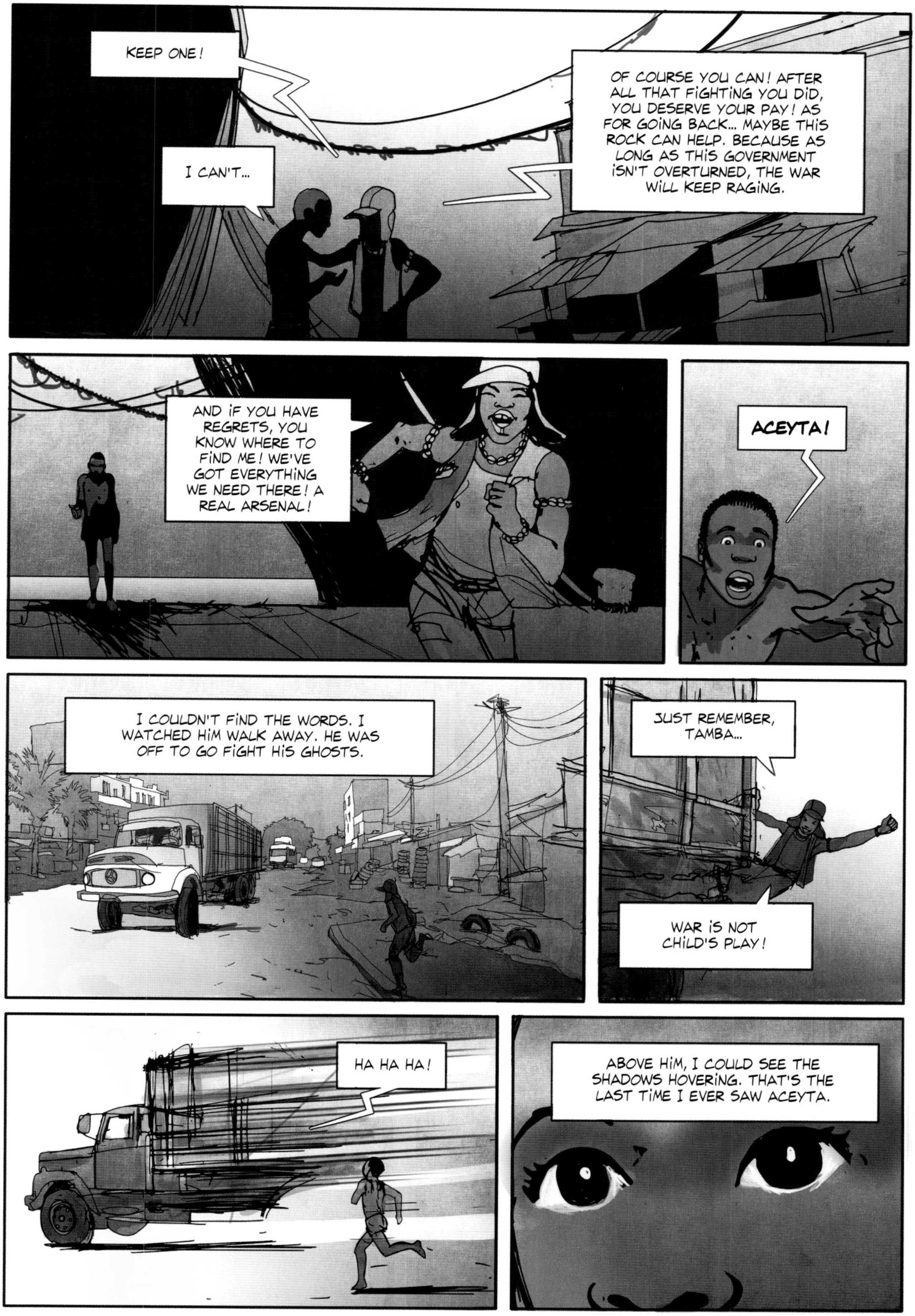
KEEP ONE!
I CAN'T...
OF COURSE YOU CAN! AFTER ALL THAT FIGHTING YOU DID, YOU DESERVE YOUR PAY! AS FOR GOING BACK... MAYBE THIS ROCK CAN HELP. BECAUSE AS LONG AS THIS GOVERNMENT ISN'T OVERTURNED, THE WAR WILL KEEP RAGING.
AND IF YOU HAVE REGRETS, YOU KNOW WHERE TO FIND ME! WE'VE GOT EVERYTHING WE NEED THERE! A REAL ARSENAL!
ACEYTA!
I COULDN'T FIND THE WORDS. I WATCHED HIM WALK AWAY. HE WAS OFF TO GO FIGHT HIS GHOSTS.
JUST REMEMBER, TAMBA...
WAR IS NOT CHILD'S PLAY!
HA HA HA!
ABOVE HIM, I COULD SEE THE SHADOWS HOVERING. THAT'S THE LAST TIME I EVER SAW ACEYTA.

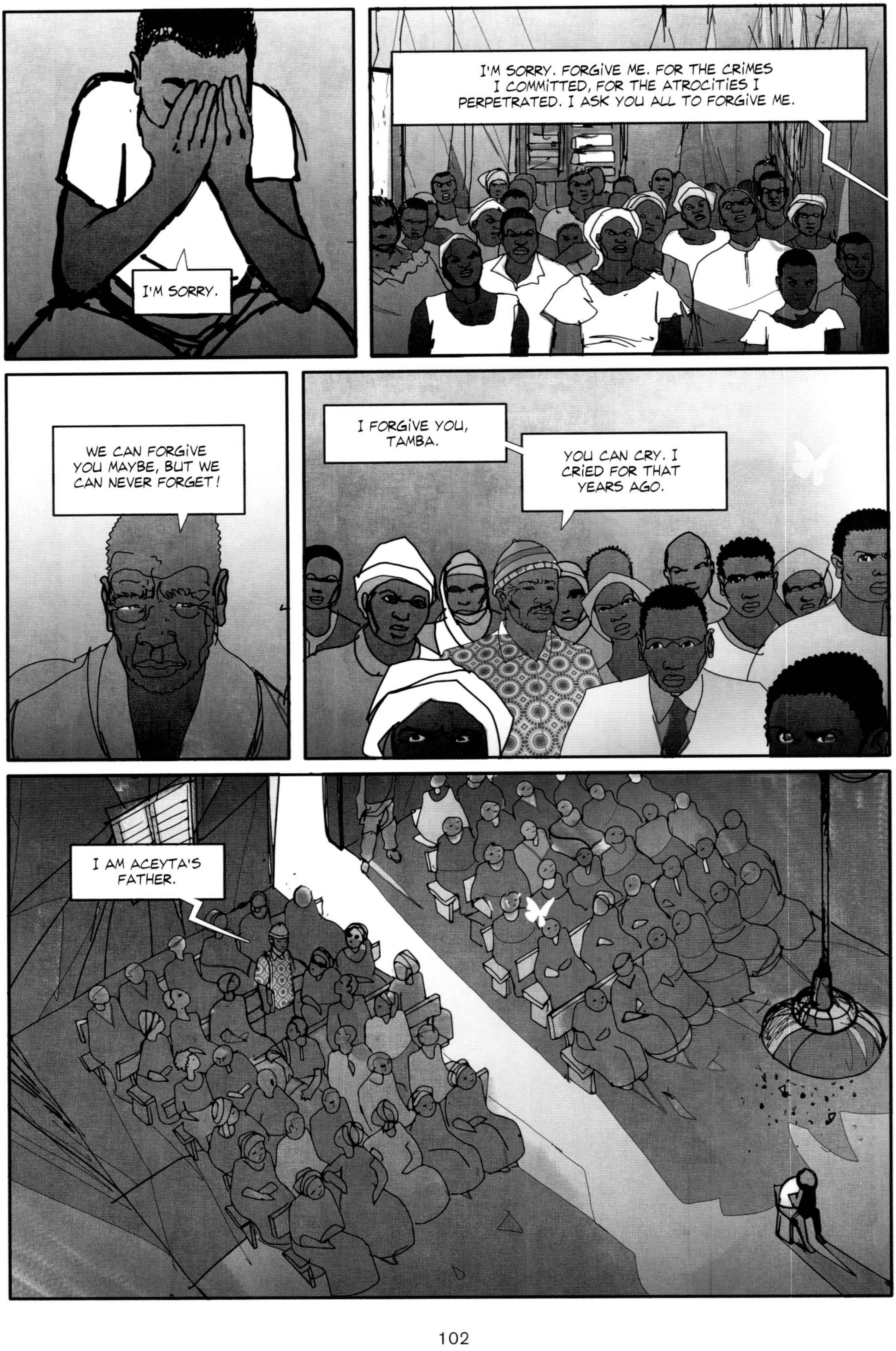
I'M SORRY.
I'M SORRY. FORGIVE ME. FOR THE CRIMES I COMMITTED, FOR THE ATROCITIES I PERPETRATED. I ASK YOU ALL TO FORGIVE ME.
WE CAN FORGIVE YOU MAYBE, BUT WE CAN NEVER FORGET!
I FORGIVE YOU, TAMBA.
YOU CAN CRY. I CRIED FOR THAT YEARS AGO.
I AM ACEYTA'S FATHER.

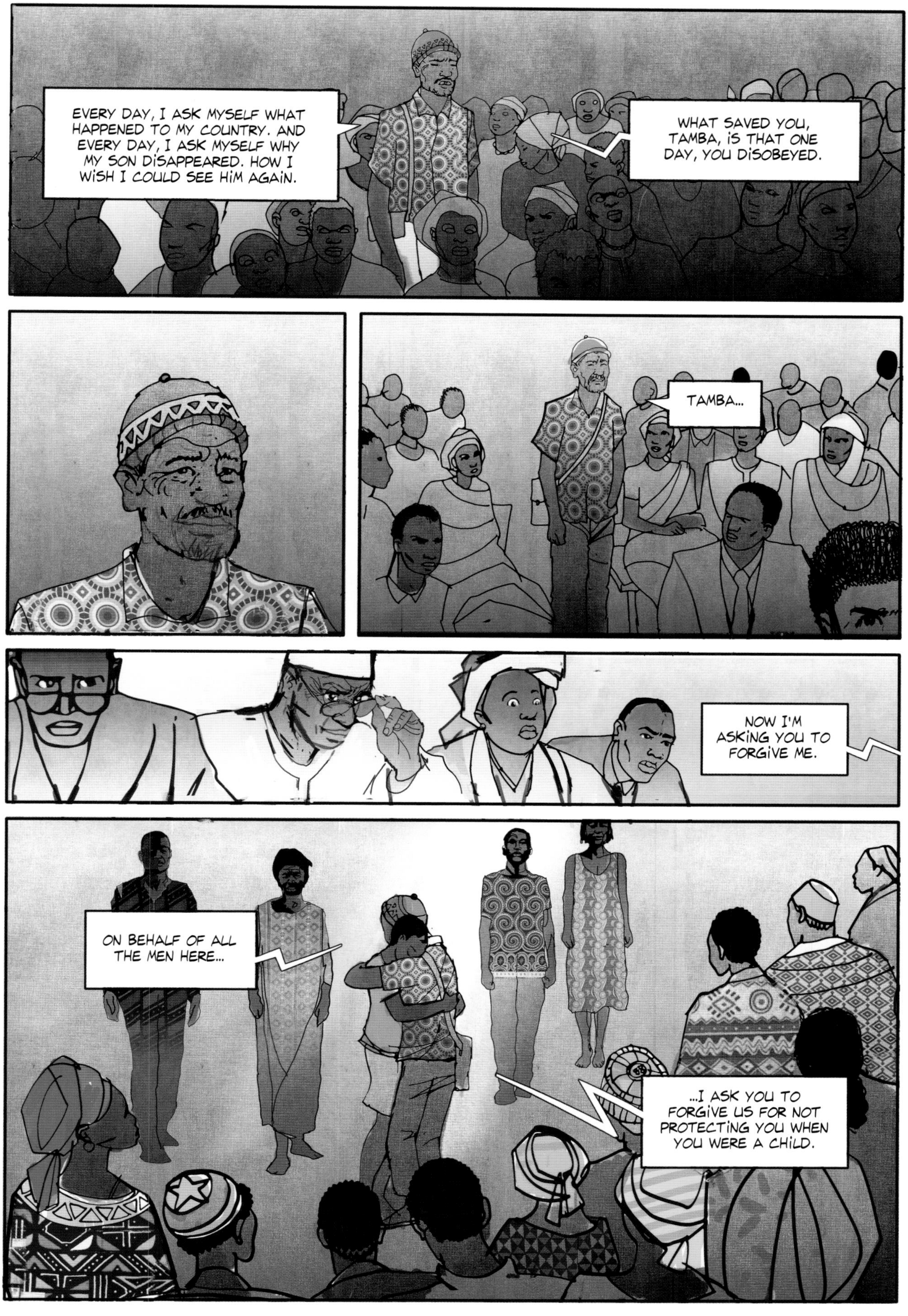
EVERY DAY, I ASK MYSELF WHAT HAPPENED TO MY COUNTRY. AND EVERY DAY, I ASK MYSELF WHY MY SON DISAPPEARED. HOW I WISH I COULD SEE HIM AGAIN.
WHAT SAVED YOU, TAMBA, IS THAT ONE DAY, YOU DISOBEYED.
TAMBA...
NOW I'M ASKING YOU TO FORGIVE ME.
ON BEHALF OF ALL THE MEN HERE...
...I ASK YOU TO FORGIVE US FOR NOT PROTECTING YOU WHEN YOU WERE A CHILD.

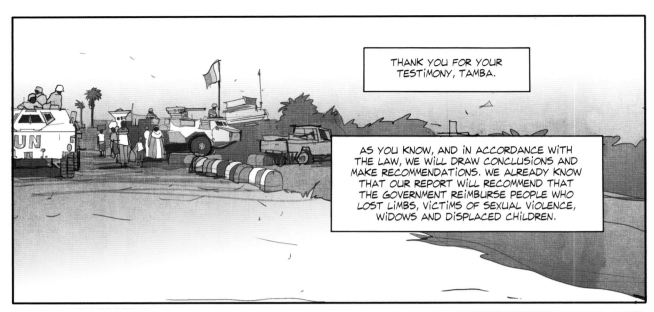

THANK YOU FOR YOUR TESTIMONY, TAMBA.

AS YOU KNOW, AND IN ACCORDANCE WITH THE LAW, WE WILL DRAW CONCLUSIONS AND MAKE RECOMMENDATIONS. WE ALREADY KNOW THAT OUR REPORT WILL RECOMMEND THAT THE GOVERNMENT REIMBURSE PEOPLE WHO LOST LIMBS, VICTIMS OF SEXUAL VIOLENCE, WIDOWS AND DISPLACED CHILDREN.

WE WILL ALSO ASK THAT EVERYTHING BE DONE TO GIVE THE VICTIMS BACK THEIR DIGNITY.

LASTLY, WE WILL ALSO ASK THAT SPECIAL ATTENTION BE GIVEN TO CHILDREN, INCLUDING CHILD SOLDIERS AND THOSE WHO WERE VICTIMS OF SEXUAL ASSAULT.

TOMORROW, WE WILL BEGIN HEARING ANOTHER TESTIMONY. THE COMMISSION IS OPEN TO THE PUBLIC. ANYONE WISHING TO ATTEND MAY DO SO. LADIES AND GENTLEMEN, THANK YOU FOR COMING.

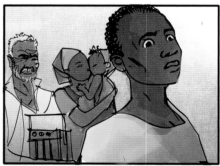

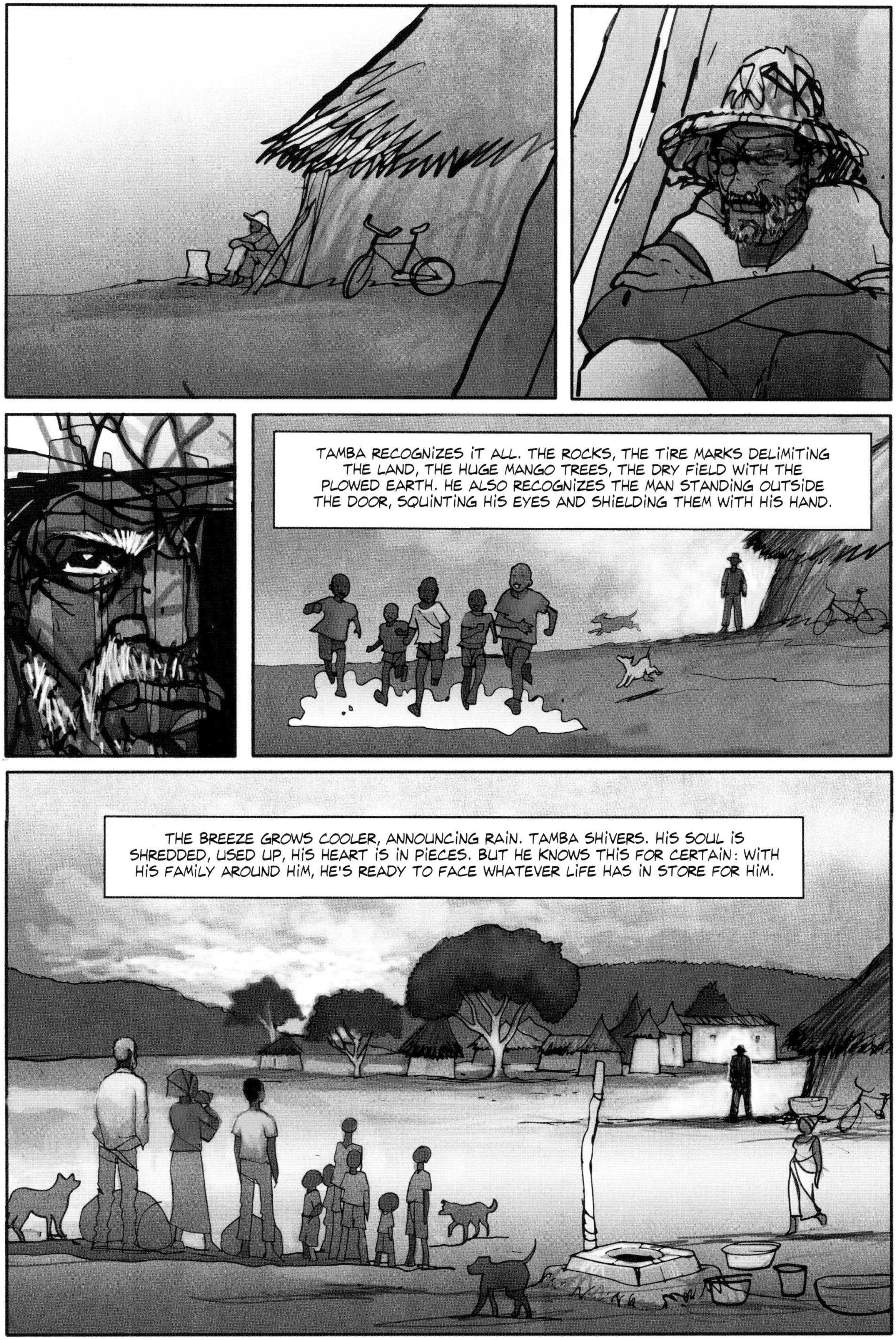
TAMBA RECOGNIZES IT ALL. THE ROCKS, THE TIRE MARKS DELIMITING THE LAND, THE HUGE MANGO TREES, THE DRY FIELD WITH THE PLOWED EARTH. HE ALSO RECOGNIZES THE MAN STANDING OUTSIDE THE DOOR, SQUINTING HIS EYES AND SHIELDING THEM WITH HIS HAND.
THE BREEZE GROWS COOLER, ANNOUNCING RAIN. TAMBA SHIVERS. HIS SOUL IS SHREDDED, USED UP, HIS HEART IS IN PIECES. BUT HE KNOWS THIS FOR CERTAIN: WITH HIS FAMILY AROUND HIM, HE'S READY TO FACE WHATEVER LIFE HAS IN STORE FOR HIM.

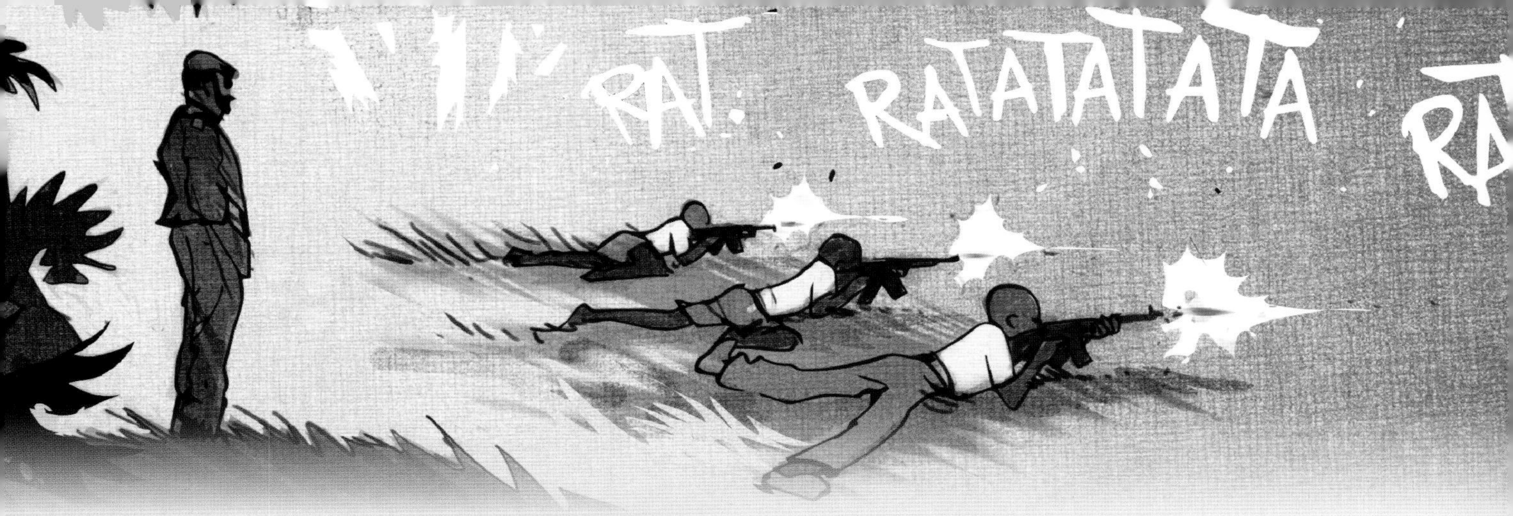
RAT
RATATATATA
RAT

CHILD SOLDIERS

How many of them are there? At least 250,000, probably more. Kidnapped, taken from their families, taken out of school, ripped from their childhood, enlisted by force or volunteers with army or rebel forces: in over fifty countries throughout the world, child soldiers fight in combat, sometimes as young as six or eight years old.

Their innocence is sacrificed for political, economic or religious ideologies, and fear leads them to commit the most unspeakable acts.

In 2000, I traveled to the Nyaedou refugee camp in Guinea-Conakry to take part in an event for «Refugee Children of the World.» Sierra Leonean and Liberian refugees were arriving by the hundreds of thousands to this forested area where the UN had built a camp to take them in. NGOs from countries everywhere were gathered in Guéckédou, a small town near the camp, each of them trying in a vast orchestration, to ensure the survival of the 300,000 refugees from the region. For one month, three other French circus artists and myself conducted workshops for a hundred children and trained eleven Sierra Leonean counselors. The aim of the NGO organizing the event was to provide refugee children with leisure time, a chance to share, and the opportunity to smile again through games, self-expression and creativity. At the end of the month, the children performed a show that toured in the surrounding camps. Some of those children were former child soldiers. They smiled like the others, laughed like the others, and, like the others, tried to survive as they went about their lives in the camp and waited for their reintegration into society... if and when the war ever ended. A few months after I left the camp and returned to France, I saw a news report on television showing Sierra Leonean rebels that had managed to cross over the border and were arriving into Guéckédou. The NGOs evacuated their personnel in the space of a few days and the 300,000 terrified refugees had no choice but to walk to the capital, over a thousand miles away.

Four years later, Sierra Leone's child soldiers were all demobilized. To this day, the existence of child soldiers remains an unbearable reality across the globe. While this graphic novel doesn't mention any one country in particular, I do however set the story in Africa, because 120,000 child soldiers are still in active combat there, which makes this continent the one most affected by this tragedy.

Marion Achard

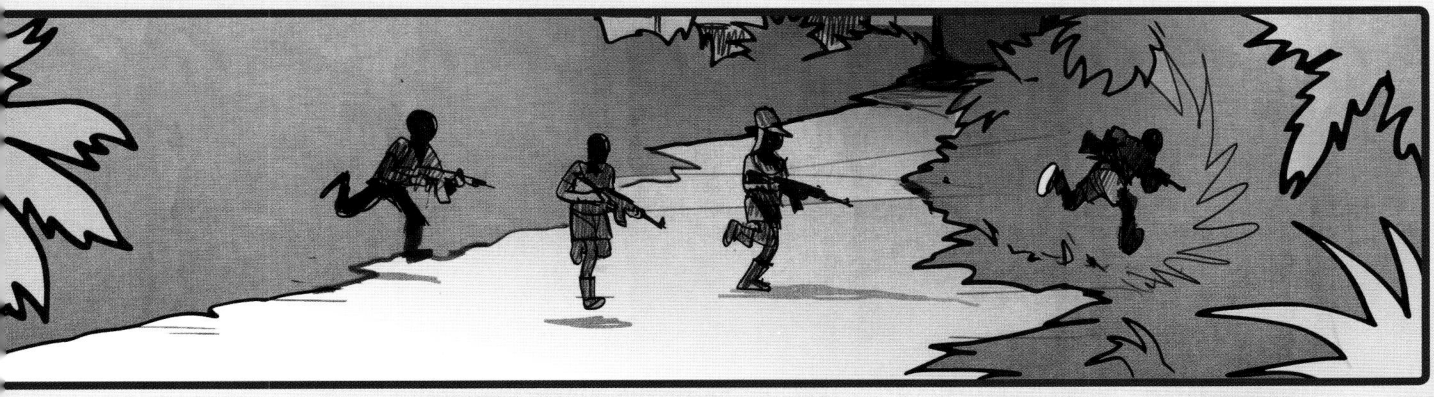

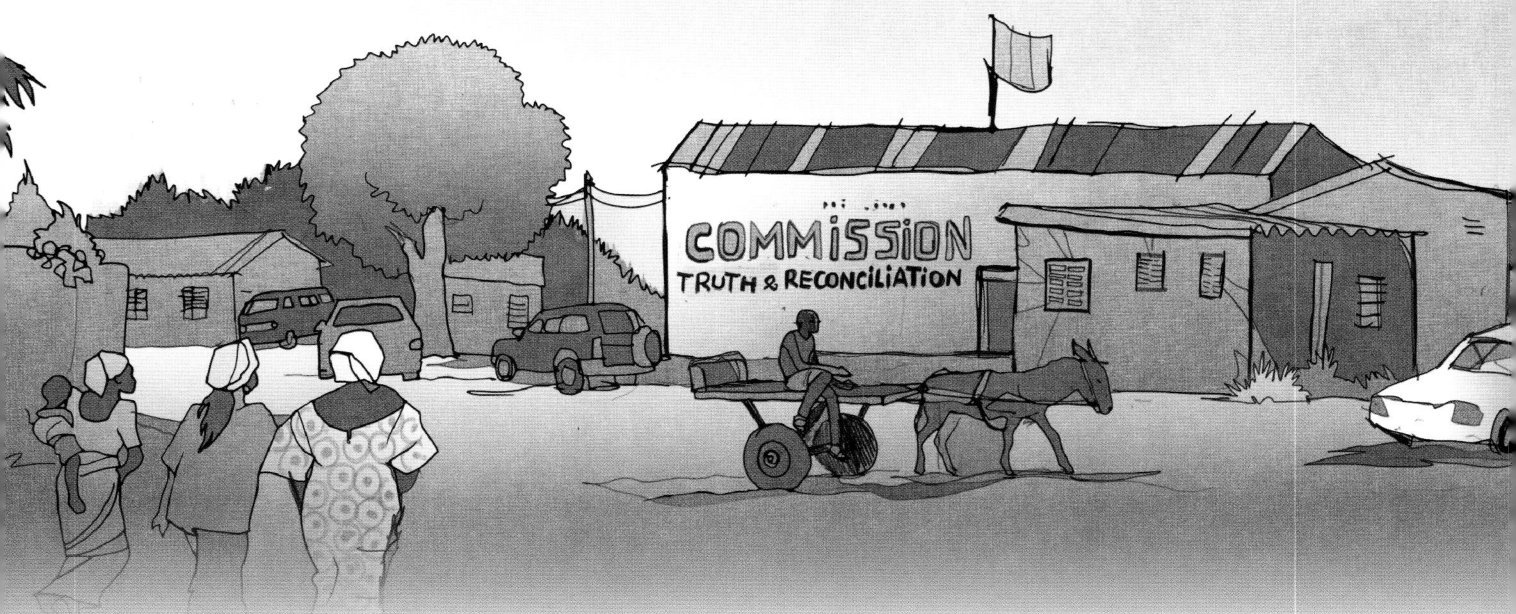
COMMISSION
TRUTH & RECONCILIATION

TRUTH AND RECONCILIATION COMMISSIONS

Countries emerging from a period of national conflict that led to massive human rights violations can seek a non-penal way in which to reconcile the different parts of society and the state. The main objective is to get out of the state of war that prevailed and to work towards lasting peace.

Since it can be impossible for justice to be served—because the incriminating facts are too complex, or too massive, or because the institution of justice itself has been decimated or compromised—the idea is to establish the truth of past facts to facilitate reconciliation. For having the truth established and the wrongs they suffered publicly recognized is one of the victims' demands, beyond their request for reparation for themselves and punishment for the offenders. These commissions understand that reconciliation, truth and justice are difficult to obtain at the same time with the same level of stringency: to aim only for justice can prevent reconciliation by ostracizing part of the population; to establish the truth without rendering justice can increase the frustration of the victims; and aiming for reconciliation at any cost can lead to dubious compromises in terms of truth and justice.

To date, around 30 Truth and Reconciliation Commissions have been created in South Africa, Germany, Argentina, Bolivia, Burundi, Chile, Congo,

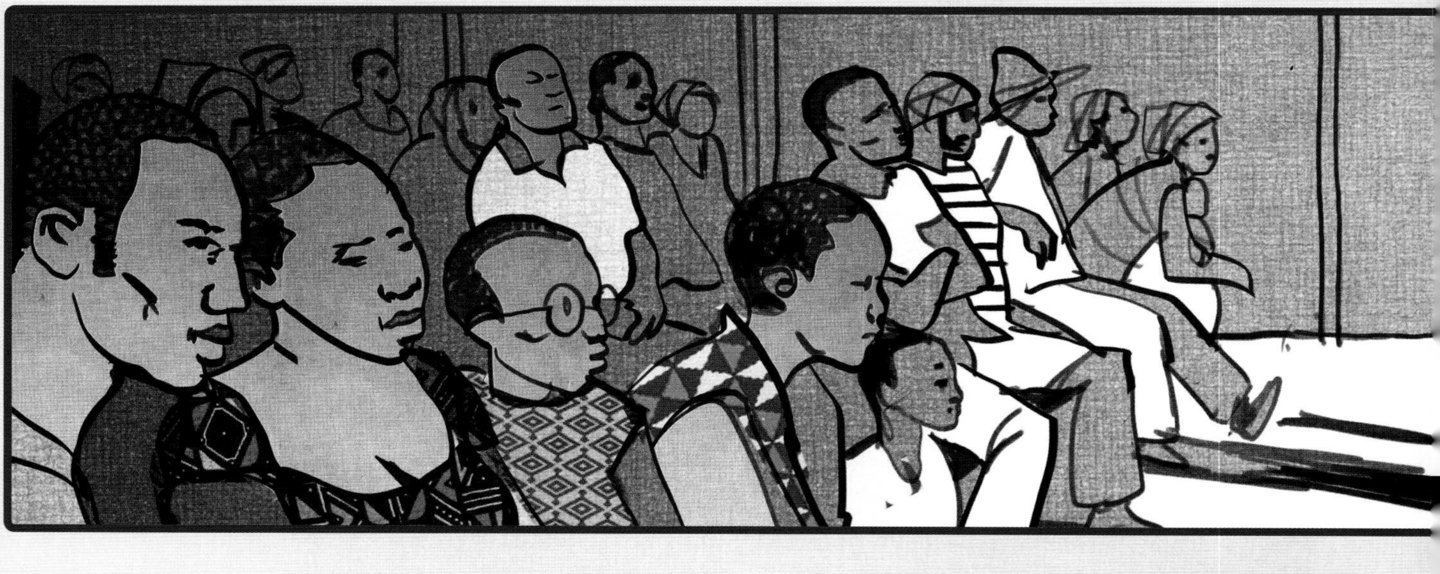

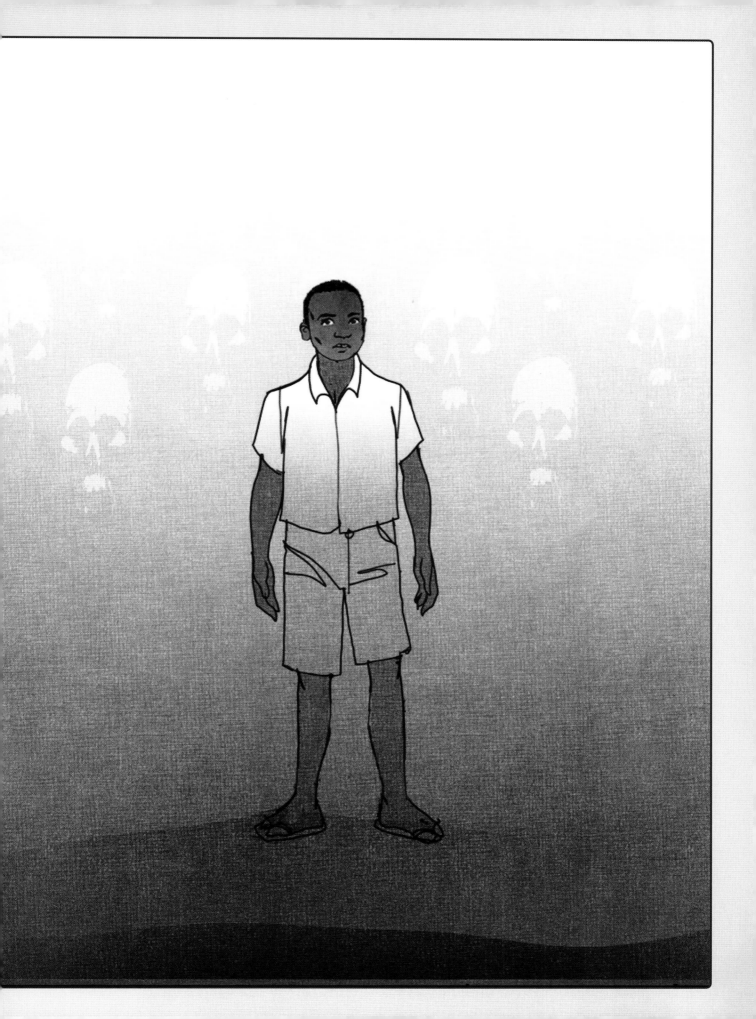

South Korea, Ecuador, and Ghana, Guatemala, Haiti, Honduras, Liberia, Morocco, Madagascar, Malawi, Nepal, Nigeria, Uganda, Panama, Peru, the Philippines, El Salvador, Sierra Leone, Sri Lanka, Chad, East Timor, Uruguay and Yugoslavia. The functioning, means, and scope of the mandate of these commissions can vary significantly from one to the next. However, they have all been established in countries emerging from violent internal conflict and embarking on a process of democratization in a context of great fragility as a state.

In these commissions, special importance is given to victims who have been invited to testify, both for ethical reasons (it is important that their suffering be publicly recognized and the culprits identified) and to allow the commission to establish the truth of the facts. The most famous and successful of these commissions is the one that South Africa created in 1995 shortly after the end of apartheid: the Truth and Reconciliation Commission. That one remains a model for all others. Created by a special law and provided with ample means, it was able to carry out investigations, locate witnesses, decide on legitimate reparations and, in certain cases, grant amnesty to the culprits. Its president, Bishop Desmond Tutu of the Anglican Church of Johannesburg, was an advocate of what is called «restorative justice,» meaning justice aimed at establishing or restoring social bonds, as opposed to a purely «retributive» justice, i.e. justice designed to punish crimes. He also emphasized the role of the request for forgiveness as an element of amnesty

for the repentant guilty party. This last point garnered mixed reactions from international bodies, in particular the Secretary-General of the United Nations, who felt that there should be no amnesty for crimes against humanity.

Opinions vary as to the success of these commissions. There is a general consensus, however, that while justice and truth are not always fully served, the goal of reconciliation and social peace is usually achieved, at least temporarily.

Source: www.un.org

THE UN HIGH COMMISSIONER FOR REFUGEES: UNHCR

Also called the United Nations Refugee Agency, this body was created in 1950 to help millions of Europeans who had fled or lost their homes. In the 1960s, the agency's action extended to other countries. The Office of the United Nations High Commissioner for Refugees was awarded the Nobel Peace Prize twice: in 1954 for its pioneering work in Europe and in 1981 for its international work on behalf of refugees.

The United Nations mandated the UNHCR to lead and coordinate international action for the protection of refugees around the world and for the search for solutions to their problems. The UNHCR now works in 130 countries to help refugees (17.2 million plus 5.3 million Palestinian refugees dependent on another UN agency), stateless people (10 million), and resettled refugees (about 190,000). It employs nearly 11,000 people, 87% of whom work in the field. Its budget in 2017 was 7.7 billion dollars.

The UNHCR's primary mission is to work to ensure the rights and well-being of refugees. To achieve this goal, it strives to ensure that everyone can lay claim to their right of asylum, seek refuge in another country and return voluntarily to their home country. In addition, the UNHCR seeks sustainable solutions to refugees' problems by helping them return home or settle in another country in a stable manner. It can also intervene on behalf of other groups: former refugees back in their homeland, internally displaced persons, stateless people or people whose nationality is controverted

The UNHCR seeks to prevent the forced displacement of populations by encouraging states and other institutions to create conditions conducive to the protection of human rights and the peaceful settlement of disputes. In all its activities, UNHCR pays particular attention to the needs of children and seeks to promote equal rights for women and girls. The UNHCR works with other UN agencies: the World Food Program (WFP), the United Nations Children's Fund (UNICEF), the World Health Organization (WHO), the United Nations Development Program (UNDP), the Office for the Coordination of Humanitarian Affairs (OCHA), the Office of the High Commissioner for Human Rights (OH-

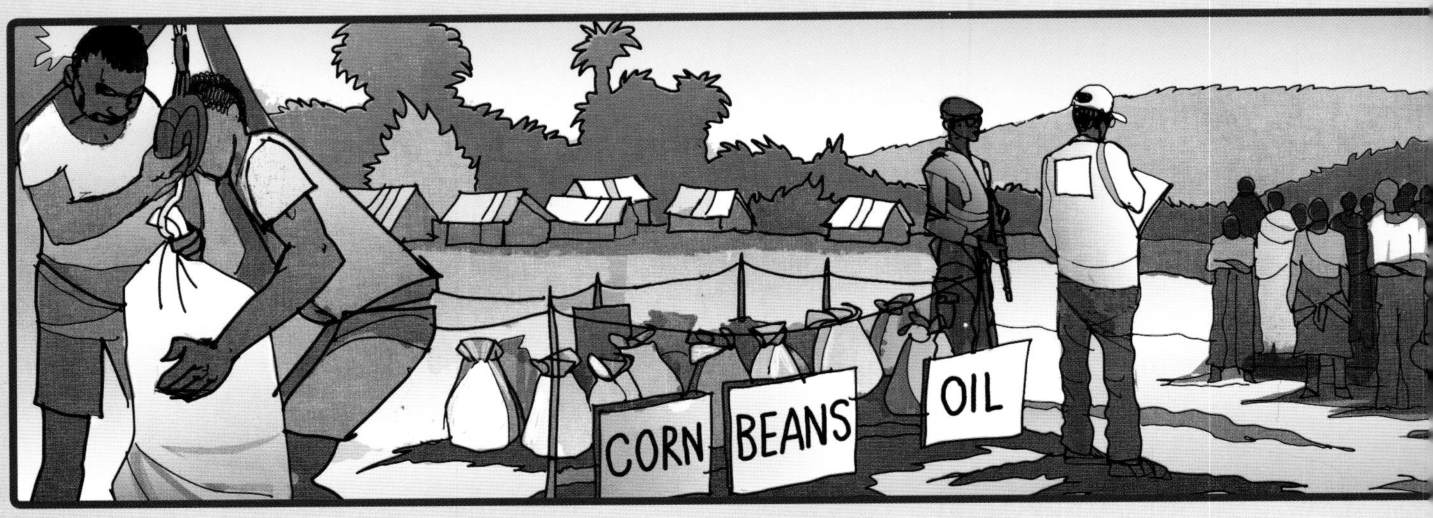
CORN
BEANS
OIL

CHR) and the Joint United Nations Program on HIV / AIDS (UNAIDS). It also cooperates with many partners, including governments, regional and international organizations, and many non-governmental organizations (NGOs). One of the key principles of the UNHCR's approach is that of participation, based on the notion that refugees and other persons benefiting from the activities of the Organization should be consulted on decisions that affect their life.

Today, 55% of refugees come from just three countries: Syria, 5.5 million; South Sudan, 1.4 million; and Afghanistan, 2.5 million. Nearly one out of every two refugees is under the age of 18. There are more than 65 million displaced people in the world. Africa is the continent that takes in the most, accounting for 30% of the total figure; 26% of them are in the Middle East and North Africa, 17% in Europe, 16% in the Americas (North, Central and South) and 11% in Asia-Pacific.

Source : www.unhcr.org

Laure Borgomano

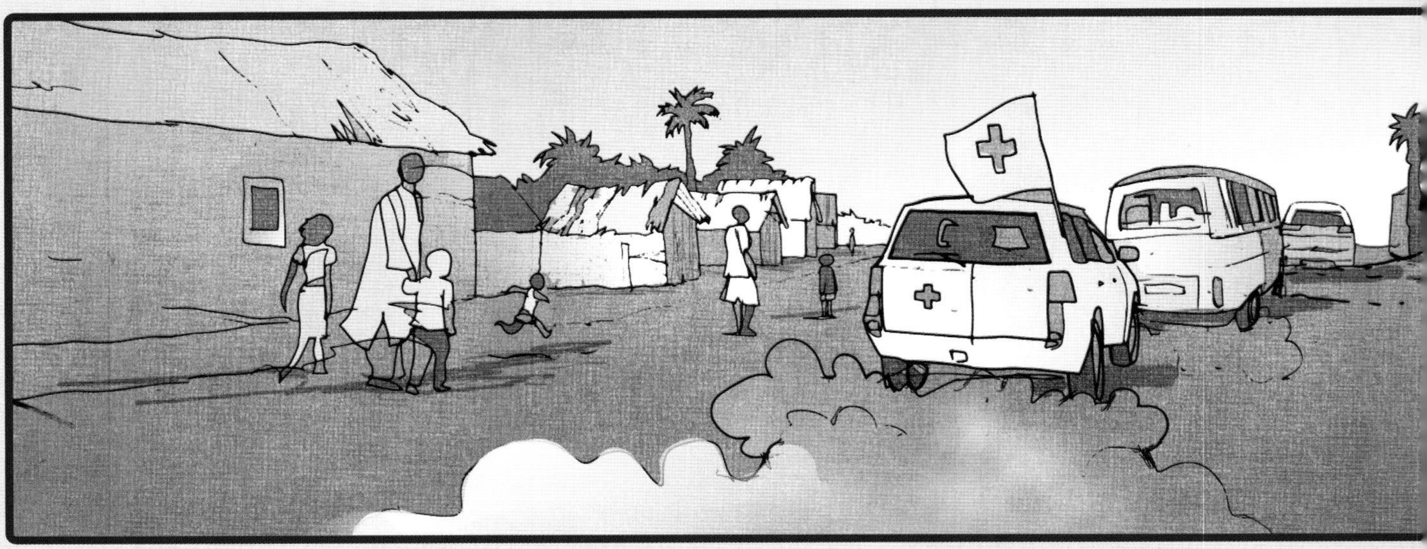

Laure Borgomano has worked in various French ministries. A Professor of Classical Literature in France, she has worked for the Ministry of Foreign Affairs in the field of cultural and linguistic cooperation in the United States and Europe. Upon graduating from France's prestigious National School of Administration, she joined the Department of Defense where she specialized in NATO security and partnership policy issues. She ended her career in Brussels as advisor to France's permanent representation at NATO. She also holds a doctorate in film semiology and has had many articles published in the field of cinema, international relations and migration.